The
AXHOLME JOINT
RAILWAY
including

THE GOOLE & MARSHLAND LIGHT RAILWAY

AND

THE ISLE OF AXHOLME LIGHT RAILWAY

by

Colin Judge

THE OAKWOOD PRESS

© Oakwood Press and Colin Judge 1994

ISBN 0 85361 441 5

Typeset by Oakwood Graphics.

Printed by Alpha Print (Witney), Witney, Oxon.

Dedicated to the people of the 'Isle'

A commercial Postcard showing the Market Cross, Epworth in front of the Mechanics' Institute building. The Mechanics' Institute was established by William Reed in 1837, in a room at the back of his printing shop in Albion House. Initially it was only a library, but within two years music and lectures were being accommodated. A news room was established in 1853 (the only paper being the *Evening Mail*, purchased second-hand from a local resident). The present premises were purchased in 1949 for £400 and now house over 12,000 books; having 140 members who have the privilege of borrowing titles for ½p per book, per week.   *Courtesy Charlie Arrand*

Published by
The Oakwood Press
P.O. Box 122, Headington, Oxford

Acknowledgements

I am extremely grateful to the following for their help in compiling this book:

J.F. Addyman
C. Arrand
Dr A.L. Barnett
The late D.S.M. Barrie
R. Belton
D. Billmore
H.D. Bowtell
Mrs S.J. Bradwell
Mrs M. Briggs
F. Casserley
H.C. Casserley
N. Coates
F. Cook
J. Edgington
L. Elvidge
F. Gee
D.G. Geldard
D. Gladwin
C.T. Goode
H. Hackney
W.G. Halkon
J. Harris
E. Harrison
B. Hastings
The late K. Hoole

F. James
S.C. Jenkins
G.L. Johnson
F. Jones
G. Horsman
F. Jux
T. Kay
Mrs B. Kirkham
The late J.M. Lloyd
B.R. Longbone
A.J. Ludlam
N. Magee
The late S. Marshall
Norma C. Neill
D.A. Peart
C.R. Potts
R. Shipley
K. Smith
P.L. Smith
I. Snell
T.T. Sutcliffe
S. Teanby
D. Thompson
R. Whitehead

Included within this list are the people of the 'Isle' who contributed so much and welcomed me into their homes. A special thank you to Eddie and Jo ·Harrison of the Mechanics Institute, Epworth who spent many hours searching, telephoning, photocopying and borrowing material for the book.
Lastly without the careful checking of Ken Plant, who spent many hours eradicating the blemishes and ensured a readable and accurate text, this volume would not have been completed. N.E. Stead supplied prints from the late Geoffrey Oates collection.

The following Institutions for their help:
Doncaster Central Library
Public Record Office, Kew
Bodleian Library (Map Room) Oxford
Fisons PLC Ltd
Mechanics Institute, Epworth
Darlington Railway Museum
National Railway Museum, York

A superb photograph of the Directors' Special that ran on 26th June, 1900 to Eastoft (the end of the G&MLR at that time) with the dignitaries posed for J.H. Bottomley's photograph. William Halkon (Chairman) is third from left (*back row*) with the flatcap. The newly acquired 0-6-0...

Contents

Abbreviations

AJR	Axholme Joint Railway
BMLC	British Moss Litter Company
BOT	Board of Trade
CW&SLR	Cawood, Wistow and Selby Light Railway
G&MLR	Goole and Marshland Light Railway
GCR	Great Central Railway
GN&GEJR	Great Northern and Great Eastern Joint Railway
GNR	Great Northern Railway
IOALR	Isle of Axholme Light Railway
IOA&MST	Isle of Axholme and Marshland Steam Tramway
L&YR	Lancashire and Yorkshire Railway
LMS	London, Midland and Scottish Railway
LNER	London & North Eastern Railway
LRO	Light Railway Order
MS&LR	Manchester, Sheffield and Lincolnshire Railway
NER	North Eastern Railway
NLLR	North Lindsey Light Railway
PRO	Public Record Office
RS Co	Railway Signal Co. Ltd
S&SYNC	Sheffield and South Yorkshire Navigation Company
TLR	Tickhill Light Railway
YDLRS	Yorkshire District Light Railway Syndicate Ltd

Epworth Gas Works in Tottermire Lane which would have received much of its supplies, via the AJR.   *Courtesy Ron Shipley*

References and Bibliography

S.E. Squires, *The Lincolnshire Potato Railways*, (Oakwood Press, 1987)

A.L. Barnett, *The Railways of the South Yorkshire Coalfield from 1880* (RCTS, 1984)

K.E. Hartley, *The Cawood, Wistow and Selby Light Railway* (Turntable Enterprises)

P. Bosley, *Light Railways in England and Wales* (Manchester University Press)

C.H. Grinling, *The History of the Great Northern Railway, 1845-1895* (Methuen, 1898)

A.L. Barnett, *The Light Railway King of the North* (R&CHS, 1992)

White's 1837 Guide, History, Gazetteer and Directory of the West Riding of Yorkshire

H.A. Steward, *The Light Railways Act, 1896* (Eyre & Spottiswoode, 1897)

R.W. Kidner, *The Light Railways of Britain* (Oakwood Press, 1947)

W.W. Tomlinson, *The North Eastern Railway: Its Rise and Development* (Newcastle; Andrew Reid, 1915)

C.R. Clinker, *The Light Railway Orders* (Avon Anglia, 1977)

E. Mason, *The Lancashire & Yorkshire Railway in the Twentieth Century* (Ian Allan, 1954)

G. Dunstan, *The Rivers of Axholme* (1858)

W.B. Stonehouse, *The History and Topography of the Isle of Axholme* (London; Longman, Rees & Orme & Co., 1839)

Read, *History of the Isle of Axholme* (1858)

T.T. Sutcliffe, *Lancashire & Yorkshire Railway Traffic Control Maps, Volume 4* (Author, 1984)

L. Bedale, *Station Master* (Turntable Enterprises, 1976)

The Isle of Axholme & Goole & Marshland Joint Railways, *The Locomotive Magazine* (15th March, 1907)

The following Journals and Newspapers:- *Railway Magazine, Railway World, The Railway Observer*, (Railway Correspondence and Travel Society), *Railway Times, The Engineer, The Railway Engineer, Branch line News, The Epworth Bells, The Crowle Advertiser, The Goole Times, The Doncaster Gazette, The Lindsey & Lincolnshire Star, The Yorkshire Evening Post*.

Lastly:-Acts for Railway Companies, Bradshaw's Timetables, Railway Clearing House Maps, Board Minutes of the AJR. Complete set of the Officers Joint Committee minutes of the AJR. Minutes of the Goole and Marshland Light Railway. Many NER and LNER official documents supplied by Ken Plant. LNER Appendices to the Working Timetables. Many documents supplied by Fisons Ltd PLC.

Another picture from local photographer J. Bottomley, marked on the back 'Epworth Cutting'. The scene depicts contractor's wagons being loaded by the steam crane (in the distance) in a cutting and the stationary engine working a hoist to lift spoil onto the wagons on the higher level, to be hauled away by the diminutive locomotive.

Courtesy Ron Shirley

Introduction

My initial interest in the Axholme Joint Railway (AJR) was kindled by stumbling across and reading the late Geoffrey Oates' booklet on the line. Although well written, it seemed only to 'précis' the line's history and it was apparent that there was much more to be discovered about the area, construction and operation of the AJR; so a file was opened some five years ago.

A stroke of luck came when a chance meeting was made with Mr Gee, who was associated with Fisons Ltd PLC and the Peat Industry. This provided me with enormous amounts of documentation on the AJR, especially relating to the early years of the line. The usual research sources were visited and other contacts made, and so an interesting story began to unfold. However, during one of my visits to the 'Isle', the people of the area became very interested in the project and opened up their hearts and photograph albums to me, this produced a wealth of superb pictures that authors dream about, in fact so many that only about half appear in this book. Many personal reminiscences were also collected to add to the ever thickening files! During this visit, the trackbed of the AJR was walked (where possible) and photographed so that a detailed personal account of the route could be incorporated.

Historically, the book would not have been completed without the endless copies of NER/LNER/L&YR and BR documentation, including plans, drawings, contracts, working agreements etc. supplied by Ken Plant, who also checked and corrected my efforts. Trevor Kay managed to unearth the original contractors' drawings for parts of the line and Noel Coates provided the facts on the signalling and operational details.

So after five years of studying, writing and re-writing from the wealth of material available, this tribute to the Railway of the Isle, (the AJR) was born. I hope you, the reader, will find the story presented within these pages as absorbing as I did whilst writing. Although the AJR's life was relatively short (as railways go), being born at the turn of the century and closing in the 1960s, I consider the story is an important one in our country's railway's history.

Finally many of the documents that came to light are unusual, so extracts have been included 'facsimile' to allow the reader the chance to study them in depth, rather than just being 'referred to', as tends to be the norm.

Colin Judge, 1994

Front Endpaper: One of the many banners constructed for the opening of the railway at Epworth in 1905. *Courtesy Colin Ella*

Rear Endpaper: A view looking from Greenhill up towards the church at Haxey at the turn of the century. *Courtesy Ian Snell*

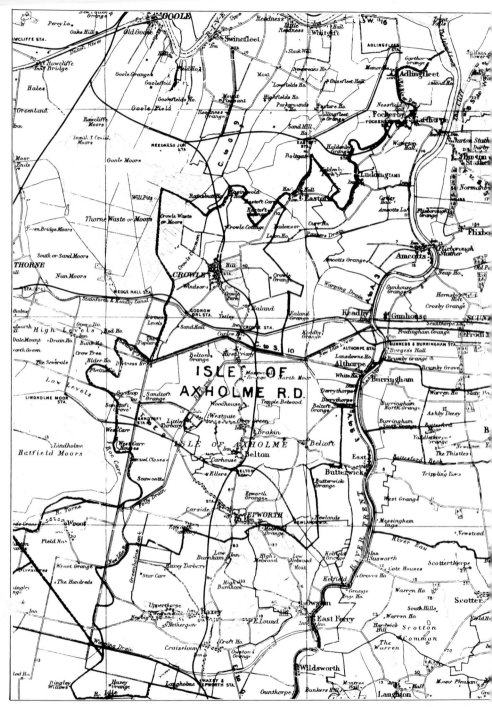

A copy of the original IOALR and G&MLR map showing the proposed branches to Adlingfleet station, Swinefleet station, Newlands station and Lindholme station plus two curves connecting the GCR line at Crowle to the IOALR.

Chapter One

In the Beginning

The Isle of Axholme, situated in the north-west region of South Humberside (previously the County of Lincolnshire), is an area of land lying to the west of the River Trent. It comprises around 38,000 acres and includes the parishes of Althorpe-with-Keadby, Belton, Crowle, Epworth, Haxey, Luddington, Owston, Amcotts, Eastoft, Wroot and Garthorpe. Axholme is an Isle due to the fact that it was (until the construction of the area drainage system) bordered by four rivers; namely the Don, Trent, Torne and Idle. Recorded in the introduction to the history of Axholme, *The Rivers of Axholme* is the derivation of the full name of Axholme. Possibly first recorded as 'Axeyholme' the *Ax* (meaning water) and given by the Celts; *Ey* (meaning island) possibly attributed to the Engles; and *Holme* (also meaning island), which is a Danish word. From this, one presumes the name has been changed in successive times of war and conquest, with each conqueror contributing an element to the name.

At one period almost the whole area was covered by a forest of oak, ash and conifer trees and modern investigations by geologists have revealed that this forest was literally drowned by general subsidence, the vegetation being preserved by a thick layer of quality peat. The rivers through the area are slow-flowing, resulting in considerable silting of their beds. Consequently, over the years, new channels or courses have been cut, making it difficult to ascertain the 'original' route of these rivers.

In 1626, King Charles I granted the 'level of Hatfield Chase' (lying to the west of the Isle) to Cornelius Vermuyden, a rich Dutch merchant. Instructions were given to drain the whole Chase (described as a badly-drained swamp). The result of the Dutch engineers' work and subsequent drainage has left the Isle of Axholme rich in soil and it is one of England's best agricultural areas. Most of the district is less than 50 feet above sea level and few hills or hillocks are visible, except around Haxey and Epworth where few are above 125 feet. The churches of the area are mainly sited on these hillocks to avoid the menace of flooding.

The town of Epworth is regarded as the capital of the Isle of Axholme, one of its celebrated occupants being Samuel Wesley, who was rector of Epworth. His son John was born in 1703 and later became the leader of Methodism. When he was refused permission to preach in his native church at Epworth, he once addressed the congregation standing on top of his father's tomb in the churchyard. Nowadays the Wesley Memorial Church is visited by Methodists from all over the world.

To the north of the Isle of Axholme is an area known as Marshland, this

1

being a low-lying area hemmed in on two sides by the rivers Ouse and Trent. In early days this area was constantly subject to flooding, but the banks and drains constructed alongside the waterways now control the problem. Again the area was rich in game, fish and wildfowl, thus satisfying the wants of early inhabitants.

The waters of the River Trent are strongly impregnated with 'earthy' particles termed 'warp'. The term warping means cutting a drain from the river, controlling it by sluice gates and then embanking and enclosing an area of land of anything up to 300 acres. Channels are then constructed from this warping drain to allow water to flood the area and so deposit the 'warp'. This is carried out repeatedly each year, finally building up levels to produce a first class soil for crops.

Marshland surrounds the villages of Adlingfleet, Fockerby, Haldenby, Ousefleet, Reedness, Swinefleet, Whitgift and the Yorkshire portion of Eastoft. It is interesting to note that several names end in 'fleet'. These derive from the many streams in the district which were called *fleot* by the Anglo Saxons. To distinguish these streams, personal names were added, hence Swinefleet, Ousefleet and Adlingfleet.

In the time of 'Railway Mania', there appeared to be a need for a line to connect these vast, richly agricultural areas and as the terrain was relatively flat it was not too long before proposals were being made. The farmers of the area had been pressing for 'rapid' transport for their products, but the railway builders had paid scant attention to their plight. The South Yorkshire Railway (later the Great Central) had followed the Stainforth & Keadby Canal, giving a railhead at Crowle, with its Doncaster to Keadby line offering a similar facility at Haxey.

The earliest known scheme for a railway to serve part of the Isle of Axholme was that of 1833, when the question of a line from London to York (and subsequently the north) was to run via Lincoln, Gainsborough and Selby. This line would have skirted parts of the Isle, but was finally rejected in favour of the present-day East Coast main line.

A further proposal, authorised but never constructed, was in the form of the Direct Northern Railway* from London to York, commencing at King's Cross (through Barnet) then on through Biggleswade, St Neots, Huntingdon, Peterborough, Stamford, Grantham, Newark, Lincoln, Gainsborough, Snaith and Selby to York. This would have passed through Haxey and then eastwards around Doncaster. The length was to have been 176 miles with a shares issue of 160,000 in 25 shilling shares.

In the next year (1846) the Great Northern Railway proposed its Isle of Axholme Extension Railway. This line would have run from Gainsborough, Haxey, Epworth, Crowle and on to Thorne, here dividing with the main line continuing to the York/Doncaster main line and also to Askern Junction on the Lancashire & Yorkshire Railway.

Railway Shareholder's Manual by Henry Tuck, 1846 and House of Lords Record office, ref. 1846/A21

Board of Trade, Session 1882.

HE TRAMWAYS ACT, 1870.

ISLE OF AXHOLME & MARSHLAND

RAMWAYS

Construction of Tramways in the Isle of Axholme, Tolls in respect thereof, Use of Steam or other Mechanical power.)

Notice is hereby given,

That application is intended to be made to the Board of Trade on or before the 23rd day of DECEMBER NEXT, under the provisions of the Tramways Act, 1870, for a Provisional Order to authorize and empower the promoters to lay down, construct, and maintain the several Tramways hereinafter described, or some, or one of them, or some part or parts thereof, respectively, with all necessary and proper rails, plates, sleepers, works, and conveniences connected therewith, that is to say :—

RAMWAY No. 1., in the Parishes of Haxey and Epworth, in the parts of Lindsey in the County of Lincoln, commencing at the Westernmost corner of a field in the Parish of Haxey, belonging to, and in the occupation of, John Brewitt Taylor, and situate partly on the Northern side of and abutting upon the Great Northern Railway Hotel at Haxey, and partly on the Northern side of Haxey Station Yard, of the Great Northern Railway, and which field abuts on the west side of the highway or main road leading from Misterton to Haxey, and passing thence to the said highway at a point opposite the North-East corner of the said field, along such highway through Craiselound. Haxey, and Low Burnham, to a point 2 chains or thereabouts, North of the South side of the Plough Inn at Low Burnham, and thence passing in and through lands belonging to William Taylor Hewitt, and Thomas Hewitt, and lands belonging to John Watkin, parallel to and abutting on the West side of the said highway and main road, for a distance of 31 chains or thereabouts, and passing thence into the said highway, or main road, to and into the Parish of Epworth, and there terminating on the said highway at the point where the occupation road divides the land owned and occupied by William Hurst, from the burial ground of the Epworth Burial Board.

TRAMWAY No. 2., in the Parish of Haxey, commencing by a junction with Tramway No. 1., at the point where Tramway No. 1. is described as entering the highway or main road, and passing in a southerly direction in front and on the South-West side of the Railway Station Hotel, at Haxey, thence into the Station Yard, and terminating at or near the East end of the Goods Shed of the Great Northern Railway, at Haxey Railway Station, aforesaid.

TRAMWAY No. 3., in the Parishes of Epworth, Belton, and Crowle, commencing at the point of termination of Tramway No. 1., and passing from thence along the highway from Epworth aforesaid to Crowle Wharf to through and into the following Parishes, Townships or Places, viz. :—Epworth, Belton, Churchtown, Braycton, Grey Green, Woodhouse, and Crowle, all in the parts of Lindsey in the County of Lincoln, and terminating at the Goods Yard of the Crowle Station of the Manchester, Sheffield & Lincolnshire Railway Company, on the Wharf of the Stable Siding at a point 2.5 chains from the end or termination of that siding.

A facsimile reproduction from the *Epworth Bells* of 19th November, 1881 of the proposed Tramways in the Isle of Axholme.

Also during 1846 a further railway was promoted by George Hudson, better known in railway history as the 'Railway King'. The Isle of Axholme, Gainsborough and York and North Midland Junction Railway was to commence at the port of Goole, passing through the townships lying to the east bank of the Trent and connecting the fertile Isle of Axholme (via Crowle, Haxey and Misterton) to Gainsborough, with a branch line to Selby. The published length was to have been 31 miles and a share issue of 12,000, 25 shilling shares was proposed. The Bill was surprisingly rejected by the House of Lords, even with the celebrated Robert Stephenson as one of the railway's engineers. It is interesting to note that it was exactly 50 years later that the Axholme Joint Railway from Haxey to Crowle was opened and constructed on a practically identical route as proposed by George Hudson.

The Great Eastern was very anxious at that time, to gain access to the Yorkshire coalfields (as well as the West Riding) and, in 1878 made proposals for a Great Eastern Northern Extension Railway. This would have taken a route from its present line to join the L&Y at Askern Junction, and would also have passed through part of the Isle of Axholme, but as before, the scheme failed.

However, before that, in 1874, the local Epworth newspaper *The Bells* made reference to the railways, with the heading, 'Suppose we get a Railway'. The article then continued reminding the reader that most railway stations in the area were at least one to two miles from the town or village they served so that 'when the day comes for Epworth to have a railway, that either a tramway will link the town to the station or that the rich railway companies will run the line through Haxey, Epworth and Belton, but in the meantime, if the tramway lines be laid, these will hasten the railways - and then the tramways and railways working together, will prove a blessing to the neighbourhood'.*

Several other abortive attempts were made at building a railway in the area and one worthy of a mention was a proposal in 1882 by the Isle of Axholme and Marshland Steam Tramway Co. Ltd[†] (registered on 5th June, 1882 with a capital of £80,000 in £10 shares).

It was to be a 3 ft 6 in. gauge tramway, running from Haxey station (on the Lincoln to Doncaster main line) to Crowle, following the route of the Gainsborough to Goole road; a short branch of 14 chains was to be constructed from Crowle High Street to the centre of the Market Place. The route mileage was to be 14 miles 19 chains of single track with eight passing loops *en route*, bringing the total track length to 14 miles 58 chains. The line was to be worked by 'animal, steam or mechanical power', subject to the full consent of the Board of Trade.

However on 27th April, 1883, an agreement was entered into between the

---

Epworth Bells, Saturday 6th June, 1874

[†]John William Denne Johnson, John Elwis, Richard Shaw Brundell and Thomas Henry Hovenden were listed as the promoters and proprietors of the Isle of Axholme and Marshland Steam Tramways.

Isle of Axholme and Marshland Steam Tramways and the Manchester, Sheffield and Lincolnshire Railway Co. to present a uniform front in opposing a further railway proposal for the area, namely the Goole, Epworth and Owston Railway.

The powers for this tramway were eventually taken over by the MS&LR in August 1883, which enabled this company to successfully oppose the Goole, Epworth and Owston Railway Act of 1882. This however was not welcomed by the local businessmen who received the news with 'surprise and bitterness', as the evidence presented had been overwhelming to the House of Lords Committee. The line was desperately needed to connect the areas of agriculture and industry to the nearest railway or canal, because at present everything was transported by wagon and horse. However one reporter closed his article by saying;

> . . . it is to be hoped, however, that the promoters will not be disheartened. Let them renew their efforts, and, as in the case of the East and West Yorkshire Union Railway, considerable success may attend their efforts on another occasion.

It was not long before the interested parties met and proposed the Isle of Axholme Railway Act, 1885 which was passed on the 25th June, 1885. This sanctioned the abandonment of the IOA&MST and authorised, for the first time, four railways especially for the area.

However, yet again this railway was abandoned without any construction taking place, by an Act of 30th April, 1888.

Another nine years passed and, in 1896, Parliament made provision for new railways in rural districts to be constructed under the Light Railways Act, thus allowing lines to be built under a Board of Trade order, alleviating the heavy costs incurred in Parliamentary dealings. There is little doubt the Goole & Marshland and the Isle of Axholme Railways were especially suited to this new Act.

The original 1896 promoters of the Goole and Marshland Light Railway were among the first to use the facilities offered by the new Light Railways Act. A public enquiry held at the Lowther Hotel, Goole, on Saturday 9th October, 1897 experienced little difficulty in recommending the proposed railway, with an estimated cost of £59,602.* The meeting before the Light Railway Commissioners (Colonel George F. Ottley Boughey RE, CSI and the Earl of Jersey presiding) made the order to the Board of Trade that the railway be built swiftly, and as the plan for this railway had been on ice for some time, that the promoters should act quickly to put their proposals before the Board of Trade. The Engineers stated that, other than several warping drains to cross, no significant engineering problems were involved. The promoting farmers' club stated that the average quantity of potatoes sent out yearly was

*Directors H.T. Bennett, B. Clegg, W. Coulman, F.J. Dupois, E.C. Foster and W. Halkon were all members of the Goole Farmers' Club, with G. Thompson becoming a further Director and H. Hobson, Secretary.

CHAPTER liv.

An Act for authorising the construction of Railways in the Isle of Axholme in the county of Lincoln to be called the Isle of Axholme Railway and for other purposes.

A.D. 1885.
——

[25th June 1885.]

WHEREAS the construction of the railways herein-after described would be of public and local advantage :

And whereas the persons herein-after named with others are willing to carry the undertaking into execution and it is expedient that they may be incorporated into a company and that the requisite powers be conferred upon them for that purpose :

And whereas by the Isle of Axholme and Marshland Tramways Order 1882 (herein-after referred to as " the Tramway Order ") confirmed by the Tramways Orders Confirmation (No. 2) Act 1882 certain promoters therein named (herein-after referred to as " the promoters ") were authorised to construct and maintain certain tramways and works therein described in the county of Lincoln (herein-after referred to as " the tramways ") and which tramways were to have commenced at or near Haxey in the county of Lincoln and proceeding in a northerly direction through Crowle to and terminating at Eastoft in the same county :

And whereas the railways herein-after described will pass through the same district as the tramways and will better accommodate the traffic of that district and when made will render the construction of the tramways unnecessary and the tramways if made could not successfully compete with these railways :

And whereas no part of the work authorised by the Tramway Order has been executed and none of the powers vested in the promoters have been exercised and it is expedient that the tramways should be abandoned and the money deposited by the promoters under the provisions of the Tramways Act 1870 should be paid to them :

And whereas plans and sections showing the lines and levels of the railways authorised by this Act and also books of reference

A.D. 1885.
——

containing the names of the owners and lessees or reputed owners and lessees and of the occupiers of the lands required or which may be taken for the purposes or under the powers of this Act were duly deposited with the clerk of the peace for the parts of Lindsey in the county of Lincoln and are herein-after respectively referred to as " the deposited plans sections and books of reference ":

And whereas the purposes of this Act cannot be effected without the authority of Parliament:

May it therefore please Your Majesty that it may be enacted and be it enacted by the Queen's most Excellent Majesty by and with the advice and consent of the Lords Spiritual and Temporal and Commons in this present Parliament assembled and by the authority of the same as follows:

Short title.

1. This Act may be cited as the Isle of Axholme Railway Act 1885.

Incorporation of Acts.

2. The Companies Clauses Consolidation Act 1845 Part I. (relating to cancellation and surrender of shares) and Part III. (relating to debenture stock) of the Companies Clauses Act 1863 as amended by the Companies Clauses Act 1869 the Lands Clauses Consolidation Acts 1845 1860 and 1869 as amended by the Lands Clauses (Umpire) Act 1883 the Railways Clauses Consolidation Act 1845 and Part I. (relating to construction of a railway) and Part III. (relating to working agreements) of the Railways Clauses Act 1863 are (except where expressly varied by this Act) incorporated with and form part of this Act.

Interpretation.

3. In this Act the several words and expressions to which meanings are assigned by the Acts wholly or partially incorporated herewith have the same respective meanings unless there be something in the subject or context repugnant to such construction the expression " the Company " means the Company incorporated by this Act the expressions " the railway " or " the railways " and " the undertaking " mean respectively the railways and the undertaking by this Act authorised For the purposes of this Act the expression " superior courts " or " court of competent jurisdiction " or any other like expression in this Act or any Act wholly or partially incorporated herewith shall be read and have effect as if the debt or demand with respect to which the expression is used were a simple contract debt and not a debt or demand created by statute.

Company incorporated.

4. John William Denne Johnson Thomas Harsley Carnochan and John Elwis and all other persons and corporations who have already subscribed to or shall hereafter become proprietors in the undertaking and their executors administrators successors and assigns respectively shall be and are hereby united into a company for the purpose of making and maintaining the railways and for other the A.D. 1885. purposes of this Act and for those purposes shall be and are hereby incorporated by the name of " The Isle of Axholme Railway Company " and by that name shall be a body corporate with perpetual succession and a common seal and with power to purchase take hold and dispose of lands and other property for the purposes of this Act.

5. Subject to the provisions of this Act the Company may make Power to and maintain in the lines and according to the levels shown on the make rail ways. deposited plans and sections the railways herein-after described with all necessary and convenient stations sidings junctions approaches bridges roads yards buildings communications and other works connected therewith and may enter upon take and use such of the lands delineated on the said plans and described in the deposited books of reference as may be required for that purpose   The railways herein-before referred to and authorised by this Act are :—

> Railway (No. 1.) 6 miles 6 furlongs and 9·25 chains in length commencing in the parish of Haxey in the county of Lincoln (parts of Lindsey) by a junction with the joint line of the Great Northern and Great Eastern Railway (Doncaster and Gainsboro' Line) near the Haxey Station and terminating in the parish of Belton in the said county at the south side of the public highway leading from Grey Green to Westgate.

> Railway (No. 2.) 2 miles 2 furlongs and 2·85 chains in length commencing in the said parish of Belton by a junction with Railway (No. 1) at the south side of the public highway leading from Grey Green to Westgate and terminating in the parish of Crowle in a field called Nettle Common or Eighteen Acres belonging or reputed to belong to George Robinson.

> Railway (No. 3.) 5 furlongs and 1·10 chains in length wholly in the said parish of Crowle commencing by a junction with Railway (No. 2) in the said field called Nettle Common or Eighteen Acres and terminating by a junction with the Manchester Sheffield and Lincolnshire Railway (Doncaster and Keadby Line) near the down platform of the Crowle Station on that railway.

> Railway (No. 4) 6 furlongs, 7·3 chains in length wholly in the said parish of Crowle commencing by a junction with Railway (No. 2) in the said field called Nettle Common or Eighteen Acres and terminating on the south side of Godknow Road leading from Crowle to Godknow Bridge

6. The capital of the Company shall be eighty-eight thousand Capital. pounds in eight thousand eight hundred shares of ten pounds each.

25,000 tons; the wheat, peas, oats, turnips, clover, hay and straw would bring the total produce available to 39,625 tons and there were 12,000 tons of peat moss litter also dispatched annually, giving a grand total of 51,625 tons of freight to move! Several members volunteered to give their land 'free' to hurry the construction.

On 16th August, 1898, the Goole and Marshland Light Railway Order, 1898 was confirmed (this being the 47th LRO for such railways to be granted) which authorised a start being made to its construction. The Engineers, Messrs Mammatt and White, were adopted and an agreement was entered into with Mr S.W. Meyer and Mr Isaac White* at the Board meeting of 2nd September, 1895 (chaired by W. Halkon), as contractors to the project, these representing the Yorkshire District Light Railway Syndicate. The LRO authorised four railways totalling 13 miles 62 chains of track and a share capital of £60,000 in £10 shares, with a further borrowing power of £20,000.

The line was to commence at a triangular junction with the NER Goole to Doncaster main line (*see original plans*) at a point about 2½ miles south-west of Goole and to run to Adlingfleet (Railways Nos. 1 and 4) via Eastoft (incidentally by the same route as was ultimately constructed to Fockerby). There were to be further branches to Swinefleet and Luddington (Railways Nos. 2 and 3 respectively). The LRO allowed five years for the line's construction and stipulated that the axle weight limit should not exceed 14 tons on any vehicle, engine or truck. It also stated that no tender engine could run tender foremost; an overall speed limit of 15 mph was to be imposed. At the same time as the LRO was being applied for, the promoters sought powers to construct a road 15 feet wide running alongside the north side of the track for a distance of two miles. It was shown that due to the shape of the fields and the various boundaries of the farms, a means of access from the very long and narrow strips of land to the railway running at their base, could only be given effectively by the proposed road. There being no objections to this proposal, the Commissioners approved the application.

The Isle of Axholme Light Railway was first mooted in 1897 with an application by T.J. Blaydes, J.H. Bletcher and E.Hirst,[†] for a light railway from Haxey station, where a junction was proposed with the Great Northern & Great Eastern Joint Railway, through Haxey, Epworth and Belton to a point near Crowle station. Here it passed over the Great Central line and a junction was proposed with this railway (to give access to Wharf sidings and the canal at Crowle), thence through Crowle to a proposed junction with the Goole & Marshland Light Railway also for two branches starting from a point between Epworth and Belton, one running west to Hatfield Moor and the other running east through a very fertile area to Newlands.

---

*Mr I.W. White for the Engineers, Mammatt and White stated the estimated cost to be £4,257 per mile or a total cost of £59,602 (*Railway Engineer* Nov. 1897)

[†]Other Directors included P.R. Meyer (brother of Sebastian Meyer and later Secretary of the North Lindsey Light Railway Company) G. Dunstan and others.

CHAPTER viii.

An Act for the abandonment of the Isle of Axholme Railway. [30th April 1888.]

A.D. 1888.

WHEREAS by the Isle of Axholme Railway Act 1885 (in this Act called "the Act of 1885") the Isle of Axholme Railway Company (in this Act called "the Company") were incorporated and empowered to make and maintain the railways in the Act of 1885 more fully described extending from Haxey to Crowle in the county of Lincoln and in this Act referred to as "the railways" and to raise a capital of £88,000 in shares and to borrow on mortgage any sum not exceeding £29,300:

48 & 49 Vict. cap. liv.

And whereas no part of the capital authorised by the Act of 1885 has been raised and none of the powers of that Act with respect to the purchase of land and the making of the railways have been exercised and it is expedient that the railways be abandoned and the affairs of the Company wound up and the Company dissolved:

And whereas the objects aforesaid cannot be effected without the authority of Parliament:

May it therefore please Your Majesty that it may be enacted and be it enacted by the Queen's most Excellent Majesty by and with the advice and consent of the Lords Spiritual and Temporal and Commons in this present Parliament assembled and by the authority of the same as follows:—

1. This Act may be cited as the Isle of Axholme Railway (Abandonment) Act 1888.

Short title.

2. The Company shall abandon the making of the railways and on and after the passing of this Act the Company shall except only as is by this Act otherwise expressly provided be absolutely freed and discharged from all obligations with respect to the making and maintaining of the railways.

Abandonment of railways.

3. The abandonment of the railways by the Company under the authority of this Act shall not prejudice or affect the right of the

Compensation for damage to land by

[*Price 3d.*]

The 'line plan' signed by Sebastian Meyer for the G&MLR. Note the station name for the terminus is 'Garthorpe' and the dotted line striking south for Crowle (the route of the IOALR).

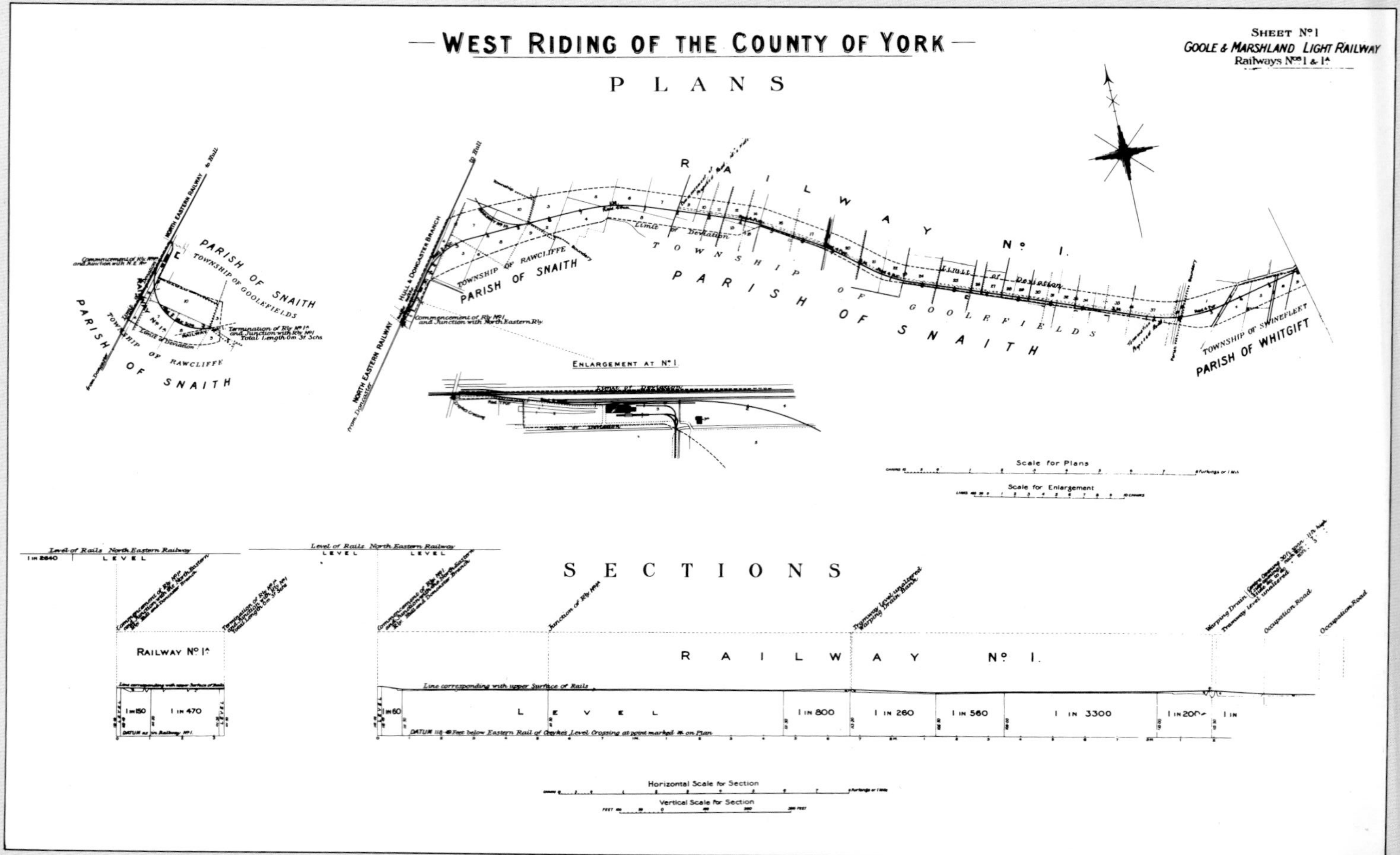

WEST RIDING OF THE COUNTY OF YORK
SHEET No. 1
GOOLE & MARSHLAND LIGHT RAILWAY
Railways Nos. 1 & 1a
PLANS
RAILWAY No. 1.
TOWNSHIP OF RAWCLIFFE
PARISH OF SNAITH
TOWNSHIP OF GOOLEFIELDS
PARISH OF SNAITH
TOWNSHIP OF SWINEFLEET
PARISH OF WHITGIFT
Limit of Deviation
NORTH EASTERN RAILWAY
HULL & DONCASTER BRANCH
to Hull
from Doncaster
Commencement of Rly No. 1 and Junction with North Eastern Rly.
Commencement of Rly No. 1a and Junction with N.E. Rly.
Termination of Rly No. 1a and Junction with Rly No. 1 Total Length 0m 3f 5chs
TOWNSHIP OF RAWCLIFFE
PARISH OF SNAITH
ENLARGEMENT AT No. 1
Scale for Plans
Scale for Enlargement
SECTIONS
Level of Rails North Eastern Railway
LEVEL
1 in 2640
RAILWAY No. 1a
Line corresponding with upper Surface of Rails
1 in 150
1 in 470
DATUM as on Railway No. 1.
Junction of Rly No. 1a
RAILWAY No. 1.
Line corresponding with upper Surface of Rails
1 in 60
LEVEL
1 in 800
1 in 260
1 in 560
1 in 3300
1 in 200
1 in
DATUM 118.49 Feet below Eastern Rail of Crayke's Level Crossing at point marked on Plan
Tramway level unaltered
Warping Drain Bank
Warping Drain
Tramway level unaltered
Occupation Road
Occupation Road
Horizontal Scale for Section
Vertical Scale for Section

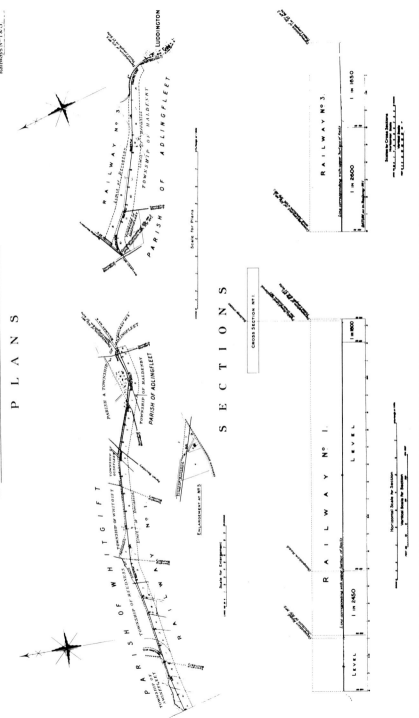

— WEST RIDING OF THE COUNTY OF YORK —

P L A N S

SHEET Nº 2

GOOLE & MARSHLAND LIGHT RAILWAY
Railways Nºˢ 1 & 3.

LUDDINGTON

RAILWAY Nº 3

PARISH OF ADLINGFLEET

TOWNSHIP OF HALDENBY

LIMIT OF DEVIATION

Scale for Plans

S E C T I O N S

CROSS SECTION Nº1

RAILWAY Nº 3.

1 in 2600

1 in 1650

DATUM of the Railway Nº1

Scales for Cross Sections
Horizontal Scale
Vertical Scale

PARISH OF WHITGIFT

TOWNSHIP OF WHITGIFT

TOWNSHIP OF REEDNESS

PARISH & TOWNSHIP OF ADLINGFLEET

TOWNSHIP OF OUSEFLEET

TOWNSHIP OF HALDENBY

PARISH OF ADLINGFLEET

RAILWAY Nº 1

ENLARGEMENT at Nº 5.

Scale for Enlargement

RAILWAY Nº 1.

LEVEL

LEVEL

1 in 2450

1 in 1800

Horizontal Scale for Section

Vertical Scale for Section

PARISH OF WHITGIFT

TOWNSHIP OF SWINEFLEET

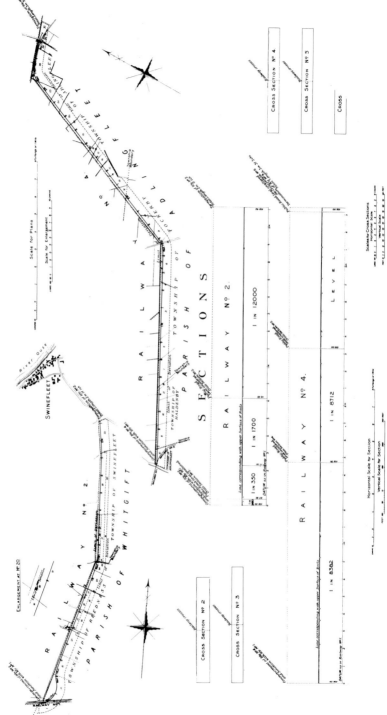

WEST RIDING OF THE COUNTY OF YORK

PLANS

SHEET Nº 3.
GOOLE & MARSHLAND LIGHT RAILWAY
Railways Nºs 2 & 4.

Scale for Plans

Scale for Enlargement

ENLARGEMENT AT Nº 20

PARISH OF WHITGIFT

TOWNSHIP OF SWINEFLEET

RAILWAY Nº 2

SWINEFLEET

RIVER OUSE

TOWNSHIP OF SWINEFLEET

TOWNSHIP OF HALDENBY

PARISH OF

RAILWAY Nº 4

TOWNSHIP OF

SECTIONS

RAILWAY Nº 2.

DATUM as on Railway Nº 1

Line corresponding with upper Surface of Rails

1 IN 350   1 IN 1700   1 IN 12000

RAILWAY Nº 4.

DATUM as on Railway Nº 1

Line corresponding with upper Surface of Rails

1 IN 8362   1 IN 8712   LEVEL

Horizontal Scale for Section

Vertical Scale for Section

Scales for Cross Sections
Horizontal Scale
Vertical Scale

CROSS SECTION Nº 2

CROSS SECTION Nº 3

CROSS SECTION Nº 4

CROSS SECTION Nº 5

CROSS

With the exception of level crossings, no part of the proposed railway would be on a public road. The total length of the line was to be just over 22 miles at a gauge of 4 ft 8½ in. and motive power was to be steam; the Engineers original estimate was £133,000 or £6,051 per mile. The capital authorised was to be £135,000 divided into 13,500 shares at £10 each, with a further borrowing power of £45,000. The line was to be mainly used for the conveyance of agricultural products, but also for iron-ore etc.*

On 4th February, 1898, the application came before the Light Railway Commissioners at the Moot Hall, Crowle and was heard by the Earl of Jersey, Mr G.A.R. Fitzgerald and Colonel Boughey. There was no general objection to the scheme and in fact local tradesmen and town people positively favoured the idea. At the close of the inquiry the Chairman stated that he expected the application would be granted.

The following submissions (amongst many others) were considered by the Commissioners;

The Sheffield & South Yorkshire Navigation Company, whose canal at Crowle would be crossed by the light railway, asked

    . . . that a swing bridge be constructed; should be left open so as to leave the

*A report in the *Lindsey and Lincolnshire Star* for 4th June, 1898 stated that 'The line starts at Goole, crosses the marshland to Crowle, where an effort is being made to revive the flax industry'

A view of the Market Cross, reproduced from a commercial postcard published by Barnes & Breeze, Epworth. The Mechanics' Institute is on the extreme right.

Author's Collection

navigation unobstructed except at such times as the bridge might be required for the passage of traffic along the railway; also that the retaining walls which served to guide the vessels into the narrower channel under the bridge should have a length of 40 yards instead of the proposed 20 yards; also that the Railway Company should provide and maintain proper lights on the bridge, not only during construction but in perpetuity; plus additionally, the Company should provide and use signals in foggy weather in order to show whether the bridge was open or not.

The Great Northern & Great Eastern Joint Committee asked that running powers over the Light Railway should be granted to them. However the Commissioners, in their wisdom, refused the GN&GE Joint Committee's request and also did not uphold the request for the canal bridge to be open constantly to the canal traffic.

The LRO was finally submitted to the Board of Trade on 27th July, 1898 and confirmed on 11th March, 1899* for the construction of 22 miles, 6 chains of railway which consisted of a line from Haxey station to join the Goole & Marshland Railway at Reedness Junction, with branches to Hatfield Moor (4½ miles) and Newlands (2 miles), both emanating from the main line near Epworth. Also as previously mentioned, a short spur siding (near Crowle) was allowed to give access to the Great Central Railway's siding at Crowle. The contracts for the construction of this railway were signed in May by Isaac White and Sebastian Meyer, who were already building the Goole & Marshland Light Railway, to the north of the area.

The independent existence of the Isle of Axholme and the Goole & Marshland Light Railways was indeed short lived. In fact right from the out-set it was agreed that the NER would work these two railways and that the NER would represent their interests at the Railway Clearing House.

By January 1900 negotiations had commenced between the two light rail-ways and the NER, and it was agreed that the latter would acquire both rail-ways. It is interesting to study the Heads of Agreement document drawn up between the NER and the G&MLR (dated 27th January, 1900) which is included in full in *Appendix One*.

It is obvious from the wording of this agreement that the NER saw great potential in the railways, both for agricultural traffic and also in routes for coal from the growing south Yorkshire coalfields.

Special meetings were called by the Isle of Axholme Light Railway Company and the Goole & Marshland Light Railway Company, the first on 2nd March, 1901 and the other on 6th March, 1901, both being advertised in *The Yorkshire Evening Post* on Monday 18th February, 1901 (*see opposite*).

The report of the Goole meeting was recorded in the *Railway Times* on

*At the first Annual General meeting held at the Reindeer Hotel, Doncaster, Mr. J.H. Bletcher presided as Chairman. Other Directors were J.T. Blaydes, E. Hirst, J. Waring (Secretary), Messrs Burtonshaw, Newburn and Everatt (solicitors to the Company) and Sebastian Meyer, representing the Engineers.

ISLE OF AXHOLME LIGHT RAILWAY COMPANY.

NOTICE IS HEREBY GIVEN, that a SPECIAL or EXTRAORDINARY GENERAL MEETING of the Proprietors of the Isle of Axholme Light Railway Company will be held at the DANUM ROOMS, DONCASTER, on SATURDAY, the 9th day of March, 1901, at half-past Three o'clock in the Afternoon, for the purpose of submitting to them for consideration and approval a proposed Bill in Parliament to be introduced:—

"A Bill to confer additional powers upon the North-Eastern Railway Company for the construction of new Railways and other works, and for the acquisition of additional lands, and upon that Company and the Midland and Lancashire and Yorkshire Railway Companies, in respect of their Normanton Station; and upon the Hull Joint Dock Committee for the execution of works and acquisition of lands; and for vesting in the Company the Goole and Marshland Light Railway and the Isle of Axholme Light Railway, and for other purposes."

Dated this 12th day of February, 1901.
JOHN HENRY BLETCHER, Chairman.
JOHN WARING, Secretary.

GOOLE AND MARSHLAND LIGHT RAILWAY COMPANY.

NOTICE IS HEREBY GIVEN, that a SPECIAL or EXTRAORDINARY GENERAL MEETING of the Proprietors of the Goole and Marshland Light Railway Company will be held at the LOWTHER HOTEL, GOOLE, on WEDNESDAY, the 6th day of March, 1901, at half-past Eleven o'clock in the Forenoon, for the purpose of submitting to them for consideration and approval a proposed Bill in Parliament to be introduced:—

"A Bill to confer additional powers upon the North-Eastern Railway Company for the construction of new Railways and other works, and the acquisition of additional lands, and upon that Company and the Midland and Lancashire and Yorkshire Railway Companies, in respect of their Normanton Station; and upon the Hull Joint Dock Committee for the execution of works and acquisition of lands; and for vesting in the Company the Goole and Marshland Light Railway and the Isle of Axholme Light Railway, and for other purposes."

Dated this 12th day of February, 1901.
WILLIAM HALKON, Chairman.
HARRY HOBSON, Secretary.

Above: Notice of meetings in *The Yorkshire Post.*

Right: Pre-IOALR advert showing the local 'busses' that connected Epworth with Haxey GN & GE Joint Railway station.
Courtesy Epworth Bells

9th March, 1901 and reads as follows:

> An extraordinary general meeting of the proprietors was held at Goole on
> Wednesday to consider the question of the sale of the undertaking to the North
> Eastern Railway Company. The purchase of the Goole and Marshland line will
> place the North Eastern Railway in direct communication, *via* the Goole and
> Doncaster branch of their line, with the Isle of Axholme Railway, and by means of
> the contemplated line from Haxey with the South Yorkshire coalfield. Mr W.
> Halkon, chairman of the directors, presided. Mr S.W. Meyer explained the negoti-
> ations which had been taking place some time with the North Eastern Railway. He
> then stated that the terms of purchase had been arranged, and they would probably
> amount to £8,000 a mile. There was general approval to sell the undertaking, and it
> was unanimously resolved to approve the proposed Bill in Parliament, which con-
> fers the power of purchase.

About this time consideration was being given to another light railway in
the area (proposed in 1899), namely The Tickhill Light Railway. This was to
run from Tickhill to Haxey (on the Lincoln to Doncaster main line) with a
connection to the Isle of Axholme Light Railway at Haxey. Plans (*see page
124*) were drawn up for a 'fly-over bridge' to be constructed here, but this
was never seriously considered. After leaving Haxey, the line was to have
crossed the GN&GE Joint line at Bawtry (where a new junction was to be
built) before proceeding due west to the South Yorkshire Joint Line at
Tickhill. The scheme was confirmed by the BOT on 7th August, 1901. Again,
without delay, the NER saw the expanding potential of this area and proceeded to draw up an agreement to acquire this new railway. The running
powers were transferred to the GNR in 1908[*] by a further LRO.

Due to bad relationships between the GCR and the GNR over the South
Yorkshire Joint Line, only the Bawtry to Haxey section was built. Being only
eight miles of single line, it did not tap into the area of coal (the original purpose of its construction) so traffic was very limited. The line was opened for
freight traffic on 26th April, 1912, but the line never carried passengers.[†]

The goods depot at Misson (the intermediate station) was the prime
source of the agricultural and sand traffic which kept the line running.
Before the Grouping in 1923 (the exact date is not known) the section from
Misson to Haxey ceased operating, with the Bawtry to Misson section
remaining open as little more than a farm siding, and officially closing on 7th
December, 1964.[#]

The Lancashire and Yorkshire Railway was greatly interested in securing
lines into the south Yorkshire coalfields as it already operated most of the rail
traffic at Goole Docks. It was therefore not surprising that the NER entered

[*]Transferred to the GNR in 1907 and confirmed by LRO 4th November, 1908
[†]A 1913 memorandum between the GNR and the AJR proposed new exchange sidings
on the AJR. These were to be built by the GNR (cost £1,000 to the AJR) if the transfer
of goods from the Tickhill Light Railway to the AJR became a problem using the existing sidings at Haxey. The scheme was never implemented.
[#]Another date recorded as the 1st April, 1965 (*Railway Magazine*)

into Agreements with the L&YR and the two light railways on 14th March, 1902, finally being sealed on 11th June, 1902. These were scheduled to the NER Act of 1902, which received Royal Assent on 31st July, 1902, giving powers for the purchase of the Isle of Axholme and the Goole and Marshland Light Railways by the NE & L&Y Railways (Joint) with effect from 2nd October, 1901.

Various extracts from this Act are relevant to the history of the Axholme Joint Railway and are shown in *Appendix Two*.

The principal feature of this Act was to allow for joint access by these two major companies to the new coalfields. However, the promotion of the South Yorkshire Joint Line rendered it unnecessary for the NER and the L&YR to purchase the Tickhill Light Railway, and as previously stated the powers were transferred to the GNR in 1908. This resulted in the construction of a railway (goods only) by the GNR from Haxey station to their main line at Bawtry.

The G&MLR had been completed by the date of the joint acquisition and the purchase price was £73,500. However the IOALR had only just started and this was bought for only £27,500.

So the new venture was born: the Axholme Joint Railway (NE and L&Y Joint) with a committee of three Directors from each of the joint owners with the chairmanship alternating yearly. The railway was destined to survive under this title for 45 years.

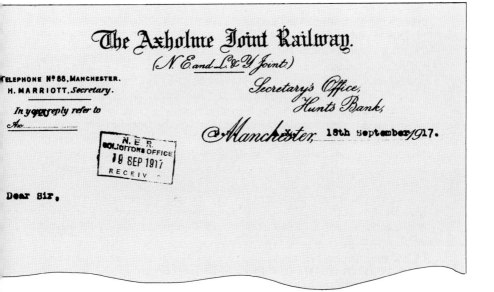

Eastoft Hall, the residence of Mr William Halkon, Chairman of the G&MLR. He died in 1923 at the age of 79 years. In 1983, the ceremonial spade (*see page 22*) was used unsuccessfully by burglars as a jemmy to try and open the safe in the house.

Courtesy Mrs S.J. Bradwell

Reproduced from the family album of the Halkon family, this gathering is reputedly carrying out the cutting of the sod for the Goole and Marshland Light Railway near Eastoft on 22nd September, 1898. William Halkon is seen second from the right.

Courtesy Mrs S.J. Bradwell

Chapter Two

Construction of the Light Railways
and Early Operations

The Goole and Marshland Light Railway

The G&MLR did not lose much time before commencing construction of its railway and the ceremony of cutting the first sod was carried out by Mr William Halkon, the Chairman, on 22nd September, 1898. The local Crowle newspaper reported as follows:

A large gathering of agriculturists and others interested in the promotion of the Goole and Marshland Light Railway, attended at Mr Bramhill's farm, Bolt-gate, Eastoft, Goole, on Sept. 22nd, to witness the cutting of the first sod for the new line, which is to be immediately constructed. The final sanction of the Board of Trade to the construction of the line was received some weeks ago, and the contracts for the work have already been let, and operations will be immediately commenced. The line, which will effect a junction with the North Eastern Railway line between Goole and Thorne at Creyke's Sidings on Goole Moor, will comprise five lines of rails, giving communication to Swinefleet, Reedness, Eastoft, Adlingfleet, and Garthorpe, is a total of 13½ miles. The authorised capital of the company, of which Mr William Halkon is the chairman, is £63,000, and it is estimated that £59,600 will be absorbed in construction. The land is for the most part level, and presents no serious engineering difficulties. Several warping drains have to be crossed, but, with the exception of the Swinefleet drain, they are of no great importance. The area which will be served, roughly speaking, stretches from the North Eastern Railway to the Trent, with a line running north of Thorne to Eastoft and Garthorpe for an irregular southern boundary, and the River Ouse for a northern boundary. The area is estimated to contain 25,000 acres, of which 15,000 are arable land, producing wheat and some of the finest potatoes in the land; 4,000 is grass land, and the balance is taken up by public thoroughfares and private roads. At the inquiry which the Earl of Jersey held last year, it was stated that the annual produce of the locality which had to be carted to Goole and Crowle Wharf stations was 51,000 tons, including the extensive traffic from the Goole Peat Moss Litter Works, and the return carriage for coal, manure, and so forth was 20,000, an amount which it is anticipated will be greatly increased when the railway is constructed, especially as through communication will be established with the Axholme Light Railway, a scheme which has already met with the approval of the Light Railway Commissioners. The engineers for the line are Messrs Mammatt and White, Leeds, and Mr W.S. Meyer, Leeds, the solicitors being Messrs England and Son, Goole, while Mr H Hobson and Mr W Everatt have acted as secretaries to the committee of the Goole Farmers' Club, which has promoted the line.
  At the outset of the proceedings Mr Meyer on behalf of the contractors, presented Mr Halkon with a beautiful spade with which to turn the first sod. In making the presentation Mr Meyer remarked that he believed the line was calculated to prove very successful. They had abandoned the original intention of light rails, and they were now going to make the rails and the line heavy enough to admit of the North-

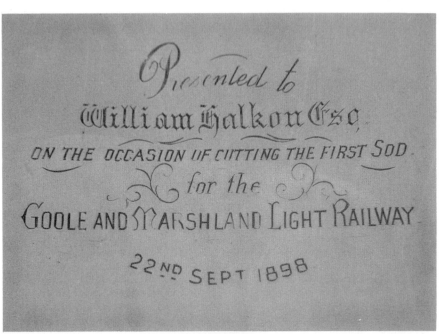

Presented to William Halkon Esq, on the occasion of cutting the first sod for the Goole and Marshland Light Railway 22nd Sept 1898

A close up of the inscription on the ceremonial spade used in cutting the first sod on the G&MLR.
Courtesy Ron Shipley

Mr Gordon Halkon of Eastoft, owner of the special spade that his father, the late William Halkon had used to dig the first sod of the G&MLR on 22nd September, 1898.
Courtesy Ron Shipley

Eastern trains running on it.

Mr Halkon then performed the task which he had been invited to discharge, and afterwards made a brief speech, in which he expressed a strong opinion that the line would be of great benefit to the neighbourhood. It was really wonderful how they had survived so long without a railway. There was no district which yielded more produce than Marshland, so that it was possible for a light railway to pay, it would assuredly pay in that district. (*Applause.*)

Subsequently an adjournment was made to the farmhouse, where various toasts were honoured, including that of 'Success to the Goole and Marshland Line', 'the Isle of Axholme Line', and 'The Officials', &c. It was stated during proceedings that this line would connect with the Isle of Axholme line, and afford through communication between Goole and Haxey.

The construction commenced on a relatively 'easy' railway to build, being almost level throughout its length.

At a shareholders' meeting in February 1899 the first Directors[*] of the G&MLR were confirmed, and it was reported that the Heads of Agreement had been drawn up with the NER. At the first Directors' meeting, held later that month it was reported that work amounting to over £1,000 had already been carried out (with request for payment from the contractors, White and Meyer), and that the signal box and signals at Marshland Junction had been constructed.[†]

The junction concerned had initially been disputed by the NER and several meetings took place between the contractors and the Traffic Committee of the NER, culminating in a letter from the latter on 15th December, 1898 stating that they had at last agreed and that the cost of the signalling and the cabin would be £784. The extra land needed (outside the existing NER boundary) would be £346 with the G&MLR paying both amounts, plus also the costs of the staff required to operate the signal cabin. A memorandum of 9th January, 1899 stated that the NER would lay the track from the junction to the points at the north end of the 'through' shunt on the G&MLR.

An award of 1,000 fully paid £1 shares was made to White and Meyer in payment for work performed, with further personal issues promised later in the year. During July 1899, shares worth £3,500 were allotted to the Yorkshire District Light Railways Syndicate (Meyer's company) in payment for more work completed. Further debentures for £5,000 (at 4 per cent) were issued to the contractors in September 1899, redeemable in a five year period. The first recorded Traffic Manager for the line was Philip Robert Meyer (relative of S. Meyer), who was paid a salary of £100 per year.

The line was constructed fairly rapidly and opened for goods traffic from Marshland Junction to Reedness Junction on 8th January, 1900. Later in the year, on 26th June, 1900, the railway ran a special Director's train, comprising

---

[*]W. Halkon(Chairman), Clegg, Bennett, Foster, Thompson and Coulman, with Harry Hobson as Company Secretary.

[†]The Agreement for this junction dated 16th February, 1899 provided for an Annual Rent of £5, payable by the G&MLR to the NER on the first day of January.

two open wagons (referred to as coaches in the newspaper reports) hauled by locomotive *Halkon*, to inspect the line as far as it had been laid to Eastoft station. The *Epworth Bells* carried the following report;

> The directors and committee of the Goole and Marshland Light Railway on Tuesday made a tour of inspection of their new line, and also had a trial run on the partly completed Isle of Axholme line, which has now reached Crowle. Starting shortly before noon from the Goole Fields Junction, where the Marshland line joins the Great Eastern Railway, the new engine, *Halkon* (named after the chairman of the directors), with two carriages, conveyed the company at a rattling speed. The trip was conducted by Mr Johnson, manager for the contractors. The most important feature of the line inspected was the steel bridge, 120 feet wide which spans the Warpings Drain near Reedness Junction. At Reedness station the party alighted for luncheon, afterwards continuing the journey to the extremity of the line (Eastoft), stopping at each station on the road. At the peat works, where the Isle of Axholme Railway joins, the train was diverted for the first trial run to Crowle, where the company was met by Mr J. Waring (the secretary to the Isle of Axholme Light Railway Company), and Mr A.W. Cundall (Messrs Burtonshaw and Cundall), joint solicitors to the Company. Refreshments were served at the Darby and Joan Hotel, where a short toast list was gone through. Col Thompson proposed the health of the Chairman, Secretary and committee of the Marshland Railway. He acknowledged the service of the Goole Chamber of Agriculture, which, he said, had proved a very tower of strength from the commencement of the scheme. A few years ago none would have thought there would ever be a railway through the Isle and Marshland, but thanks to combination this big undertaking had been achieved. In a few years those living in the district would see a wonderful success. Up-to-date the traffic on the Marshland line had been enormous, and he hoped the Isle of Axholme line, when completed, would likewise be supported. After being photographed in front of the engine the party commenced the homeward journey.

In December 1900, a survey of the G&MLR was carried out for George Gibb, the General Manager of the NER at York (by their Southern Division Engineer, Mr H. Copperthwaite) prior to the NER's purchase and his report is included in full:

York
10th December, 1900

My dear Sir,

GOOLE AND MARSHLAND RAILWAY

From the junction with the Hull & Doncaster branch to Luddington station, the line is now open and goods traffic being worked, and it is expected that the line will be laid to Garthorpe* in about three weeks. Many things, however, remain still to be done, and in the event of the railway being taken over by the North Eastern Railway Coy. the following matters should be required:-

The stations at Reedness Junction, Luddington and Garthorpe should, *mutatis mutandis*, be finished after the plan of the Eastoft Station, with proper sidings, wharves, roads, weighing machines, offices, and station masters' houses with garden ground attached.

---

*Named Fockerby station later.

All the carting roads should be properly formed with 6 inches of pitched stone, covered by 6 inches of metal (say) Belgian granite, broken to 2 inch sizes, and the whole rolled down with the steam roller. About half the line is unfenced; this must be completed with creosoted Baltic pine, similar in sizes and quality to that already put down.

Side drains 18 in. x 12 in. must be cut three feet within the fences for the whole length of the line where sufficient drains do not already exist.

Many of the culverts and drains across the Railway are too short, and should be lengthened and the pipe ends protected with brickwork or stone-pitching.

The Tramway from the Goole Peat Moss Works which crosses the line should be provided with gates and protective points.

All buildings and houses should be built with damp proof courses, and be erected according to the plans furnished to Mr Cudworth.

Public Road level crossings must be provided with the usual gates and signals.

Occupation level crossings must have the usual gates with locks and keys, and the crossings must be formed with old sleepers laid between the rails, and for at least two sleepers in width on each side outside the rails.

Between Eastoft and Reedness the land appeared to be too narrow for two lines of way, and in fencing, sufficient should be taken in.

Reedness Junction appears the most suitable place for locomotive water supply, and here a tank to contain not less than 5,000 gallons should be erected over an engine house and tool house: the pump to be of sufficient power to fill the tank in two hours, and to be properly fitted up and connected. It is suggested that a petroleum gas-engine should be supplied to work the pump, and that two water cranes be provided, one for the main line, and one in the station sidings.

All ditches should be dug with slopes of 1½ to 1.

At present the rail points are only fitted with two stretcher rods; three should be provided and fitted.

As to signalling nothing has been done. I think Reedness Junction should be made a block station and signalled in the manner usual for an ordinary Railway. The line from Reedness Junction to Garthorpe, if worked on the single engine system, will not require any signalling, but for this and any other portion of the line, any requirements of the Board of Trade must be carried out at the cost of the Goole & Marshland Company.

Lifting cranes may not be necessary.

Before the line is taken over by the North Eastern Company, it should be inspected and passed by an Engineer of that Company, and final payment made on his certificate.

Yours faithfully,
H. COPPERTHWAITE

George S. Gibb Esq.　　　　　　　　　　　　　　　　　　　　　YORK.

The report and accounts for the G&MLR for the year ending 31st December, 1900 were submitted to the half-yearly General Meeting of the shareholders held at the Lowther Hotel, Goole on 27th February, 1901. Shareholders were told that the works on the railway had commenced in February 1899, and that since then substantial progress had been made by the contractors. The accounts showed that of the authorised £60,000 share

The Goole and Marshland Light Railway Company.

Report and Accounts

FOR THE

Year Ending December 31st, 1900.

THE GOOLE AND MARSHLAND LIGHT RAILWAY.

Notice is Hereby Given, that the Ordinary HALF-YEARLY GENERAL MEETING of the Goole and Marshland Light Railway Company will be held at the Lowther Hotel, Goole, on WEDNESDAY, the 27th day of February, 1901, at 11-30 o'clock in the Forenoon, for the transaction of the General Business of the said Company.

WILLIAM HALKON,

Chairman.

HARRY HOBSON,

Secretary.

William Halkon

SWINEFLEET, FEBRUARY, 1901.

ROBINSON & SON, Printers, 49½, Briggate, Leeds.

This facsimile of the G&MLR Report and Accounts is personally signed by the Chairman, William Halkon.

The Goole & Marshland Light Railway Company.

Directors.

WILLIAM HALKON, Esq., Fockerby, Goole, Chairman.
HERBERT THOMAS BENNETT, Esq., Goole.
BENJAMIN CLEGG, Esq., Adlingfleet Grange, Goole.
WILLIAM COULMAN, Esq., Eastoft Hall, Goole.
EDWARD CLARK FOSTER, Esq., Waterton Hall, Goole.
GEORGE THOMPSON, Esq., Field House, Goole.

Report of the Directors

To be submitted to the Proprietors at the HALF-YEARLY GENERAL MEETING, to be held at the LOWTHER HOTEL, GOOLE, on WEDNESDAY, the 27th day of FEBRUARY, 1901.

1.—The Accounts of the Company for the Year ending the 3 st day of December, 1900, prepared in the form required by Statute, are annexed.

2.—The Works of the Railway were commenced in February, 1899, and since then substantial progress has been made by the Contractors.

WILLIAM HALKON,

Chairman.

SWINEFLEET,
GOOLE, 14th February, 1901.

The Goole & Marshland Light Railway Company

Year ending 31st December, 1900.

No. 1.—Statement of Capital Authorised and Created by the Company.

Acts of Parliament or Certificates of the Board of Trade.	Capital Authorised.			Capital Created or Sanctioned.			Balance.		
	Stock and Shares.	Loans.	Total.	Stock and Shares.	Loans.	Total.	Stock and Shares.	Loans.	Total.
	£	£	£	£	£	£	£	£	£
The Goole and Marshland Light Railways Order, 1898, Sections 45 and 57	60,000	20,000	80,000	60,000	20,000	80,000	—	—	—

No. 2.—Statement of Stock and Share Capital created, shewing the proportion received.

Description.	Amount Created.	Amount Received.	Calls in Arrears.	Amount Uncalled.	Amount Unissued.
	£	£	£	£	£
Shares ...	60,000	45,000	—	—	15,000

No. 3.—Capital Raised by Loans and Debenture Stock.

	Raised by issue of Debenture Stock at 4 per cent.		
	£	s.	d.
Existing at 31st December, 1900	13,800	0	0
Existing at 31st December, 1899	13,800	0	0
Increase	—	—	—
Decrease	—	—	—
Total amount authorised to be raised by Loans and by Debenture Stock in respect of Capital created, as per statement No. 1	20,000	0	0
Total amount raised by Loans and by Debenture Stock, as above	13,800	0	0
Balance, being available Borrowing Power	6,200	0	0

No. 4. Receipts and Expenditure on Capital Account.

	Amount Expended to 31st December, 1899.			Amount Expended during Year ending 31st December, 1900.			TOTAL.		
	£	s.	d.	£	s.	d.	£	s.	d.
Dr. To Expenditure—									
On Lines in course of construction	21,591	11	7	37,903	1	3	59,494	12	10
							59,494	12	10

	Amount Received to 31st December, 1899.			Amount Received during Year ending 31st December, 1900.			TOTAL.		
	£	s.	d.	£	s.	d.	£	s.	d.
Cr. By Receipts—									
Shares as per Account No. 2	21,500	0	0	23,500	0	0	45,000	0	0
Debenture Stock, as per Account No. 3							13,800	0	0
By Balance							694	12	10
							59,494	12	10

No. 5.—Details of Capital Expenditure, Year ending 31st December, 1900.

Lines in Course of Construction—	£	s.	d.
Construction of Railways	37,300	0	0
Printing and Stationery	2	7	11
Miscellaneous Expenditure	30	0	0
Directors' Fees	92	10	0
Salaries and Wages	183	6	8
Auditors' Fees...	1	1	0
Law Charges	195	5	0
Rates	4	4	2
Debenture Interest	95	0	0
Rent Charges	11	17	6
	37,915	12	3
Less Bank Interest	12	11	0
Total Expenditure	37,903	1	3

No. 7.—Estimate of further Expenditure on Capital Account.

	Further Expenditure.		
	During the Year ending 31st December, 1901. £	In subsequent Half-Years.	
Lines in course of Construction, Equipment, &c.	12,000	Uncertain.	Uncertain.
Total Estimate further Expenditure of Capital			Uncertain.

No. 8.—Capital Powers and other Assets available to meet further Expenditure as per Account No. 7.

	£	s.	d.
Share Capital created, but not yet received, as per Account No. 2	15,000	0	0
Borrowing powers, as per account No. 3	6,200	0	0
	21,200	0	0
Less Balance of Capital Account, as per statement No. 4	694	12	10
	20,505	7	2

No. 13.—General Balance Sheet.

To Sundry Outstanding Accounts	£	s.	d.		£	s.	d.
	744	16	5	By Cash at Bankers	50	3	7
				By Capital Account—Balance as per Account No. 4 ...	694	12	10
	744	16	5		744	16	5

WILLIAM HALKON, Chairman.
HARRY HOBSON, Secretary.

Auditors' Certificate.

We hereby Certify that the Accounts proposed to be issued contain a full and true statement of affairs of the Company.

GEO. WM. TOWNEND, C.A.,
JOSEPH H. GLOVER, A.S.A.A., } Auditors.

N.B.—Forms Nos. 6, 9, 10, 11, 12, 14, and 15 Scheduled to the 31 and 32, Vic., Cap. 119, have been omitted, as they are not at present applicable to this Company.

Swinefleet, 14th February, 1901.

capital, only £45,000 had been issued. An additional sum of £13,800 had been raised by the issue of Debenture Stock. Expenditure on the line in course of the construction had been £21,591 11s. 7d. (up to 31st December, 1899) and £37,903 1s. 3d. during 1900 which broke down as shown in the preceding fac-simile reproduction of the Accounts:

The balance sheet showed that the company had just £50 3s. 7d. at the bank; not a healthy situation when the line was nowhere near being complete.

A serious collision occurred on Friday night, 4th January, 1901 between the two contractor's locomotives *Halkon* and *Elgie*. It was a terrible night, with thick fog laying between Reedness and Eastoft, on the Fockerby line. *Elgie* running light engine collided head-on (near to Eastoft) with *Halkon*, which was in charge of a goods train consisting of three ballast wagons and four open goods wagons. Both engines were badly damaged. The crew of *Halkon* jumped clear before the impact and helped in the rescue of driver Hemsworth and his stoker who were trapped in *Elgie's* cab, both badly scalded from the burst boiler tubes. The story relates that they were carried to a nearby farmhouse and early next day taken by farm cart the seven miles to Goole hospital; one can imagine the journey! Mr Hemsworth unfortunately died at noon on the same day without regaining consciousness, but the fireman lived for a few days before he to succumbed to his burns.

The driver of *Elgie* was blamed for the accident and a verdict of accidental death was recorded at the subsequent inquiry.

A full list of all accidents between 1905 and 1916 is included in *Appendix Seven*.

At a Board meeting of the NER at York on 1st March, 1901, the General Manager reported,

The negotiations for the purchase of the G&MLR are now complete. The railway consists of 8 miles 73 chains of line, as shown in the plan submitted and the price arranged for the undertaking is £73,500 or £8,246 per mile.

The works have been thoroughly inspected by Mr Copperthwaite who has set out in memoranda, dated 10th December, 1901, a schedule of everything that remains to be done to complete the railway for traffic and the Light Railway Company have covenanted that they will, before the date of transfer, complete the works. The agreement having been submitted in duplicate, resolved . . .

On 26th June, 1901 a further special train was organised hauled again by locomotive *Halkon* but this time pulling two first class carriages and one open truck.

The Crowle Advertiser reported:

On Thursday afternoon, a large gathering of the most important landowners in the Isle and Marshland, and the best farmers in England, took place at the Darby & Joan

The Directors' Special train which ran over the G&MLR on 26th June, 1901. It is seen here at Eastoft station with 0-6-0 Manning, Wardle locomotive *Halkon* and dignitaries posing for the camera. Note the open wagon coupled to the two first class carriages.

Courtesy H. Garside, Goole

J. Bottomley's series of masterpieces continue with this scene capturing the 0-6-0 locomotive *Elgie* standing on the newly constructed steel bridge over Swinefleet Warping Drain near Reedness Junction on the G&MLR. The photograph carries the inscription 'The Artistic Touring Photographic Company, Arthur Vivian, Manager, 1900'.

Courtesy Mrs S.J. Bradwell

Hotel, Crowle, in response to a cordial invitation from the directors of the Goole and Marshland Light Railway, who also invited the directors and friends of the Isle Railway to meet them, and join in a tour of inspection of the two lines. The day was most propitious for the occasion, and over 50 gentlemen took advantage of the trip, which proved to be in every way enjoyable. It is just about a year ago that the esteemed secretary, Mr H Hobson, issued invitations for a similar trip, and since that time many improvements have been made. The same engine *Halkon* (named after the Chairman of Directors), was in readiness at Reedness Junction, and two first-class carriages and an open compartment behind were provided for the party. A goodly number entrained here, and the journey commenced, calls having been made at all stations on the line for the purpose of taking on board expected passengers. When the full complement had been picked up, the train sped away to Creyke siding, and from there the inspection commenced, not only of the line, but of the crops. At Garthorpe, a pause was made for the purpose of holding a short 'discussion' at the Bay Horse Hotel, after which the journey resumed, and Crowle was the final landing stage. The inspection gave the utmost satisfaction, the permanent way being remarkably good, owing to the large amount of traffic that had been dealt with during the past year. On alighting from the carriages, the company adjourned to the Darby & Joan Hotel, where Hostess Cranidge had awaiting them a delightful *recherché* repast, at which all seasonal delicacies were in evidence. The tables looked cool and refreshing, they being very tastefully adorned with choice plants and flowers, lending a charming effect to the whole. Hostess Cranidge fully upheld the prestige she has gained for her first-class catering, and her forethought in providing cooling and very palatable salads, &c., (for the day was warm), was appreciated by all. After dinner, when the goblets had been handed round, the Chairman made a few appropriate remarks about the inspection, and in doing so, expressed a hope that all had passed an enjoyable time. It gave him the greatest pleasure to meet such important body of gentlemen, and he hoped they would live long to enjoy the fruits of their labours, and the benefits the Light Railway would confer on them. 'Success to the Goole and Marshland and Isle of Axholme Light Railways' was then enthusiastically honoured. In complimentary terms Mr Yewdall proposed 'The health of the Directors and Secretaries of both Railways' and an able response was made by Mr Halkon. In proposing the health of 'The Visitors', who comprised the leading farmers of the district, Mr W Brunyee made pleasing allusions to their presence that day. It had indeed been a 'festival', and they would all agree that the impressions received that day portended a bright and successful future for the Light Railways. The Directors were thanked on behalf of the visitors for their kind invitation, which had proved so pleasureable to all. The company then walked down to the station, where the *Halkon* was soon in attendance. The open compartment was freely patronized, and about 6 pm Stationmaster Watkin dispatched the express on its homeward journey.

As previously mentioned in *Chapter One*, the special meeting of proprietors was held on 6th March, 1901 at the Lowther Hotel, Goole where it was unanimously agreed to sell the railway to the NER; thus ended the short-lived existence of the Goole and Marshland Light Railway.

The Isle of Axholme Light Railway

The Isle of Axholme Light Railway, unlike its northern neighbour, made much of the occasion of cutting the first sod at Epworth (as can been seen from the accompanying photographs).

The *Epworth Bells* for Saturday 22nd July, 1899 included the following lengthy report which captures the day's activities well:

Epworth is not likely soon to forget the events of Thursday, for they were without parallel in the history of the old historic town. Never before, in the memory of the oldest inhabitant, has there been such high carnival as on that day. A railway through the Isle is the millennium for which the inhabitants of this district have been looking for close on half-century, and almost every body laid their work aside and took part in the proceedings. Not only was the entire populace of Epworth *en fete*, but visitors poured in from all parts of the Isle, and added to the busy appearance of the streets. The town was gaily decorated; bunting was displayed everywhere, flags fluttering from cords hung high aloft across the streets and from windows, while there were quite a number of triumphal arches, which gave evidence of a considerable amount of enthusiasm, skill, and hard work on the part of those responsible for their erection. They all bore mottoes indicative for the most part of the general feeling of the inhabitants. One very elaborate design of this description was opposite Mr W. Maw's. It was the work of local artist, Mr S. Hudson, and represented a North-Eastern engine steaming to Epworth station and drawing trucks laden with coal from South Carr colliery, upon each of which was a separate letter, which when read one after the other spelled 'Welcome'. Other arches were erected at the Belton and Burnham road ends, near the *Epworth Bells* office, and near the Rectory. These bore the inscriptions, 'After fifty years, suspense ended - patience rewarded', 'Progress', 'Prosperity' and 'Success to Agriculture'. A large portrait of the late Mr Barnes, who was one of the most active of those progressive residents of the town who strove years ago to obtain railway facilities was displayed on one. This had been executed by Mr J. Bottomley. Over the triumphal arch leading into the field in which the first sod was to be cut were the appropriate words, 'The dawn of a New Era', while on another on the opposite side of the road was 'Success to our Work'.

One of the greatest difficulties - we might say the greatest difficulty - with which Isle of Axholme farmers have had to contend in the past has been their inability to get their crops on to the markets, and in return to be able to get a plentiful supply of manures and other fertilizers at a rate which would allow them to compete with agriculturists in more highly-favoured districts. Several schemes have been promoted at various times to provide this inaccessible district with a railway, and one project in particular, the Goole and Owston Railway received Parliamentary sanction, but got no further. In 1883 a tramway scheme was sanctioned, but came to nothing. The passing of the Light Railway's Act once more roused the energy of the people of Epworth, and thanks to the well directed efforts of Messrs J.H. Bletcher, T.J. Blaydes, and E. Hirst, the directors, and others connected with the present scheme, there hopes are to be realized. The railway will be constructed from Haxey station, through Haxey, Epworth, Belton, and Crowle, and there are arms reaching out from about the centre near Belton to the Levels on the west, and Newland on the east. Principal stations will be established at Haxey - the village being a mile and a half from the existing railway - at Epworth, Belton, and Crowle. It is proposed to

A posed gathering for Mr J. Bottomley, showing the enormous crowd assembled at Epworth to witness the cutting of the first sod of the Isle of Axholme Light Railway by Miss Bletcher on 20th July, 1899.   *Author's Collection*

The High Street at Epworth depicting the celebrations for the cutting of the first sod. The gentleman second from the left is Mr Coggan and the 'white aproned' gent just behind the left support is Mr Wray. The man wearing a dark apron on the path on the right is Mr Jennings.   *Edwin Harrison Collection*

give similar accommodation to that provided by the Cawood, Wistow, and Selby Light Railway. Wherever the new line crosses a public road of any importance, sidings are to be constructed for the reception of produce and goods, and at the stations there are to be sidings and loading docks for dealing with large quantities of agricultural traffic.

A junction with the Marshland Light Railway is to be affected about two miles out of Goole, thereby getting into direct communication with the Hull and Doncaster branch of the North-Eastern system. A light engine of 25 tons will be provided, capable of drawing twenty ordinary trucks. The line will be of full gauge, so that traffic can pass between it and existing railways without any reloading. The carriages for passengers will be constructed after the tramcar pattern, rather than in the simple style of the ordinary railway coach. These will be more convenient for getting in and out, and in every way suitable for short journeys.

The engineers are Messrs Mammatt and White, of Leeds, who made the necessary survey some two years ago, and the estimated cost was £135,000. Since then, however, the price of material and labour have gone up, and the contract was let at the Reindeer at Doncaster - where all of the meetings of the committee have been held - to Messrs S.W. Meyer and White, of Leeds, for £175,000.

The engineering difficulties are by no means severe. The most difficult work is the construction of a bridge over the Great Central Railway and the canal, which run side by side at Crowle, and must be covered with a 50 ft span and two side openings. With the exception of one or two small hills the country is quite flat, and the stiffest gradient is only one in 70 or 80. A new source of traffic is not unlikely to spring up in the course of time at the southern extremity of the line. Four workable seams of coal have been discovered at South Carr, one at a depth of 682 yards, and another, said to be 8 ft 8 in. thick, at a depth of 1,052 yards. Arrangements for sinking shafts are in progress, and should the result justify expectations, Lincolnshire will have developed an entirely new industry. The estimate allows for the purchase of land, roughly set down at £50 per acre. Naturally there is no opposition from landowners, and the directors do not therefore anticipate having to pay extravagant prices to people whose estates they are going to benefit.

The comprehensive Celebration Committee, under the presidency of Mr Hirst, with Mr Gorbutt as secretary, had arranged a full day's programme, and the manner in which it was carried out reflected the utmost credit upon the organising ability and executive skill of all concerned.

THE PROCESSION

which assembled in the Market Place was far larger and more imposing than any before seen in Epworth. It started from the Market Place and proceeded up Albion Hill, along Mowbray Street, down Queen Street, and as far as Scawcett lane end; turning round there, and proceeding to the field where the sod was to be cut. It was almost a mile long, and close on a quarter of an hour elapsed between the passing of the first and last items from Market-Place. The position of each section having previously been allotted, everything was quickly arranged, and shortly after the stated time the procession moved off.

Upon reaching 'Maw's Flat', where the great ceremony of the day, the cutting of the first sod of the new railway, was to take place, the cavalcade drew up in the roadway, but the crowd who had accompanied it came into the field and took up their position round the roped enclosure within which the ceremony was to take

Epworth village High Street crossroads prior to the cutting of the first sod, decorated with banners and arches proclaiming the coming of the railway 'At Last'. Even Miss Hill's bicycle-wheels were decorated. Today the crossroads has a set of traffic lights. The building (*left*) in the top photograph is the 'White Bear'.

(Both) Courtesy Edwin Harrison

place. Round the flagstaff there gathered a distinguished company, including the directors, Messrs J.H. Bletcher, E. Hirst, and T.J. Blaydes; the Misses Bletcher (2); Mrs Alfred Taylor, Mrs Blaydes, Mr and Mrs Tom Bletcher, the Local Committee, Mr J. Waring, secretary; Mr W. Standring, the Rector, Rev. J. Greaves; and others.

The proceedings commenced with prayer, offered up by the Rector, after which Mr J.H. Bletcher said that they were met together that day to make a formal beginning of the Isle of Axholme Light Railway, which, he hoped, would be of great benefit to the district. It had been been a long time in coming, but he was thankful to say they had got it at last. As Chairman of the Directors he begged to introduce them to Mr Meyer, one of the contractors, who was under agreement to make that line, and he hoped they would go ahead and finish the line as soon as possible.

Mr Meyer said that he had much pleasure in asking Miss Bletcher to be kind enough to cut the first sod of the Isle of Axholme Light Railway. The Chairman, Mr Bletcher, to whose energy and industry they were all very much indebted, and whose business capacity had helped to bring about the beginning of those proceedings and to get the railway on its legs, had referred to the fact that the railway had been a very long time coming, and nobody who had been through the village, and read the inscriptions to be seen there could doubt that as a general rule things had been delayed for a very long time. But things delayed sometimes tasted a little sweeter when they did come, and they hoped that that would be the case in regard to the Isle of Axholme Light Railway. (*Hear, Hear*). When in London, a few weeks since, he heard Lord Salisbury referring to a railway which we were making in South Africa, and which had been stopped owing to the lions and other wild beasts eating the platelayers. He hoped that that would not be the experience in the Isle of Axholme. (*Laughter*). He was one of those who thought they could not commence any undertaking with any promise of success unless it was supported and graced by the presence of a lady, and he hoped that it would be a good augury for them and bring them prosperity. He was very much obliged to Miss Bletcher for coming there to perform the ceremony. (*Applause*). He would now ask her to perform the important ceremony which she had been kind enough to undertake.

Mr Wm Standring having loosened the turf, a handsome silver spade with ebony shaft was handed to Miss Bletcher. It bore the following inscription:

ISLE OF AXHOLME LIGHT RAILWAY.

"Presented to Miss Bletcher on the cutting of the first sod of the above railway at Epworth - 20th July, 1899."

Miss Bletcher then stepped forward, and Mr Meyer handed her the handsome presentation spade mentioned above. In a clear voice she addressed the large assemblage. She said that she had much pleasure in turning the first sod of the Isle of Axholme Light Railway with the handsome spade kindly presented to her by Mr Meyer, and she heartily wished the undertaking every success. Miss Bletcher then gracefully performed the ceremony of turning the first sod with the silver blade.

Mr Waring, the secretary of the company, then broke a bottle of champagne over the upturned sod.

Mr T.J. Blaydes said the pleasurable duty devolved on him of being the first local man to speak upon this now historic ground. The duty he had to perform was to move that their best thanks be given to the lady who had turned over the first piece of soil. He asked them to record their thanks by giving three cheers for Miss Bletcher and her father. The response was hearty and Mr Bletcher briefly returned thanks.

LUNCHEON

was subsequently provided in a marquee on the ground. The catering was entrusted to Mrs Copeman, of the Red Lion Hotel, and was efficiently and satisfactorily carried out. A very large company sat down, including not only officials, but a large number of prominent residents of the town and district, and others from a distance. The menu was as follows:

FISH
Salmon and Cucumber
JOINTS
Roast Lamb Roast Beef Ham Tongue
POULTRY
Roast Duck Roast Chicken Pigeon Pie
SWEETS
Fruit Tarts Custards Jellies Pastry
CHEESE SALAD

MR J.H. BLETCHER presided, and gave the toast of the Queen.

The CHAIRMAN proposed loyal toasts, which were enthusiastically received.

The toast of the day, 'The Isle of Axholme Light Railway', was submitted by Mr P.G. Skipworth, who contrasted the state of affairs that day with that of 20 or 30 years ago, when out of 250 candidates at a civil service examination, as recorded by Mr Peacock, not one knew of the Isle of Axholme, or had ever heard of it. (*Laughter*). The effect of their development and the introduction of the railway would bring them into closer contact with the outer world, and, he trusted, add to their individual and collective prosperity. (*Applause*).

MR T.J. BLAYDES in responding, first informed the company that he had drunk the toast in ginger ale. (*Laughter*). He had great pleasure indeed in responding to the toast. One of the sayings that had been applied to the proposal had been 'Hope deferred maketh the heart grow sick'. There were many in this marquee who had felt their hearts grow sick over the question of railway or no railway. There had been several occasions on which heart sickness had been their lot, but to-day they rejoiced as the first practical step towards the completion of the railway had been taken. (*Cheers*). To-day his mind reverted to one portrait before all others - that of the late Mr Barnes - who had always advocated and worked hard to establish a railway in the district. He had often said to him, 'Mr Barnes, you go on talking about it, and I will try to get the needful'. He only wished Mr Barnes had been spared to be present to-day. He (the speaker) thought he could claim some share in the making of this railway, which he believed would be a great blessing and boon to the district. He believed it would bring nothing but blessings. He knew of no means whereby agriculture could be improved so much in this district as by this railway, and many of those interested in agriculture were looking forward to it as a great help. In Epworth there was an undercurrent of feeling - or a too over-fondness - for taking the trade away from the place. He knew it had been said that he went away for a little cheese a long time ago. (*Laughter*). He knew he should rejoice the hearts of some, but should touch those who took away their share of commercial trade of the place, when he reminded them that if a Light Railway was to prosper they must purchase home products. (*Applause*). Patronise the home tradesmen and the demand would create the supply. In reference to the preface quoted by Mr Skipworth he remarked that probably had the 250 students been asked where Epworth was they could have replied. In the wilds of Africa the name of Epworth was becoming known to thousands. He trusted that the establishment of the railway was the beginning of better days for Epworth, and that he might be spared to share in the advantage with all of them.

MR Wm STANDRING then proposed the 'Directors and Officials'. In reference to the directors, and taking the chairman first, he said perhaps many of them were not so well acquainted with Mr Bletcher's business capacity as he was. He had known him for many years, and he knew him for one of the best business men in the district, and one who was always courteous, kind, and generous to all with whom he came in contact. With regard to the other directors he could not tell them more than they already knew. They were men of sound business habits, men who not only had a sound grip on their own business, but were also well versed in public matters. He took it that the highest compliment was paid to them when it was said 'This is a Bletcher and Blaydes railway'. (*Applause.*) They had taken this business up as it had never been taken before, and had pushed it forward to the successful issue they saw to-day. They had become responsible for large sums of money, while those who spoke disparagingly were probably those who dared not come forward and undertake the same responsibility. He hoped every one present representing the town and district would join heartily in drinking the health of the directors.

MR E. HIRST in responding for the directors, said it was their intention to see the line carried out to the best of their ability, and they hoped it would be a success. They depended upon the Epworth people and the people of the district through which the line was to go for support. He thought the gathering to-day was evidence of the great interest taken in the railway.

MR G.H. NEWBORN, in proposing 'The Contractors', expressed the hope that Mr Meyer would give them if he could an intimation as to the time they might expect the railway to be opened for traffic - the sooner he fixed the time the better they would like it. (*Laughter and hear, hear*).

MR MEYER, in his response, said the present scheme was not connected with any of the great railway companies, but was entirely free. When it was made, however, they would make arrangements for through rates, etc. It was being made under the Light Railways Act, but of metals heavy enough to take the heaviest coaches or trucks in use on the main line. As to the invitation of Mr Newborn, he did not like to pose as a prophet, but he hoped the rail from Haxey to Epworth would be open for traffic by this time next year. (*Loud applause*). The further length would take more time on account of the very heavy work at Crowle and elsewhere, but it would be completed as quickly as possible.

MR F.J. SOWBY, Gainsborough, said he had had the privilege of visiting Epworth frequently for something like 30 years, and he thought he could claim to know something of the business of the town. He had often been mystified as to the manner in which so many of the people were engaged in the higher and more expensive forms of agriculture managed so successfully to conduct their business considering the great difficulties they had to face of getting their produce to their markets. This Light Railway would add greatly to the future prosperity of Epworth, and of the Isle of Axholme. (*Applause*).

The RECTOR, who was all day ready in the highest of spirits to wave his mortar board as if he were still an undergraduate, was properly complimentary in toasting the chairman.

TEA

A free tea was served in the Temperance Hall, where there about 400 children sat down. Adults were served in the Wesleyan, New Connexion, Primitive, and Baptist

Schoolrooms, and a large number attended. At the Wesleyan schoolroom there were as many as half-a-dozen sittings.

SPORTS

were held in the Thurlow croft after tea, and were witnessed by close on fifteen hundred spectators. The fancy dress football match caused a lot of amusement, but there were only about a dozen players, who fagged early on, and the latter part was rather tame.

The sports over, the company adjourned to the King's Head croft, where a display of fireworks were given by Messrs Payne of Manchester.

For the occasion of the cutting of the first sod, a commemorative medal was struck and then presented to the children as a reminder of the event. The *Epworth Bells* for 9th September, 1899 records;

The Contractors of the Light Railway have remembered the promise made at the luncheon on the occasion of the sod cutting to have medals struck in commemoration of that remarkable event. On Tuesday evening the Market Hall was besieged by a crowd of eager youngsters, and about four hundred medals were distributed by the Secretary, Mr Gorbutt, and his assistants (Messrs W. Maw and F. Newborn). The medals are very pretty, and about the size of five shilling piece. On one side within a floral border are the words, 'Isle of Axholme Light Railway. MANUS JUSTA NARDUS', and on the reverse, 'In commemoration of the cutting of the first sod of the railway at Epworth by Miss Bletcher, 20th July, 1899'.

By the end of the 1900 construction had barely commenced just at the time the NER decided to purchase the company. In the *Doncaster Gazette* of

11th November, 1900 a report read;

> This means the light Railways will be light no more! They have, as a matter of fact, been constructed as heavy lines and are capable of carrying heavy mineral traffic. The G&MLR will as far as the traffic of its own immediate district is concerned, remain a largely agricultural line. The Isle of Axholme, which will connect with it at Reedness Junction will be a mineral line as well as an agricultural one and will carry most of the coal for South Carr Colliery. The ramifications are not to be confined to the G&MLR and the IOALR. The NER have desired direct access to the Derbyshire coalfields and they intend to ask Parliament to sanction the acquisition of powers already granted by the Light Railway Commissioners for a light railway from Haxey to Tickhill.

On 2nd March, 1901, the second AGM of the IOALR took place at Doncaster with,

> Mr J.H. Bletcher presiding. There were also present Messrs T.J. Blaydes, E. Hirst, and W. Maw (directors); Messrs W. Everatt, W. Burtonshaw, and G.H. Newborn (solicitors); Mr S.W. Meyer (contractor); and Mr Waring (secretary). The report stated that the construction of the railway was proceeding satisfactorily, both in Haxey and Crowle districts, and the details of expenditure, read by Mr Meyer, the contractor, of Leeds, showed general interest, £109; £650 had been paid into court pending the completion of purchase; construction of railways and stations, including land, absorbed £51,300; surveyor's fees, £96; preliminary expenses, £50; stationery, etc., £4; total expenditure up to December 31, £52,210. The total receipts amounted to £33,249, leaving a balance of £18,961 8s. 5d. due to the contractor. The Chairman moved the adoption of the report, which was seconded by Mr Maw, and carried. Mr Meyer, proposing a vote of thanks to the chairman, said that the company was greatly indebted to him. Mr Maw seconded. The Chairman, in replying, said he hoped at the next meeting they would be able to give further particulars of the negotiations with the North Eastern Railway Company.

Just after this Board Meeting at 3.30 pm the special extraordinary General Meeting took place to consider and approve the NER's acquisition of the IOALR.

However locally in Epworth concern was growing as to the slow progress of the line and also to the reasons why the NER was so interested in the line. The *Epworth Bells* carried the following report on 13th April, 1901;

> A large representative public meeting was held in the Temperance Hall, Epworth, on Thursday afternoon, in support of the Bill now being promoted in Parliament by the North Eastern Railway Company.
>
> Mr G.H. Newborn said the reason the meeting had been called so early was to allow the inhabitants of the Trent-side villages to attend.
>
> Several Epworth gentlemen were asked to take the chair, but as they were not agreeable, Mr Hirst proposed, and Mr W. Standring seconded that Mr L.G.

Epworth railway bridge in Sandtoft Road on the south side of the station under construction and, *below*, the completed bridge. The locomotive would have descended a steep gradient from track level to the base of the bridge. *Courtesy Edwin Harrison*

Lowthorpe take the chair.

Mr Newborn then explained the purpose of the meeting, and stated that the bill was to grant permission for the North Eastern Railway Co. to take over the Goole and Marshland, Isle of Axholme, and Tickhill Light Railways. The terms of the Isle of Axholme Light Railway are not yet settled, but the bill has the approval of all whom it may concern. This railway will be much better worked by a large company than it could possibly be by a small amateur one. The Isle of Axholme Railway Company have had the advantage of entering into several companies, the North Eastern being the one chosen. Unless a company is powerful we cannot get beneficial rates, and this company is certainly a powerful one. The bill is being opposed by the Great Northern and Great Central Railway Companies, as well as mineral interests in the West Riding.

Mr Standring asked if when the North Eastern take over the line will the agriculturists receive the same benefit as arranged for them by the Isle of Axholme Railway Co. Mr Newborn replied that the arrangements will be carried out as proposed by the Isle of Axholme Railway Co., and there was not any chance of the Company abolishing such privileges.

Mr W. Moody, Haxey, said that when the line was passed it was stated that there was not to be a level crossing at Haxey, but since then a level crossing had been arranged, and at Epworth a bridge was to be erected over the highway. It was, he contended, unfair for any parish to be favoured. Mr Newborn said it was unfortunately the formation of the district, and a level crossing at Haxey could not be avoided. It was either a level crossing or no railway.

Messrs W. Standring, Blaydes, and E. Hirst spoke of the inconvenience the district had suffered through not having a railway, and they were pleased to have a railway whether bridges or level crossings. They also alluded to the bad treatment received from the Great Northern and Great Central Railway Companies, and they felt sure the North Eastern was the company to best serve the interests of the district, not only regarding fair rates but also a good service, and the meeting could do no better than support the bill. Several others spoke in favour of the railway being taken over by this company.

The Chairman asked if a siding could not be made at Graizelound, and stated he had done a great deal in favour of a railway being constructed. Mr Newborn said they would no doubt be glad to make a siding at Graizelound if it could be proved that it was needed.

Mr Standring proposed, and Mr J.M. Hill seconded 'That this meeting of the Inhabitants of the Isle of Axholme having considered the proposals in the North Eastern Railway Bill, 1901, so far as they relate to the acquisition of the Light Railways between Goole and Haxey, and the extension of the railway to Tickhill and the collieries beyond, are unanimously of opinion that such proposals, if carried out, would be for the advantage of the District'.

Messrs Blaydes, Hirst, and W. Standring were appointed to appear before the Committee in support of the bill.

The Rev. J. Greaves proposed, and Mr R. Brown, West Butterwick, seconded that the Hon. Seymour Ormsby-Gore be asked to support the bill.

A vote of thanks to the Chairman brought the meeting to a close.

The wooden station buildings and the long station approach road at Epworth station captured on film before the opening of the line. Note the slotted signal with the cross affixed and the contractor's locomotive in the lower photograph. This road is where the locomotive would have run down to the base of the bridge in the previous picture. The upper photograph shows the distant position of the large, newly constructed station master's home (*right*) and Epworth cutting in the far middle distance.

Courtesy Edwin Harrison

By August 1901, Meyer (whose address was then 13, Bond Street, Leeds) was discussing with W.J. Cudworth of the NER prices for work that he had already carried out, and for the construction still to be done. The memorandum stated: Bridge-work already supplied; price to be 15 per cent above the actual invoiced price. Bridge-work to be done would be in accordance with the schedule arranged. Permanent-way material already paid for by the IOALR to be 15 per cent in excess of the prices actually paid. Permanent-way material contracted for, but not paid for, to be 10 per cent in excess of prices actually paid and any additional permanent-way material above what was contracted for to be supplied by the NER.

At a NER Board meeting of 9th August, 1901, the following report was submitted;

> The General Manager reported that the Isle of Axholme Railway had been constructed from Reedness Junction as far as Crowle and that he had provisionally agreed the price of that section of the line at £24,781, with an addition for a share of preliminary expenses not yet ascertained. Also that the line from Crowle to Haxey was in course of construction and that the total expenditure of the Light Railway Company up to the present amounted to about £50,000. The total estimated cost, including the completed portion is £125,000. He further reported that a specification and schedule of prices with respect to the line from Crowle to Haxey had been agreed between Mr Cudworth and the Contractors who are constructing the line, and stated that it was desirable that the construction of this portion of the line should be proceeded with without waiting for the Parliamentary sanction of the purchase of the Undertaking by the North Eastern, or by the North Eastern and Lancashire & Yorkshire Companies as the case may be. In order to enable this to be done the Light Railway Company require a payment on account of £30,000 and it will be necessary to make some arrangement for providing further money for the construction as it proceeds.
>
> RESOLVED, That Mr Tennant be authorised to arrange with the Bankers for the payment to the Light Railway Company of the sum of £30,000 and such further sums as Mr Cudworth shall from time to time certify to have been properly expended in the construction of the line from Crowle to Haxey and to guarantee the repayment of the same to the Bank, the Light Railway Company issuing and registering in the joint names of Mr Tennant and Mr Wharton Ordinary Shares paid up in the Undertaking of that Company to the amount of the sums guaranteed, and this Company indemnifying Mr Tennant and Mr Wharton.
>
> *A. Kaye Butterworth, Esq*

Attached to this memo were several hand written notes, probably from the solicitors, relating to the way the monies were to be paid. One relevant note read;

> The NER to pay £27,500 (plus interest) thereon from October 1st, 1901 for payment and to take receipts of the Crowle section from the same date (this is their full liability - for they retain £21,490 for a debenture debt; also the amount of arrears of interest (if any) up to 1st October, 1902 - and after that date they will retain the

£21,490 against the debt and accruing interest up to the redemption). The NER to pay for the Southern section by monthly instalments according to the schedule of prices (no question of interest - they advance the money to the Isle of Axholme as required and take shares - the Isle of Axholme find no money themselves and pay no interest.)

Work continued at a 'leisurely' pace and the local population became impatient, one member putting pen to paper and summing up his feelings in a poem, published in the *Epworth Bells*.

The Good Time Coming
We are waiting, patiently waiting,
For the Parliamentary train,
Which for our modest sixpence
Will take us to Haxey and back.

Not all the joys of Lamps and Lovers' Seats,
Can bring us equal gain,
To seeing our friends alighting,
From the Isle of Axholme train.

Of course these things are very good:
We all want More Light (for our eyes)
Especially the Railway Directors,
Who told such awful lies.

In ninety-nine 'twould be a year:
Two years later, eighteen months was the guess:
If that Paddy's Mail had smash'd the lot,
We shouldn't have had a saint less.

Whilst the construction in 1901 was not considered 'rapid', several employees were seriously hurt during the days leading up to the first train to Epworth. May saw George Eastwood (aged 14 years) run over by a wagon, cutting his leg in several places and in September, Thomas Lindley (aged 15 years) picked up a detonator which exploded, shattering his hand.

However the big day came when the first train ran into Epworth, crossing the road by means of the 'new bridge'. The occasion was captured on film by local photographer Mr J. Bottomley and accompanied the following report on 30th November, 1901 in the *Epworth Bells*:

Epworth, on Monday, was *en fete* on the occasion of the first engine crossing the road in High Street. It had been publicly announced that this notable event would take place at one o'clock. For some time before this hour people began to gather

The crowd posing for the camera on 25th November, 1901, when locomotive *Epworth* hauled an open wagon of officials into Epworth station to 'try out the track' and Station Road bridge.   *Courtesy T. Kay*

near Mr J. Tonge's field, and at the time stated for the crossing there would be fully 400 people anxiously looking for the engine which started from the Carrside road. Almost to the minute, the fine engine, *Epworth*, steamed over the road, and up the embankment near 'Maw's mill', where the passengers alighted on a stage specially prepared. The engine was decorated with flags, etc., and was in the charge of Mr Fry, the foreman, to whom great credit is due for the excellent way in which he carried out the admirable arrangements. Those on the engine were Mr P. Carney, foreman fitter; M. Marney, driver; F. Greenslade, rope-runner. After looking round, the party again entered the carriage, and after it had moved out a little way, three shots, which had been previously prepared, were fired, thus showing the process of blasting the rock.

The engine then proceeded to the Carrside road, where the passengers alighted upon a platform specially arranged, and thus terminated a pleasant ride. Mr Glover, the engineer, was unfortunately away, being in London. On the north side of the road leading to the cutting near 'Maw's mill' an archway had been erected over the line, bearing the words, 'Success to the work', in attractive lettering.

Through the generosity of several residents in Epworth, a scheme had been promoted by Mr W. Maw for entertaining with refreshments, the workmen who travel by the 'Mail' to their work down the line. The usual time for their return is about 5.20, and at this hour quite a large number of people from all parts of the town were waiting the arrival of the 'Mail'. Mr Fry had sent down an engine to which was attached a wagon conveying a flash light, and this was in working order when the

'Mail' arrived. The men, about 100 in all, proceeded to Mr J. Tonge's shop, which had been kindly lent for the occasion, where the refreshments were served. Mr Standring invited the men to partake of what had been so generously provided, which consisted of beer, tea, plum bread, cheese and tobacco. After the men had done justice to the excellent repast, Mr Standring, on behalf of Mr Fry, who through a severe cold was unable to speak, thanked the generous donors, and also alluded to the unity of capital and labour, which combination worked admirably in the construction of the present line. The refreshments were served by Mrs J. Tonge, Mrs W. Maw, Miss Tonge, Mr R. Chamberlain, and several others, in an admirable manner. This brought to a close a very interesting and memorable day.

During 1902, as work continued on the various cuttings, embankments and bridges (especially Crowle Swing Bridge), various incidents occurred, many involving the 300 or so navvies (many Irish) employed on the construction work.

At the beginning of the year, an accident befell a juvenile named Samuel Hinchcliffe (aged 15 years) who was employed by the contractors as a 'point-turnover'. A large rock hit the boy whilst blasting operations were being carried out in Haxey cutting, causing him multiple injuries. He was 'rushed' by cart to Haxey station on the GN & GE Joint Line and thence by the 4.06 train to Doncaster, but, after being operated on, the boy died from his injuries.

In February, the Highways Committee of the Lindsey County Council received a report to the effect that the Isle of Axholme Light Railway was considering diverting the line north of Epworth for the purpose of avoiding

Construction of the Haxey cutting north of the station, with the navvies, steam and human, posing for the official photograph. This was the deepest of earthworks on the Isle of Axholme Light Railway. The man holding the horse is Mr Cooper of Westwoodside. *Courtesy Westwoodside Heritage Society*

Another superb photograph by J. Bottomley of a different steam navvy working on Epworth cutting. Note the railway along the top of the cut-a level crossing at the foot of Hoggarth Hill, and proposed bringing the railway through Hoggarth Hill and constructing a bridge carrying the main road (without altering the gradient) which was to be 35 feet wide between the parapet walls. The clerk of the Council was instructed to prepare a legal agreement with the IOALR to relieve them of all responsibility in connection with the construction of this bridge and future maintenance costs.

The local area too received its fair share of 'increase in crime' due to the large influx of workmen, with theft, drunkenness and violence being the main problems the local constabulary had to deal with. On 1st February, 1902 the *Epworth Bells* reported:

> George Prade, was charged with stealing an accordian, value 3s., the property of John Henry Spencer, of Sandtoft, on the 20th of January. Mrs Spencer said that prisoner called at the Reindeer Inn, Sandtoft, about 4 p.m. on the day in question, and was supplied with a pint of beer. He stayed until 5.30, and when he had left, the accordian was missing from the mantelpiece in the tap room. - George Jarvis, employed on the Light Railway, stated that he purchased the accordian from prisoner for 1s. 6d. Prisoner was arrested on his discharge from Lincoln prison, and on being charged he replied 'It's quite true, its no good telling any lies about it'. Defendant pleaded guilty, and was fined 10s. and costs, or in default 14 days.

Whilst on a lighter note, the navvies (playing under the name of the Light Railway Club) played local sides at football. March saw a game against Epworth Rovers (played at Haxey) with the final score of four to one, in favour of Epworth.

Not far away from this event, in the Haxey cutting, one of the enormous steam crane/diggers (steam navvy) fell over and the driver was entangled within the mechanism and levers. He was taken to his lodgings in Haxey by ambulance, and luckily made a full recovery.

During the summer, the cutting at Epworth was progressing at 'full speed' and it was recorded that 388 wagons were filled by the large crane/digger (called a Rushton Navvy) on one Monday and by noon on the Tuesday 200 had been filled at the same place.

This spoil was being moved to the Haxey side of Epworth station and being used to construct the huge embankment needed to bring the track level up to the required height of the embankment being made at the Haxey end. It would not be long before the whole route from Haxey to Epworth would be joined up!

Football matches continued with a 2-all draw against Gainsborough Working Men's Club in September, on a ground near Burnham village.

In November, 1902 a further fatality occurred on the line, again involving a 15 year old lad. The *Epworth Bells* reported;

> William Woodhead, aged 15, died in the Infirmary from injuries received at

The steam navvy at work in the cutting at Epworth; the photographer is standing on a contractor's line on the top of the embankment. *Courtesy Ian Snell*

Haxey cutting being excavated with a similar steam navvy, this time the contractor's locomotive (*left*) is being used to take away the wagons of spoil. *Edwin Harrison*

Epworth by being run over on the railway now in the course of construction. - It was stated that on Wednesday morning the deceased, who had been in the employ of the contractors for 15 months, was working on the line. His duty was to hold a point of the railway back for the purpose of the waggons passing over it. In front of the last waggon was a coupling chain, and the chain appeared to have been out of repair, and a temporary arrangement was made by which the last waggon was fastened to the waggon immediately preceding. The coupling chain had fallen down below the waggon, and as it was passing over the point it caught the striking rod. At the end of the coupling chain there was a hook, and the chain by means of the hook caught in the stretching rod, causing the lever to be suddenly pulled, throwing deceased on the line. One of the firemen partly pulled him off, but he put his foot back again, and the engine and a carriage went over it. The following was the chief evidence taken: John Richard Bailey, Belton, stated he was a rope-runner on the line in question. He had been at this work about 18 months. He saw the deceased on Wednesday morning about 8 o'clock, who was holding the points for the purpose of allowing twelve waggons which were coupled together to pass over the points. Witness was riding on the engine with the driver and fireman. As the waggon was passing this point, witness heard the foreman shout 'My God, Stop'. The driver pulled up as quickly as possible within a waggon's length. The engine was then travelling about three miles an hour. When the engine was stopped witnessed noticed deceased being pulled from beneath engine, which had passed over one of his legs a little distance above the ankle. Witnessed alighted, and the engine was still coupled to the waggons. Deceased said, 'Where's my brother?' Witness did not hear the foreman make any remark at that time. Deceased was conveyed on the engine to Epworth, saying on the way 'My arms hurt'. Witness blamed no one for the accident. George Peck, residing at Epworth, foreman on the railway, deposed that he had been on the railway about eleven weeks, but his experience of the work extended over a period of 27 years. Corroborative evidence was given, witness stating that he pulled the lad back, and deceased pushed his feet out on to the rails. When deceased fell his hands were between the two waggons. When the deceased was raised up one of his feet went on the rail and a waggon passed over it. Witness tied a handkerchief above deceased's knee and placed him on engine. When falling he cried out 'Oh, master; oh, master'. The jury returned a verdict of 'Accidental death', adding 'we think there is negligence on the part of some unknown person, but the company's to blame'.

By the end of 1902, the section from Reedness Junction to Crowle station had been completed and an agreement to its purchase by the NER for the sum of £27,500 was reached, to be paid on 1st October, 1903. On that date the Joint Companies would also pay all liabilities and debts in respect of the remaining uncompleted railway (still under construction).

As can be appreciated, by the beginning of 1903 the NER & L&YR had taken control of the two light railways. Thus the independent existence of the IOALR and the G&MLR was truly short lived. As previously mentioned, the G&MLR had completed all its lines whereas the IOALR had only constructed the section from Reedness Junction to Crowle and from Epworth to

Haxey Junction, where the IOALR adjoined the GN&GE Joint station with its own single platform station.

An interesting memorandum from a meeting of Staff Clerks of the NER at York on the 23rd June, 1903 stated:

> *Item 2:* Stationmasters. The present stationmasters at Eastoft, Luddington, Fockerby and Crowle who are receiving £78 per annum with a free house, which is more than it is considered the positions are worth at present, to be removed when the opportunity arises, the L&Y to provide for the Crowle and Eastoft Agents and the NER for the Luddington and Fockerby Agents.

Already the squeeze on cutting costs was being implemented as both major companies had spent more on the purchase of these two light railways than they had intended.

As the Isle of Axholme Light Railway was still not finished, the NER issued a specification to contractors for the completion of the architectural works. Thanks to Mr K.P. Plant this document has been included in full as *Appendix Three* as many readers may never have had the chance to see such a document before. Also included are Sebastian Meyer's estimates written on one of the forms supplied with the specification. The legal Deed of Contract was executed on 19th November, 1903 by Meyer, the L&Y and the NER. Most surprisingly the whole of the works was sub-contracted to Messrs James Bryant & Sons of York, the contract price being £4,231 8s. 5d.

The Joint Railway opened part of the system to passenger and goods traffic on 10th August, 1903 with the following stations and sidings operational: Reedness Junction, Eastoft, Luddington, Crowle and Fockerby with sidings; Corner's, Smith's, Gossop's, Goole Fields, Blacker's, Whitgift, Bramhill's, Peat Moss Litter and Spillman's.

Apparently, although rousing great interest in the area at the time, no opening ceremony took place. The published timetable follows:

	a.m.	Weds. and Sats. only	p.m.	p.m.
Goole ....dep.	7 45		12 58	6 15
Reedness Junction ......arr.	7 58		1 11	6 28
Reedness Junction ......dep.	7 59		1 12	6 56
Eastoft .... ,,	8 8·		1 21	7 5
Luddington .... ,,	8 12		1 25	7 9
Fockerby................arr.	8 16		1 29	7 13
Reedness Junction ......dep.	8 42		1 20	6 29
Crowle...................arr.	8 51		1 29	6 38

	a.m.	Weds. and Sats. only	p.m.	p.m.
Crowle ....dep.	8 55		1 37	6 42
Reedness Junction ......arr.	9 4		1 49	6 51
Fockerby ....dep	8 20		1 33	7 17
Luddington .... ,,	8 24		1 37	7 21
Eastoft .... ,,	8 28		1 41	7 25
Reedness Junction ......arr.	8 37		1 50	7 34
Reedness Junction ......dep.	9 5		1 55	7 35
Goole ....arr.	9 18		2 8	7 48

The first train is reported to have comprised a L&Y tank and three L&Y coaches.

The first meeting of the members of the new Joint Board was held at York on Thursday 23rd October, 1902 and Mr Tennant (for the NER) was appointed Chairman. The revenue from the section open was to be divided equally between the two companies. Several other matters were raised and two cheques were drawn on the York City and County Banking Co. Ltd, York. One was for £8,750 to pay the Yorkshire District Light Railway Syndicate Ltd for work done and the other for £37,000 to pay the Goole and Marshland Light Railway.

At the second meeting of the Axholme Joint Railway (AJR) held at the NER Company's office in Westminster, London on Wednesday 17th February, 1904, the name of the railway was resolved as the Isle of Axholme Joint Railway (NE and L&Y Joint), this being approved by the following Directors who had just been appointed for the year; Sir George Armytage, Bart., E.B. Fielden, MP, J.H. Stafford (for the L&Y) and The Right Hon. Sir Edward Grey, Bart., MP, Frank Stobart, Henry Tennant (for the NER). Also present were Messrs Aspinall and Bayley for the L&Y and Messrs Gibb, Butterworth, Cudworth and Burtt for the NER.

The appointed Secretary was Mr H. Marriott at a salary of £50 per annum. The superintendent of the line, Mr M. Woodhouse was appointed at a salary of £275 per annum.

By March 1904, the whole of the line of the IOALR was completed with exception of the swing bridge over the canal at Crowle. During this year also the Board of the light railway held its last Directors' meeting before being wound-up. The line from Crowle station to Haxey Junction was opened for freight traffic on 14th November, 1904* and the Directors and other dignitaries of the Joint Railway inspected the line in a special saloon which ran on 9th December, 1904 stopping at Epworth for lunch. The *Epworth Bells* reported the goods opening as follows;

The opening of the Axholme Railway from Crowle to Haxey for goods traffic took place on Monday last. The gates were opened at 7 am and within three-quarters of an hour, a cart loaded with produce had been deposited at the entrance in readiness for entering the station yard. There was a good company present and the first consignment was 216 bags of potatoes consigned by Mr William Maw to a Mr William Crocroft of Mexboro'. Two trucks of hay were consigned by Mr John Standring, two waggons of corn by Messrs Hirst and Hodgson and a truck of carrots by Mr William Gravill. Five waggons of coal were on sale and the first load being sold to Mr G. Harrison for 10s. a ton, this being about 6s. below the usual price. It was interesting to see men and women unloading the carts of produce and Mr William Maw presented each person on his consignment with a sum of money in commemoration of the event. The present rates are said to be exceptionally high, but this state of things will, it is expected, be quickly altered. Preparations are in hand for the opening of

*It was hoped that passenger services could have commenced as well, but damage to the swing bridge by a crane only allowed it to open manually.

AXHOLME JOINT RAILWAY. COPYRIGHT
JAN 2 1905
WAITING FOR FIRST TRAIN

the line for passenger traffic which is expected to take place in a few weeks. The fare to Haxey Town is already fixed at 3d., Haxey Junction 4½d., Crowle 6½d., and Goole 1s. 3d.

The BOT inspected the whole line and after several modifications passed the line fit for passenger service. On Monday 2nd January, 1905 the line saw its opening day. Large numbers of people were carried and the first train from Goole (7.18 am) was reportedly full when it arrived at Epworth at 8.01, reaching its destination of Haxey Junction at 8.14. A special party of over 100 people had arranged to take the 1.09 pm service to Goole and these were seen off by about 400 spectators at Epworth station, many of whom came back to see the party return at 6.14 pm. Of the 325 tickets sold on the first day 201 were from Epworth station with the 'party excursion' being arranged by Mr William Maw who 'had done much to promote the line'. The full timetable for the opening day was;

AXHOLME JOINT RAILWAY.

TIME TABLE OF PASSENGER TRAINS.

From	a.m.	a.m.	p.m.
Goole (depart)	7.18	11.50	5.30
Crowle	7.41	12.14 p.m.	5.54
Belton	7.54	12.27	6.7
Epworth	8.1	12.34	6.14
Haxey	8.10	12.43	6.23
Haxey Junction (arr.)	8.14	12.47	6.27
Returning from			
Haxey Junction	8.20	12.55	6.32
Haxey	8.25	1.0	6.37
Epworth	8.34	1.9	6.46
Belton	8.41	1.16	6.53
Crowle	8.54	1.29	7.6
Goole (arrive)	9.18	1.53	7.31

The Axholme Joint Railway was now operational after 5½ years from the cutting of the first sod. The contractors had laid over 11 miles of drainage pipes, excavated 820,000 cubic yards of earth on the Epworth to Haxey section alone, with another 200,000 cubic yards moved from the surrounding land to build the embankments around the Crowle swing bridge. Over 11,000 cubic yards of bricks were needed and 8,000 cubic yards of concrete used to cement the materials together. For a 'light railway' these figures were somewhat high.

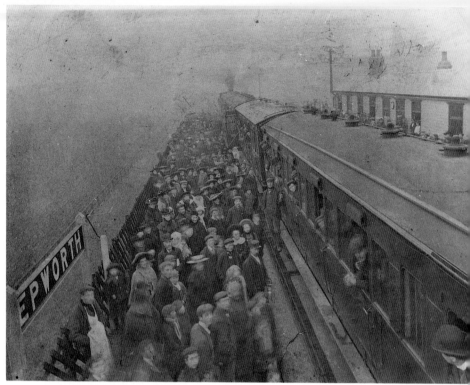

The arrival of the 12.00 pm from Hull on the first day, with passengers from Doncaster and surrounding district. It was a memorable day for the 'Isle'. Note the carriage gas lamps and the communication cord running the length of the coaches over the doors.

Courtesy Edwin Harrison

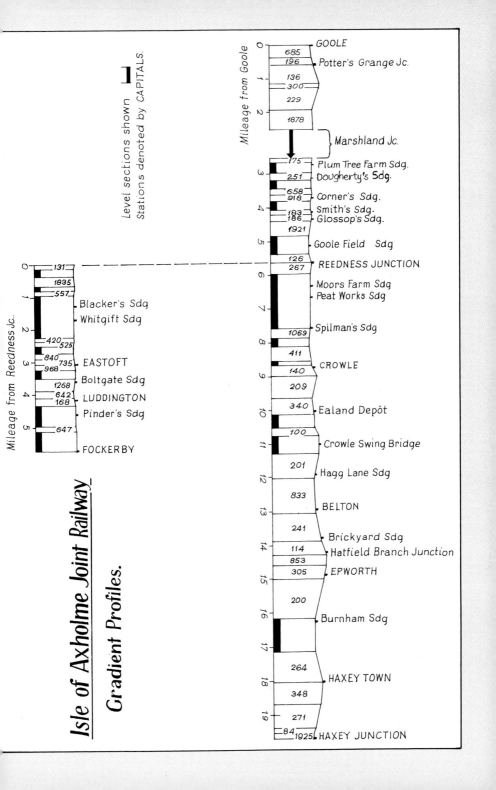

Isle of Axholme Joint Railway

Gradient Profiles.

Level sections shown
Stations denoted by CAPITALS.

Mileage from Goole

GOOLE
685
196 — Potter's Grange Jc.
136
300
229
1878

} Marshland Jc.

175 — Plum Tree Farm Sdg.
251 — Dougherty's Sdg.
658 — Corner's Sdg.
918
183 — Smith's Sdg.
186 — Glossop's Sdg.
1921

Goole Field Sdg
126
267 — REEDNESS JUNCTION

Moors Farm Sdg
Peat Works Sdg

Spilman's Sdg
1069

411

140 — CROWLE

209

340 — Ealand Depôt

100

Crowle Swing Bridge

201 — Hagg Lane Sdg

833

BELTON

241

Brickyard Sdg
114 — Hatfield Branch Junction
853
305 — EPWORTH

200

Burnham Sdg

264

HAXEY TOWN

348

271
84
1925 HAXEY JUNCTION

Mileage from Reedness Jc.

131
1835
557 — Blacker's Sdg
Whitgift Sdg

420
525
840 — EASTOFT
735
968
1268 — Boltgate Sdg
642 — LUDDINGTON
168
Pinder's Sdg

647
FOCKERBY

AXHOLME JOINT LINES

HATFIELD MOOR BRANCH

Epworth Junction to Sandtoft (Goods Yard)—2 Miles 71 Chains.

Epworth Junction to Hatfield Moor Depôt—4 Miles 78 Chains.

This is a reciprocal (triangular) distance table. Each station name appears on the diagonal; the figures give the distances (in miles) between each pair of points. The stations, in order, and their distances from GOOLE are:

GOOLE	—
Potter Grange Junction (Potter's Grange Loop)	0.38
Marshland Junction (Hull and Doncaster)	2.35
Duckle's Siding	3.3
Corner Siding	3.55
Smith's Siding	4.3
Gossop's Siding	4.18
Goole Fields Siding	5.5
Reedness Junction	5.48
Reedness (for Fockerby)	5.58
Reedness (for Crowle)	5.51
Blacker's Siding	7.2
Whitgift Siding	7.32
Eastoft Station	8.55
Bolgate Siding	9.30
Luddington	9.70
Pinder's Siding	10.19
FOCKERBY	11.24
Moss Litter Company's Siding	6.61
Spilman's Siding	7.38
CROWLE	8.50
Ealand Siding	9.70
Hagg Lane Siding	11.76
Belton	12.77
Epworth Junction (Axholme Jt., Hatfield Moor Branch)	14.43
Epworth	14.74
Burnham Lane Siding	16.31
Haxey Town Station	17.78
HAXEY JUNCTION STATION	19.42
End of Line	19.47

NER Reciprocal Distance Tables, 1915.

Chapter Three

Along the Line

The Main Route

Marshland Junction

The Axholme Joint Railway was single track throughout, although sufficient land had been purchased to enable a double track to be laid should the loadings warrant it. All the embankments and bridges were made for single lines with exceptions at the Crowle Swing bridge and the cuttings and bridges between Haxey and Epworth. The line was 17miles, 12chains in length and numerous passing places were allowed for *en route*, mainly at stations.

The line commenced at a junction with the NER main line between Goole and Doncaster, at a point near the 9 milepost from Staddlethorpe Junction.

The junction of the G&MLR was single (*see page 62*), but later a head shunt was added and a double line laid to hold a full train before entering the single line section. The junction also had a single slip to allow a crossover on to the up and down main lines. The land for this junction was purchased for £160 17s. 6d., from Ralph Creyke of Rawcliffe Hall by the Yorkshire & District Railway Syndicate, for whom Sebastian Meyer executed the contract on 17th March, 1900. Ralph Creyke had also entered into an agreement with the NER on 24th April,1876 for the sale of land for their main line.

The cost to the light railway for the use of the NER junction was £5 per annum, payable in January each year, the agreement being signed by Harry Hobson for the G&MLR and J.G. Beharrell for the NER on 16th February,1899. The plan originally called for a triangular layout at this junction but, only the northern connection was constructed, so in consequence all traffic had to be dealt with via Goole only.

Marshland Junction was the name selected by the G&MLR, who paid for the signal box, which was sited on NER land to the west side of the Goole to Doncaster main line (*see page 64*).

Just after the junction and situated on the down-side* of the track, the first siding was encountered which later became named Plumtree Farm Siding. In 1919, a local farmer, Mr J.W. Firth of Plumtree Farm applied to be allowed to load his 'goods' directly into the wagons on the siding alongside the main line. On 26th March, 1919 the Joint Officers of the railway issued the following statement (No. 580):

Suggested alteration of the siding at Marshland Junction and the transfer of the Buffer Stops from Marshland Junction to Reedness Junction.
Loading of traffic by Mr W. Firth at Marshland Junction.
Mr W. Firth of Plumtree Farm, works land on both sides of the Joint Line (near

---

*The line was 'down' from Marshland Junction to Haxey and Fockerby.

61

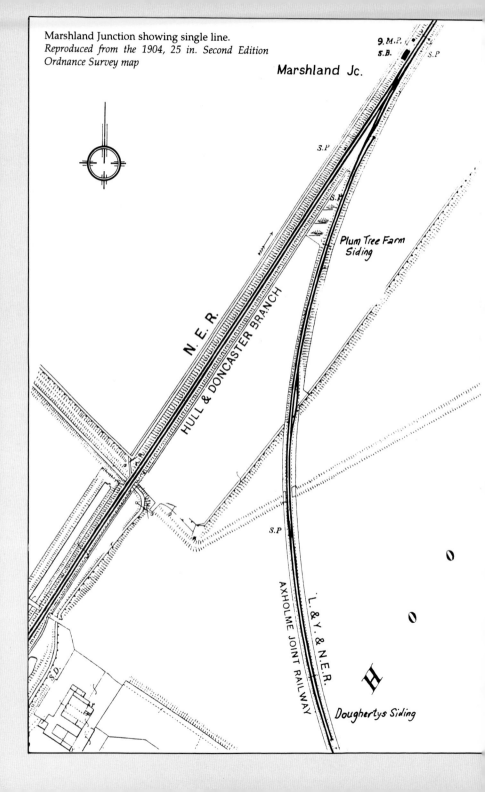

Marshland Junction showing single line.
*Reproduced from the 1904, 25 in. Second Edition
Ordnance Survey map*

Marshland Jc.

9. *M.P.*
S.B.
S.P

S.P.

S.P.

Plum Tree Farm
Siding

N. E. R.

HULL & DONCASTER BRANCH

S.P

AXHOLME JOINT RAILWAY

L. & Y. & N.E.R.

S.D.

Doughertys Siding

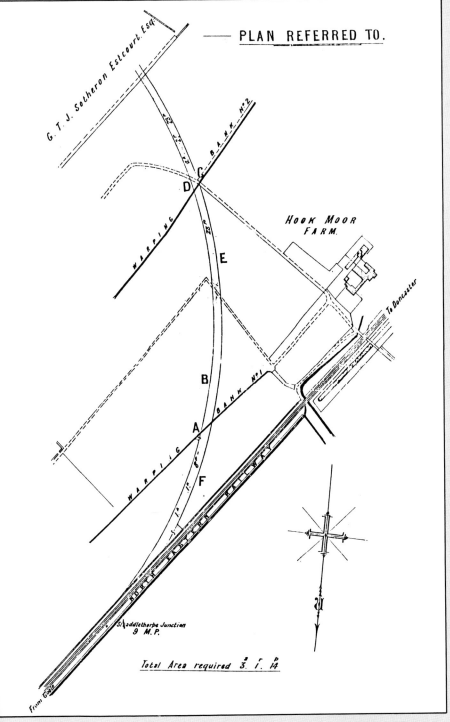

Original plan for the purchase of land for the junction and trackbed of the G&MLR at Marshland Junction.

N.E.R. HULL AND DONCASTER BRANCH.

GOOLE AND MARSHLAND LIGHT RAILWAY.
PROPOSED JUNCTION.

A view from the brake van of a train on the AJR just joining the Doncaster to Goole main line at Marshland Junction; the signal box is visible.

C.T. Goode

The plan showing the proposed junction and signal box. However line 'A' was not put in.

A

N.E.R.^{CN} BOUNDARY

TP.

To Doncaster

N.E.R.^{CN} BOUNDARY

From Goole

Proposed New Signal Box

This view taken from a steam railcar, looks back along the NER Goole-Doncaster line towards Marshland Junction. The AJR forks left and Marshland signal box can only just be seen behind the outline of the railcar, which has just come off the AJR *en route* to Goole. Note Hookmoor Farm just to the left of the slotted-post NER bracket signals.

Real Photographs

Marshland Junction) and desires to load his traffic direct into wagons on the Committee's siding at that place so as to avoid cartage to Goole or Rawcliffe. It was agreed to recommend that the privilege be granted and that the place be designated 'Plumtree Farm Siding', Mr Firth to sign an indemnity freeing the Joint Companies from all responsibility. It was pointed out that the southern portion of this siding is not now required and was agreed to recommend that the permanent way be taken out as and when required by the Engineering Dept. and used for maintenance and renewal purposes on the Joint Line, the buffer stops to be removed and re-fixed, at the estimated cost of £40, at the end of No.10 siding at Reedness Junction, where there have been several derailments owing to the absence of proper stop-blocks.

Moving a further ¼ mile down the line, the next siding reached was Dougherty's Siding(called originally Duckell's Siding)* and this was to the left of the running line, just 100 yards from the junction's outer signal and on the left-hand curve of the main line. It had a facing point and was 240 ft in length.

A further ½ mile on came Corner's Siding which consisted of a parallel track to the main line (on the left-hand side) connected just over halfway

*When the G&MLR was taken over, there appeared on the reports, a claim by P. Dougherty for £65 compensation for loss of his potatoes and bags (being burnt) in 1903, caused by sparks from a contractor's locomotive. This did not seem to have been paid or resolved.

along by a trailing crossover, thus allowing a headshunt. The relevant agreement between the G&MLR and Charlotte Wait (plus others) was drawn up on 20th June, 1901.

Only a ⅓ of a mile further on, but this time entered by a trailing point was the short Smith's Siding situated at Smith's Bank, again on the left-hand side of the running line. This particular siding gave considerable problems to the NER and on 6th October, 1902, a meeting took place to discuss the British Moss Litter Company's tramway (established in 1896 before the railway) which crossed just 150 yards further on from Smith's Siding. It was proposed that the tramway crossing (*see opposite*) should be taken out and a further siding inserted for a cost of £260, with the tramway being cut in half and then running alongside both standard gauge sidings. This would have been cheaper than a tunnel or a bridge, both of which were considered.

This proposal did not come into being and on 15th August, 1903, a ground frame was installed to control the tramway crossing (1 mile 1180 yds from Marshland Junction (*see the Circular opposite*). Apparently the tramway was used by the BMLC approximately 12 times a day. During 1904, Inspector Connell from Hull made a complaint against Farmer Smith, inferring that he was using the crossing as an 'occupation crossing' for horses to and from his fields, stating that he had his own private road for this operation. A charge of £2 9s. 1d. had been incurred for the attendance of a platelayer at the crossing gates whenever the horses were crossing (period 19th November, 1903 to 14th January, 1904). On 30th January, 1904, Sebastian Meyer wrote to Mr Cudworth* and stated that Farmer Smith's lease gave him certain rights over the crossing and the matter seems to have been dropped.

In February 1905, Smith's Bank and Goole Grange Farm came into the limelight again when the NER and L&Y drew up a deed of agreement to construct a subway 10 ft wide and 8 ft deep under the Joint line and requiring that the tramway be diverted to run through it (*see opposite*). The gradient of the tramway[†] was not to exceed 1 in 20 at any point; the landowners were to pay £150 for the rights and also have a level crossing constructed over the AJR with access by wicket gates (these to be made not wide enough to allow the passage of carts).

---

*W.J. Cudworth was Chief Engineer of the Southern Division of the NER.

[†]Board minute 173, dated March 1907, refers to this tramway being unauthorised.

173. TRAMLINE LAID BY MR SMITH ON JOINT PROPERTY BETWEEN MARSHLAND JUNCTION AND REEDNESS JUNCTION

Mr Smith, of Goole Grange Farm, has without any arrangement with the Joint Companies recently laid down a tramline through the Joint Companies' fence and alongside the siding provided in accordance with the arrangement recorded in Joint Committee Minute 103 for the purpose of facilitating the loading and unloading of traffic.

The encroachment has been pointed out to Mr Smith who now admits the mistake, and it is recommended that the arrangement be agreed to on the understanding that Mr Smith bears the cost of providing a suitable gate, and that acknowledgement of 1s. per annum be paid for the privilege.

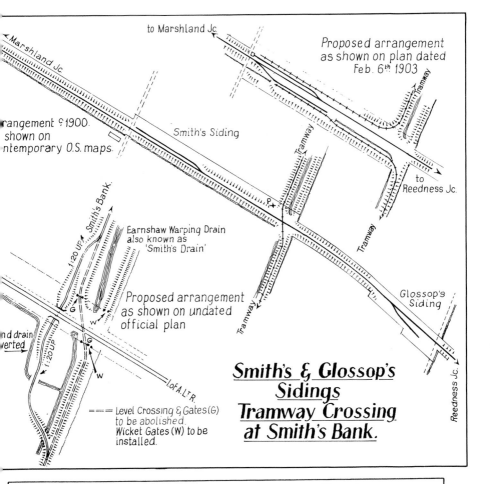

Smith's & Glossop's Sidings Tramway Crossing at Smith's Bank.

Tramway Crossing. Smith's Bank,
Between Marshland Junction and Reedness Junction.

A new ground frame has been fixed at this Crossing (1 mile 1180 yards from Marshland Junction), from which the following Signals are worked :—

Up Stop Signal.

A single armed signal fixed on the Up Side of the Line about 20 yards from the ground frame.

Down Stop Signal.

A single armed signal fixed on the Down Side of the Line about 20 yards from the ground frame.

The frame and the crossing gates will be kept locked, and will be opened when the crossing is required by the Permanent way Inspector or Platelayer who will work the signal levers.

These signals are provided for the protection of the Tramway Crossing when it is being made use of for traffic purposes, and Drivers must be careful to satisfy themselves when proceeding in either direction as to whether the stop signals are at "DANGER" or in the "ALLRIGHT" position.

Immediately the Main Line has been crossed the levers must be put to the normal position and locked by the Permanent Way Inspector or Platelayer who will also lock the gates.

The Tramway must not be used when it is seen that a Train is approaching.

Instructions to be observed at Reedness Junction in regard to Trains approaching.

Until further notice Trains approaching Reedness Junction from any direction must be prepared to stop at the outer home signal, which if the section is clear, will be lowered to allow the Train to proceed in the direction required.

M. WOODHOUSE,
Joint Superintendent.

Extract from AJR Circular No. 2, dated 15th August, 1903.   *Collection K.P. Plant*

Just 120 yards from the problematic Smith's Tramway crossing, and this time on the right-hand side lay Glossop's Siding, equipped with a facing point and a single 225 ft spur. After approximately ½ mile yet a further siding was reached, namely Goole Fields Siding, which ran a considerable length along (and parallel) to the main line right up to the Swinefleet Warping Drain bridge, where it turned left and ran beside the drain. This siding had a tramway connection (situated on a mound) for loading, which was agreed in 1907. The main line continued its way by crossing a steel bridge, which was of girder construction, 120 ft in length and incidentally the main engineering feature of the G&MLR.

Reedness Junction

Reedness Junction was the first station* on the AJR after its commencement at Marshland Junction and was the point where the Fockerby branch joined the main route from the east. The station had one platform for each of the routes; one near the junction and the other further away along the Fockerby branch (*see page 70*). The station master's house was situated between the two running lines, with two wooden huts, one used as a booking office and the other for the single line signalling apparatus cum signal box. A fine NER water column (No. 457) stood between the lines.[†] Access to the goods sidings and loading facilities were entered from the Fockerby branch line. It is obvious that passenger revenue at this station could have never been substantial as the station was situated right in the heart of the sparsely populated Marshland, only serving a handful of farms and homesteads. The nearest villages of Swinefleet and Reedness were 3 and 4 miles away respectively!

In 1906, an application was submitted from a Colonel Thompson for permission to be given to his female potato gathers (about 16) to walk through the Reedness Junction goods yard, walk along the main line and then cross the warping drain bridge to gain access to the road running along the bank of the drain to the fields, thus saving considerable distances of walking around the fields. After a heated Board meeting, it was agreed to comply with the application on the understanding that Colonel Thompson would indemnify the Joint line against accident to the ladies. The tall water tower (*see page 72*) which was built of brick, could be seen for a considerable distance and served the three water columns at the junction. The water supply to the junction was the subject of several Board discussions and in September 1907 the following minute was recorded:

> Attention was called to the engine delays which had been caused at various times in consequence of the failure of the water supply at Reedness Junction. Since the opening of the Joint Line a tank has been erected at the Pumping Station at Shipcote Drain, 1¼ miles from Reedness Junction, to be used in the event of the tank at the

*There is some doubt to the exact name of this station. Some tickets say REEDNESS (RCH Map confirms) however others say REEDNESS JCT (NER Public timetables and handbills agree). The station never appeared to carry a nameboard so the 'exact' name remains debatable.

[†]There were two other water columns at the junction, one on the Crowle platform (NER No. 410) and the other on the branch platform (NER No. 411).

Reedness Junction showing Swinefleet Warping Drain.

Reproduced from the 1906 25 in. Ordnance Survey map

REEDNESS JUNCTION

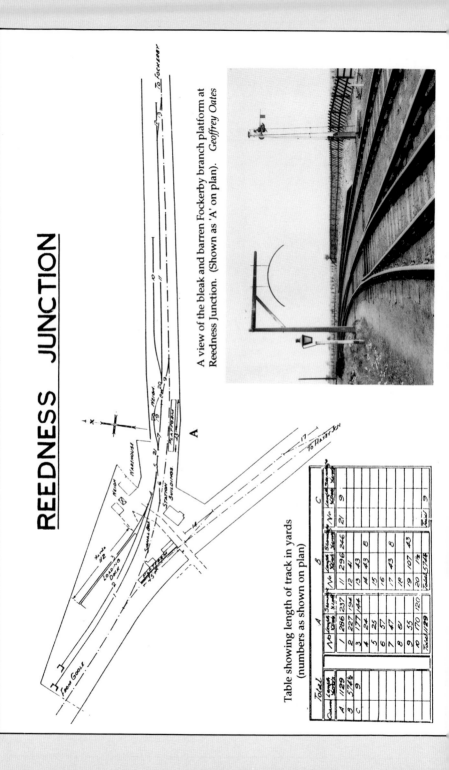

A view of the bleak and barren Fockerby branch platform at Reedness Junction. (Shown as 'A' on plan). *Geoffrey Oates*

Table showing length of track in yards
(numbers as shown on plan)

AMENDED NOTICE.

AXHOLME JOINT RAILWAY

(Lancashire and Yorkshire and North Eastern Railways.)

JOINT SUPERINTENDENT'S OFFICE,

CROWLE,
15th August, 1903.

CIRCULAR No. 2.

Reedness Junction.

The following Signalling arrangements at REEDNESS JUNCTION were brought into use on 8th August, 1903.

A new ground frame fixed mid-way on the Platform at which trains to and from CROWLE are dealt with, was brought into use, and the following SIGNALS worked from it :—

Down Outer Home Signal—For trains approaching from Crowle.

A single armed semaphore fixed on the Down Side of the Line 130 yards from the ground frame.

Down Home Signal—For trains approaching from Crowle.

A single armed semaphore fixed on the Down Side of the Line 20 yards from the ground frame.

Up Outer Home Signal—For trains approaching from Fockerby.

A single armed semaphore fixed on the Down Side of the Line 130 yards from the ground frame.

Up Home Signal—For trains approaching from Fockerby.

A single armed semaphore fixed on the Down Side of the Line 20 yards from the ground frame.

Down Starting Signal—For trains proceeding to Marshland Junction.

A single armed semaphore fixed on the Down Side of the Line 130 yards from the ground frame.

Up Home Signal.

A single armed semaphore fixed on the Up Side of the Line 150 yards from the ground frame.

Down Direction Signal—To Fockerby.

Up Direction Signal—To Crowle.

A double armed bracketed signal fixed on the Up Side of the Line 80 yards from the ground frame to read

1. **To Fockerby.**
2. **Crowle.**

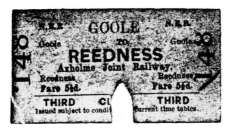

A 12 vehicle goods train from Haxey, headed by an Ivatt 2-6-0 running tender first, is ready to depart for Goole.   *Geoffrey Oates*

Reedness Junction on 14th September, 1963 with an RCTS brake van Special hauled by No. D2611 heading for Fockerby. The main line runs to the left of this view which shows the prominent brick-built water tower. Number D2611, a 204 hp Gardner-engined 35 ton 0-6-0 diesel mechanical locomotive was built by the Hunslet Engine Co. Ltd, Leeds, in 1960 (works number 5660). Later becoming BR class '05', it was withdrawn from Goole shed in November 1967, sold in May 1968 to the National Coal Board, Yorkshire Main Colliery Doncaster, where it was scrapped about December 1976.   *Harold D. Bowtell*

A view from Reedness Junction's main line platform looking north-westwards towards Marshland Junction on 14th September, 1963. Note the assortment of signals. The gradient is rising to the bridge in the distance which passes over the Swinefleet Warping Drain. *John Edgington*

A 1930s photograph of Reedness Junction with a steam railcar standing taking water on the main line from Haxey, *en route* to Goole. The Fockerby branch swings to the left. *Real Photographs*

Junction becoming empty. Difficulty is experienced in keeping the Reedness Junction tank full on account of the small and inadequate connecting pipe, 2 in. in diameter, from the Pumping Station to the tank. To improve the supply it will be necessary for a 4 in. cast-iron main to be laid from the tank at the Pumping Station to the tank at the Junction, at a cost of £517 (£310 Revenue, £207 Capital).

After discussion the Traffic Officers came to the conclusion that the delays which had been experienced by the engine having to run the extra distance on the occasions of the failure of the Reedness Junction tank, were not sufficiently serious to justify the expenditure above named.

Comparison of the 1906 Ordnance Survey map and the 1923 track diagram shows an additional loop south of the junction on the main line and extra sidings alongside the loading-dock,* with a wagon weighbridge facility (at a cost of £120) added to the extra sidings on the Fockerby branch.†

A former station master, Len Bedale, wrote of his experiences whilst at Reedness Junction# and the account is as follows:

The Hull District covered quite a large area and among the most difficult parts to reach was that traversed by the Axholme Joint line. In the case of Reedness Junction it was necessary to make one's way from Goole by road, a distance of some six miles. I used my cycle on these journeys, and in winter it was quite a tough proposition. Although the road was generally flat, the country was open to the full blast of everything the weather could offer. The final two miles were the worst and loneliest stretch. Short of Swinefleet village one turned very sharply right and, after roughly a further mile, it was then possible, on a clear day, to see the high water-tower at Reedness Junction from which the water cranes were supplied. The electric tablet and Tyer's Patent block instruments were at Reedness station office, the headquarters of the line. The main line split sharply, some 40 yds or so before reaching the lever box. The track to the left led to Fockerby terminus, which was in close proximity to the river Trent. Running over this 6½ miles long branch was governed by train staff (one engine in steam). The other branch of the fork ran to Epworth (Lincs), where the line terminated, the connection to Haxey Junction (Great Northern & Great Eastern Joint) having been severed some time previously. The electric tablet sections were from Marshland (on the Doncaster to Goole main line) to Reedness, Reedness to Crowle, Crowle to Belton and Belton to Epworth. There was no signalman at Reedness, or Epworth, and the station masters, or station clerks, who had been passed in the Rules and Regulations, were responsible for working the block instruments, points and signals. The goods shunter stationed at Reedness travelled on the goods train to both Epworth and Fockerby, to assist the guard. In 1960 there were three station masters on the branches, one each at Reedness Junction, Crowle and Epworth. Very soon the Crowle man was withdrawn, and some time later the Epworth station master, Mr Johnson, and his wife, who was clerk at the station, suffered the same fate.

This left the station master at Reedness, Mr G. Little, in full charge, with his wife

*BOT document MT6 1559/2 Reedness Junction dated 12th February, 1907, states that 'on the downside of Reedness Junction, a new facing siding in the up direction has been added.

†These additional sidings for 45 wagons and the Fockerby branch carriage stock siding were agreed by the Board in March 1906 at a cost of £620.

#From *Station Master* by Len Bedale, published by Turntable Publications, 1976.

The photographer is standing with his back to Marshland Junction, looking at Reedness Junction station. The Fockerby branch curves away to the left with its platform just past the water tender standing in the siding. The 'main line' to Haxey bears off to the right and its low platform can be seen clearly. Completely dwarfed by the station master's house are the signal cabin and ticket office.   *Geoffrey Oates*

A last look at Reedness Junction, this time from the main line platform, looking towards Marshland Junction. The date is 14th September, 1963 (Brakevan Special). Note the platform-mounted signal cabin (*middle*) and the station building (*right*), with the water tower in the distance.   *Harold D. Bowtell*

as part-time clerk. The station house at Reedness was very isolated, with no piped water supply, or electric light.

During the summer months traffic was fairly light, but from October to about late Spring there was quite a large quantity of agricultural traffic, both forwarded and received, in addition to domestic and coal inward and peat outward traffic. From end to end the Axholme Joint line boasted a large number of private sidings, and in the sugar beet season it was quite a job arranging wagons for loading and picking up, bearing in mind that some points to the main line faced one way and others the reverse. In this matter one had to rely on the travelling shunter and, of course, on phone messages from the traders.

It was at Reedness Junction where there occurred 'The Unusual Case of the Locomotive that was Pushed to Start'. The time was late afternoon towards the end of October. Much shunting had been done and most of the siding space was occupied by loaded wagons of sugar beet awaiting despatch, many requiring labelling and checking. The heavily-laden train from Epworth was not long arrived when, after the first shunt, the driver of the six-coupled diesel locomotive announced with dismay that the engine had stalled. He was unable to restart and he wanted the diesel fitters to be sent from Goole Motive Power Depot. This was indeed a nasty one, it was almost five o'clock and I knew that the fitters at Goole would be on their way home. To send for them would mean long delay, as, in addition to collecting the men from their homes, transport to Reedness would have to be arranged. Seeing a fair number of agricultural workers engaged in loading sugar beet at the loading dock, an idea came into my head. I asked the driver whether he thought the engine would start if the locomotive were moved in gear. He said it might, but who would be likely to move it? I said that I would see what could be done and went across to the dock to ask the farm men if they would help me, after briefly explaining the position to them. There was ready agreement and, propelled by the united strenuous efforts of fourteen determined men, the recalcitrant monster started to move. With masterly judgement of the moment when 14 m.p. (i.e. manpower!) had reached maximum velocity, the driver let in the clutch and the engine burst into life with a mighty roar. It was a pleasing demonstration of what could be done, given the will, and, after thanking the men for their efforts, one of them laconically remarked that this was the first time that he had helped to push a railway engine. It was quite a new experience for me too!

Continuing a further third of a mile down the main line from the junction, a further siding was situated on the gentle southwards curve of the running line. This was a trailing siding called Moor's Farm, serving the farm of the same name.*

On a further mile, an important trailing siding was encountered, namely Peat Moss Works Siding. This line came into the main line on the level and served the Yorkshire Peat Works of the British Moss Litter Co. This complex had a considerable narrow gauge tramway system coming in from the vast peat fields thus serving the works, and finally the AJR with freight. This tramway still survives today, but the product is transported from the works by road. On southwards and at the 7¼ milepost was Spilman's Siding which again was trailing and 45 yds in length being authorised by an agreement of

*BOT file, MT6 1922/6 dated 27th September, 1910 (PRO Kew).

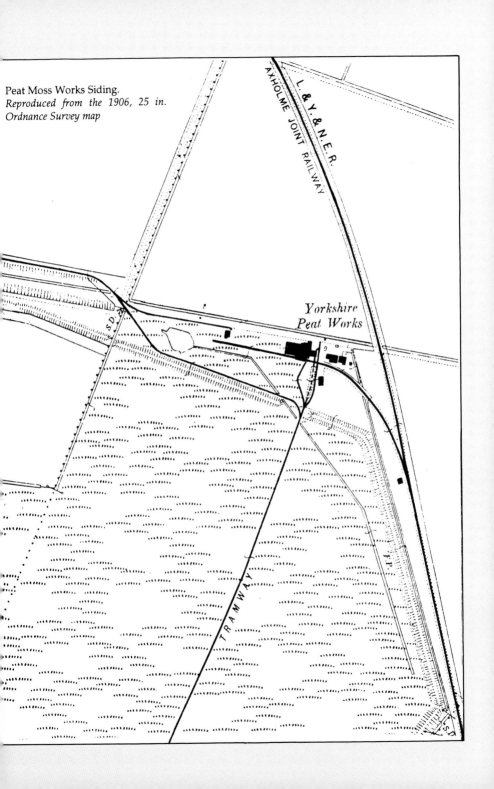

Peat Moss Works Siding.
Reproduced from the 1906, 25 in.
Ordnance Survey map

Yorkshire Peat Works, Swinefleet Mill with the 3 ft Peat Moors tramway curving into the site.   *Courtesy Stan Marshall*

The curved portable track of the Peat tramway being used to join the tramway 'main line' to the portable track laid into the peat cutting area. The 90° angle was made up of three portable 6 yard curved lengths. Many miles of this tramway was used on the moors to feed the mill.   *Courtesy Stan Marshall*

This 'crude' locomotive seen here at the British Moss Litter Company on the 28th May, 1957 at Swinefleet, is thought to be by J.F. Howard Ltd of Bedford. It was purchased from a quarry around 1951 and arrived at Swinefleet Mill sometime in late 1954, where it was used on most of the tramways, being sold for scrap locally in 1960. Further interest in the photograph centres on the late Jack Oughtibrige (standing next to the cab) who was a foreman at Swinefleet Mill and instigated the use of mechanisation to the moors. On this occasion he had just taken a teacher and his pupils on a 'local studies' trip to the peat moors. *Courtesy Stan Marshall*

The 'new' steel-caged wagons purchased from Robert Hudsons, seen here full awaiting a bumpy trip on the tramway to the British Moss Peat works.

Courtesy Stan Marshall

16th August, 1901 between Henry Strickland Constable and the IOALR, for agricultural use. In 1908, Mr C. Stone of Rainsbutt Farm (which was near the siding) made an application for the 1.30 pm train service from Crowle and the 5.30 pm service from Goole, to stop here (on Wednesdays) just for the use for his wife and himself. Needless to say the Board of the AJR declined the application. Just south of this siding was situated an ungated crossing (Maw Crossing) near Crowle cottage, where the railway and a by-road formed a 'Vee'. In March 1930 an alarming incident occurred with the newly introduced steam Sentinel railcar (working the 5.25 pm from Haxey). Mr Farnsworth in his Crossley 16 hp car did not see the railcar which hit the motor car and carried it a considerable distance down the line. The driver and his son were injured but Mrs Maw was unharmed. The crash had fractured the steam brake pipe and so the railcar could not be moved; a bus had to be supplied by Mr Watkins (the Crowle station master) to take the five passengers on to Epworth and Haxey.

Crowle

At the time of the Norman Conquest the village of Crowle was one of the most populous and valuable 'Manors' within the Isle of Axholme. *Crul*, or *Croule*, derives from the Dutch word *KROL* - a shed or small habitation of some kind. The population at the 1851 census was 3,008. The area was once an ancient forest girded by the fertile fields of Crowle on all sides. This was destroyed leaving extensive peat moors, marshes and bogs. In the early days before the conquest, the river Don gave the people of Crowle free access to the river Humber and was the means by which an early Christian missionary visited the village and dedicated the church to St Oswald (early Saxon). The village was one of the first in the area to have a gas works installed (1854) and at the time of the coming of the railway, supported two breweries; James Fox & Son (to the north of the town) and the New Trent Brewery, owned by John Dymond. Old advertisements show that John Dymond was 'Brewer, mineral water manufacturer and bottler of ale and stout'. Whether the gas works obtained their coal via the AJR cannot be established, but in March 1906, it was reported that the Trent Brewery was sending all its output by the AJR, on a six-monthly, recurring agreement, as from the 1st October,1905 (finally ceasing in June 1909). Other companies with accounts on the AJR at this time, were James Fox and Sons and the British Moss Litter Co. Certainly the gas company used the canal wharf at Crowle and had a permanent unloading facility in use.

Crowle station was situated near the 8¾ mile post and provided the first passing loop on the line. It boasted two low platforms, plus adequate sidings

Cross Street, Crowle *c.* 1920.

Courtesy Ian Snell

Mr M. Woodhouse Superintendent
of the AJR 1903-1926.

Mrs S.J. Bradwell

The three sons of Mr M. Woodhouse, who was the
joint superintendent of the AJR.
Left Mathews Woodhouse, employed by the NER in
the timetable office at York, following in father's
footsteps who also started his working days in this
office.   *Mrs S.J. Bradwell*
Middle Frank Woodhouse, station master at
Epworth until leaving in 1937. He had many mean-
ingful discussions with his brother Bernard who
was employed by the LMS, whereas Frank worked
for the LNER.   *Mrs S.J. Bradwell*
Right Bernard Woodhouse who was station master
at Belton and then Fockerby.   *Mrs S.J. Bradwell*

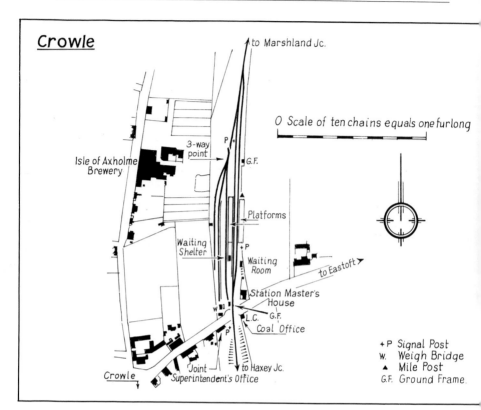

Crowle

to Marshland Jc.

O Scale of ten chains equals one furlong

3-way point

G.F.

Isle of Axholme Brewery

Platforms

Waiting Shelter

Waiting Room

to Eastoft

Station Master's House

L.C. G.F.

Coal Office

W

+P Signal Post
w. Weigh Bridge
▲ Mile Post
G.F. Ground Frame.

Joint Superintendent's Office

to Haxey Jc.

Crowle

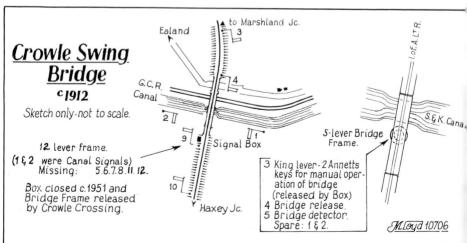

Crowle Swing Bridge
c 1912

Sketch only - not to scale.

Eoland

to Marshland Jc.

G.C.R. Canal

I. of A. L.T.R.

3

4

Signal Box

2

9

1

S. & K. Cana.

5-lever Bridge Frame.

10

Haxey Jc.

12 lever frame.
(1 & 2 were Canal Signals)
Missing: 5.6.7.8.11.12.

Box closed c.1951 and Bridge Frame released by Crowle Crossing.

3 King lever - 2 Annetts keys for manual operation of bridge (released by Box)
4 Bridge release.
5 Bridge detector.
Spare: 1 & 2.

JLloyd 10706

Not the Axholme Joint Railway, but relevant, as this pre-1900 view shows Crowle station on the GCR line which would have been the junction of the two railways if the two curves had been constructed from the AJR down to the GCR. Note the 'Keel' barge on the canal roughly where the AJR swing bridge was to be constructed. In the lower view the same station building (*left*) as in the above view shows how close the AJR was; with the embankment and brick arches clearly visible in the distance.

(Top) Edwin Harrison; (lower) Mrs Ella

for goods traffic,* including a public weighbridge.

The booking office was situated at the station master's house and consisted of a wooden single-storey office (with a clock); a waiting room was provided near the down platform. Although the AJR station was to the north of the village, it was far more convenient to the residents than that of the rival GCR station (south of the village) on the Doncaster to Cleethorpes line. This station is still in use today, but is in fact in the village of Ealand, some distance south of Crowle. The Ordnance Survey map of 1906 shows only one siding whereas both the original IOALR survey and the 1923 track diagram show two.

The superintendent of the AJR was based at this station and from the opening Mr M. Woodhouse served the railway for 23 unblemished years. On his retirement, in 1926, the local newspaper reported that this man 'was always approachable by all, always courteous and considerate and studied the best interests of the railway'. He was presented with a 3 valve wireless set (an Axophone) made by the local Axholme Wireless Works at Crowle (including a license and loudspeaker).

Mr Woodhouse was the only superintendent on the AJR, as the post was discontinued on his retirement. The permanent way inspector was also based at Crowle and during this period was Bill Barnes (whose son was at one time the station master at Belton on the AJR).

During World War I nearly all the male staff were called to arms, leaving the AJR short of employees and so several wives were pressed into service on the line. Mr Woodhouse, being short of staff in the main office asked his wife Mary to help and she, being of a 'forceful nature', apparently took over. It was rumoured that on Sundays, after services ceased she would use the permanent way trolley to visit friends at Spilman's Siding (north of Crowle); some effort would have been needed, if the account is to be believed.

After crossing the main A161 Eastoft to Crowle road, the line curved slightly and ran into a cutting (now a nature walk) and on down to Mill Road crossing, which at one time was in the capable hands of Johnny Chafor. A further straight stretch of track followed before another level crossing was reached, Field Road Crossing. On 8th March, 1924 a fatal accident occurred when Mary Clynes (aged 60) wife of Jas Clynes, who was the resident platelayer, was killed by a train whilst she was opening the gates for the 8.14 pm service. The inquest found that the gates had to be opened in a sequence to operate the warning bells which she had unfortunately not done; this was duly changed so that the bells would ring however the gates were operated. The doctor certified her dead 'between the tracks'; her distraught husband never returned to duty. Later a Mr George Fields lived in the house and his wife operated the crossing gates.

The line continued south-eastwards and on to the village of Ealand. The joint superintendent of the AJR had on several occasions (prior to 1908) been

*Crowle siding was increased by 60 yds in October, 1904 at a cost of £60 for the increase in coal traffic to the station.

A view (looking north) of Crowle station photographed in the late 1930s. The low platforms some way from the waiting room can be seen in the distance, whilst the large station master's house and booking office is on the right. The goods yard is on the left.

Geoffrey Oates

Crowle AJR station looking north towards Reedness Junction. The ground frame can be seen just beyond the 'low' platforms. These platforms must have satisfied the Board of Trade because the Light Railways Act stipulated that 'platforms shall be provided to their satisfaction unless all carriages in use on the railway for the conveyance of passengers, are constructed with proper and convenient means of access to and from the same, from and to the level of the ground on the outside of the rail'. Later, however, to facilitate alighting at the low station platforms, brass handrails were fitted to the inside of the lower part of the carriage doors and short portable steps were provided at each station to assist the aged and infirm.   *Real Photographs*

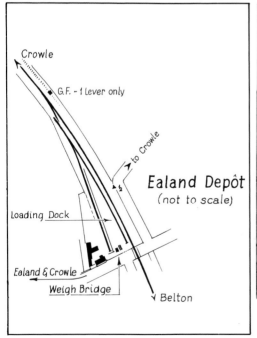

The entrance to Ealand Depot seen from the front of a dmu.   *Stan Teanby*

approached by farmers and others in the Ealand district, on the question of siding accommodation for handling the ever increasing goods traffic around Ealand crossing. The bulk of the traffic had been carted from local farms on the east side of the line over the level crossing to the nearby GCR station (about ⅔rds of a mile as against nearly two miles to the AJR station at Crowle). If siding accommodation were to be provided it was estimated that the AJR could benefit from 5,000 tons of freight traffic being secured from rival routes.

The rail distance from Crowle to Ealand was about 1½ miles and, after careful consideration, the Joint committee agreed to provide siding accommodation for 22 wagons at a cost of £1,000, excluding the land purchase of a third of an acre needed.

It was necessary to appoint a senior porter at this depot, to work under the direction of the Crowle station master with all the clerical work being processed at Crowle. The depot sidings were on the west side of the main line and consisted of two tracks protected by a catch point.*

After passing the goods depot, the line began to rise on an embankment to enable the Stainforth & Keadby Canal (Sheffield & Yorkshire Navigation) to be crossed by an opening swing bridge, whilst leaving sufficient clearance for smaller craft to navigate the canal. The bridge (called Crowle Swing Bridge) was the major engineering achievement on the whole railway and was needed to allow the very tall Yorkshire 'Keels' to journey up to Thorne in full sail. This stipulation was laid down by the Sheffield & South Yorkshire Navigation, which was incorporated in an Act of 1889, to allow the purchase of the Sheffield Canal, River Dun, Dearne and Dove Canal plus the Stainforth & Keadby Canal.

The approach to the swing bridge by the railway was over three brick-arched spans, crossing a minor road and then a drainage channel before reaching a 52 ft trussed iron girder bridge which spanned the GCR (Scunthorpe to Doncaster main line) consisting of three tracks, finally traversing a further brick arch. The line ran on to the 104 ft-long hog-backed open webbed-truss girder bridge built at a cost of some £20,000 by the Cleveland Bridge & Engineering Company Limited of Darlington. The total length of this complex was well over 330 feet.

The 1885 Act clearly stated the terms of construction for this bridge:

The railway shall be carried over the railway of the Sheffield Company by means of a girder bridge the piers or abutments whereof shall be parallel with that railway and shall have a single span of not less than fifty feet measured at right angles with the abutments thereof and shall have a clear height or headway over the rails of the railway of the Sheffield Company of not less than fifteen feet.

* *The operators of the sidings (in conjunction with local villagers from Ealand) requested a passenger station in March 1908, but this was declined by the Board due to the proximity of the other stations.

A panoramic view of the AJR main line looking east from the Ealand main road and showing the Crowle Swing Bridge and signal box. The Ivatt 2-6-0 is propelling its train of assorted freight vehicles towards Epworth. Provision was made in the Sectional Appendix for freight wagons to be propelled between Marshland Junction and Epworth with or without a brakevan. In the reverse direction when it was necessary to propel and pull wagons at the same time, the number to be propelled was restricted to 20. On the Fockerby branch propelling was permitted in either direction in clear weather only with a maximum of 10 wagons; when propelling towards Eastoft the brakevan in which the guard was riding had to be the leading vehicle. The houses on the left were for the signalman and swing bridge foreman.   *Geoffrey Oates*

This time looking west with a southbound freight crossing Crowle Swing Bridge with a class '2MT' in charge. The structure crosses a 10 ft drain, the Stainforth Keadby Canal, GCR main line, a further drain then the Ealand village road.   *Geoffrey Oates*

The second viaduct south of the Crowle swing bridge was a nine-arch substantial brick-built structure which took the AJR over South Engine Drain and Folly Drain with a track to North Moor Farm. This again was constructed to carry double tracks.

Geoffrey Oates

In this view an Ivatt 2-6-0 sets off, tender first with a loaded train for Goole. The first viaduct south of the Crowle swing bridge was a 12-arch brick-built structure which carried the single track AJR over the New Torne River, Double River, the A18 Althorp road and then further drains.

Geoffrey Oates

This view of the construction of the Crowle Swing Bridge centre-drive mechanism was an official picture used by the Cleveland Bridge and Engineering Co. Ltd of Darlington in an advertising brochure of the time. They constructed bridges all over the world, their most spectacular creation being the railway bridge over the Zambesi at the Victoria Falls. *Courtesy The Darlington Railway Centre and Museum*

A period photograph of Crowle Swing Bridge in the open position allowing one of the very tall 'Keel' barges to pass through. This view also clearly illustrates that the bridge was built for double track, although only one line was ever laid.

Courtesy Peter L. Smith

The railway shall be carried over the canal of the Sheffield Company by means of a bridge having one opening span on the swivel-principle of at least forty feet clear width measured at right angles with the abutments thereof and with a clear headway above the ordinary water level of the canal of at least twenty feet and the piers of the said bridge shall be parallel with the centre line of the canal.

The Company shall at all times and for ever after the completion of the bridge over the canal of the Sheffield Company cause to be hung out or exhibited in a conspicuous situation on each side of the opening span of that bridge every night from sunset to sunrise a good and sufficient light to be kept burning by and at the expense of the Company for the navigation and safe guidance of boats and vessels using or navigating the said canal which lights shall if necessary be from time to time altered by the Company in such manner and be of such description and be so used and placed as the principal engineer for the time being of the Sheffield Company shall reasonably require and in case the Company shall neglect to exhibit and keep any such light burning as aforesaid they shall for every such neglect be liable to a penalty not exceeding ten pounds which may with full costs be recovered by the Sheffield Company from the Company in any court of competent jurisdiction.

The Company or any person or persons acting under them shall not detain at the said bridge over the canal of the Sheffield Company any vessel barge or boat navigating that canal and having masts or chimneys from any cause not then capable of being lowered with safety to the vessel or without risk of damage to the cargo and in case the company or any person or persons acting under them shall wilfully or negligently detain any such vessel barge or boat contrary to the provisions of this Act or demand take or receive any toll or charge for the passage of any person or persons vessel barge or boat through or under the said bridge the Company and every person so offending shall for every offence be liable to a penalty not exceeding the sum of ten pounds which penalty shall be recoverable by summary process in the manner directed by the Railways Clauses Consolidation Act 1845 for the recovery of penalties incurred by the Company but nothing in this Act shall prevent any remedy for damages which any party may sustain in respect of any such detention as aforesaid.

Originally, design work on the swing bridge was carried out by the Yorkshire District Light Railways Syndicate of Leeds. However Mr F.S. Wheat the resident Engineer worked to the designs of W.J. Cudworth* of the NER, who in turn was under the supervision of Mr W. MacDmalt of York, then the NER's resident Engineer.

It is interesting to note that the working and maintenance of this swing bridge, with the exception of the girders and the brick and stone work but including all the machinery and gear for working the bridge, together with the staff employed thereat, was taken over by the L&YR from 1st July, 1905.

The following reprint from the *Goole Times*, 23rd September, 1904 sums up the technical specification of the works;

*Cudworth wrote to Meyer on the 17th September, 1901 stating that the NER would pay 5% in addition to the accepted tender, for the iron and steel work already carried out on the bridge. These prices were to be settled between the NER and Meyer when the final drawings were completed and approved by the canal company.

The structure swung on a circular centre-hollow pier on one bank of the canal and this housed the control mechanism and the turning engine, being 20 hp Crossley diesel oil engine (there being no electricity available at the time). The whole structure could be turned by hand in case of engine failure and was similar in design to the bridge spanning the Doncaster to Cleethorpes Railway. The weight was transferred by a special cross girder to a circular box girder which was bolted to the upper roller path; the outer edge being in the form of a tooth and rack into which a pinion was driven by the engine. In order to adjust the span the canal had been narrowed at the bridge to a width of 26 feet. The bridge had a 10 mph speed limit imposed on it for safety.

During the construction of the bridge, the *Goole Times* gave details of an accident which occurred on 10th October, 1904.

An accident, which will seriously delay the completion of the large swing bridge for the Isle of Axholme Railway that is to span the Keadby Canal at Crowle Wharf, occurred on Friday afternoon. A large steam crane, fixed close to the parapet of the bridge, was being used to place the sections of the steel work in position, when it overbalanced whilst hauling one of the main girders weighing about four tons. With the engine and girder, it fell crashing over the side of the bridge into the Soak dyke below. The dyke is both wide and deep and the engine fell head foremost,

This view shows the detailed construction of Crowle Swing Bridge and the central support. Note the small corrugated hut next to the central pier housing the standby diesel unit.   *Geoffrey Oates*

being nearly submerged, both being damaged. It is expected that a new girder will have to be manufactured and the delay in completing the bridge will be considerable. The brickwork was also torn away but luckily no one was injured.

During its life several attempts were made to ensure the bridge became fixed, as the railway was supposedly losing trade to other routes thanks to the constant opening for the canal traffic and so holding up its own freight, but these efforts failed. One such appeal was reported on 31st October, 1914 in *The Star*. A Mr John Rusling of Hull, the owner of sloops and keels trading along the Stainforth and Keadby Canal, sought an injunction to stop the Joint Companies fixing the swing bridge but the judge ruled against Rusling. He appealed in February 1915 but lost the appeal. During all its existence, a speed limit of 10 mph was enforced upon the bridge.

REGULATIONS FOR THE WORKING OF TRAINS
OVER
BRIDGES AND VIADUCTS.

CROWLE SWING BRIDGE.
(AXHOLME JOINT RAILWAY.)

Working Arrangements between the Signal Box and the Bridgeman's Box.

1.—The signalman will be the look-out man for canal craft.

2.—When the signalman requires the bridge to be opened he must give to the bridgeman's box one beat on the bell, and after acknowledgment must, provided no train is in sight, pull the release lever ; the indicator in the box will show that this has been done, whereupon the bridgeman, after making the necessary lever movements, will swing the bridge and lower the canal signals.

3.—When the bridge is to be closed the signalman will give two beats on the bell, and after acknowledgment, the bridgeman will, after seeing craft is clear, close the bridge, which he must always do as soon as possible ; he will then give three beats on the bell which the signalman will acknowledge and at once lock the bridge with his lever.

4.—Before anything is done to the machinery at the bridge which will in any way interfere with the wedge blocks or wires, the releasing lever in the bridge box must be pulled over.

5.—Telephonic communication is provided so that the signalman can whenever necessary communicate with the bridgeman and vice versa.

Special Instructions in force during Foggy Weather or Snowstorms.

1.—During foggy weather or snowstorms trains must not be allowed to leave Crowle or Epworth until information has been received from the bridgeman that the bridge is in position for trains to pass over it.

2.—If the signalman has allowed a train to leave either Crowle or Epworth he must not interfere with the bridge or signals in any way until he is satisfied that the whole of the train has passed over the bridge.

Extract from the Regulations covering the working of Crowle Swing Bridge in the NER Appendix of 1st January, 1905.

Just over a quarter of a mile to the south, and beyond the swing bridge at North Moor, there was a further 12-arch brick viaduct locally known as Crowle Arches which crossed the A18 road, the Hatfield Waste Drain, North Engine Drain and the River Torne, then just another half mile along a further nine-arch brick viaduct spanned the South Engine Drain and Folly Drain plus a farm track. From this point the railway started to fall to the level of the surrounding countryside and reached, after half a mile, an important siding (situated on the left-hand side of the running line) called Hagg Lane. This siding was controlled at one time by Mr Wardle who lived in the gatehouse alongside the track. Initially this spur was subject to an agreement with J.H. Bletcher of Wroot, one of the astute local farmers who had worked on the construction of the railway. Dated 21st March, 1910, this agreement was to build a loading dock at Hagg Lane alongside the siding and it is interesting that Mr Bletcher was subjected to the following conditions

IN CONSIDERATION of your providing a Loading Dock for the accommodation of five wagons at Hagg Lane Siding near to Bolton, I the undersigned John Henry Bletcher of Worlaby in the County of Lincoln hereby undertake and agree that in the event of the total amount of traffic received at or forwarded by me after the completion of the said Loading Dock from the said Siding in any year or part of year ending the 31st day of December being received and forwarded at the rate of less than 2,500 tons per annum I will pay to you in respect of such year or part of a year as the case may be a yearly sum equal to 6% on the cost of the said Loading Dock (not exceeding £200) as certified by your Engineer and so in proportion for any loss time than a year. Provided that this undertaking shall operate so long only as I shall occupy or continue tenant of the North Moors Farm.

In December 1920, Bletcher decided to lay his own tramway from Hagg Lane to serve his own farmland (*see NER plan opposite*). Stewart Squires describes the layouts of these tramways in his book *The Lincolnshire Potato Railways.**

A quantity of Army-surplus 2 ft gauge track was purchased and, by 1920, 1¼ miles of it laid on North Moor Farm, from Hagg Lane Siding on the Axholme Joint Railway, due east into the fields, and north to North Moor Farm. It was then extended eastwards from North Moor Farm, and south and east from Hagg Lane Siding to a point east of Old Farm, forming the shape of a capital letter 'E', with a total length of some three miles. In addition, lengths of track were kept at the end of the central stroke of the 'E' to be temporarily laid into the fields wherever needed.

The line was always horse-worked, the poor state of some of the second-hand track with its rusty metal sleepers precluding the use of a locomotive. For the opening, a number of four-wheel flat trucks, Army-surplus, were provided. Sides were built on to these by farm labour. Towards the end of its days, additional second-hand trucks were purchased from another, recently closed line, although which one is not known.

At Hagg Lane, the line ran up on to a dock from which produce was trans-shipped

*Published by the Oakwood Press, 1987

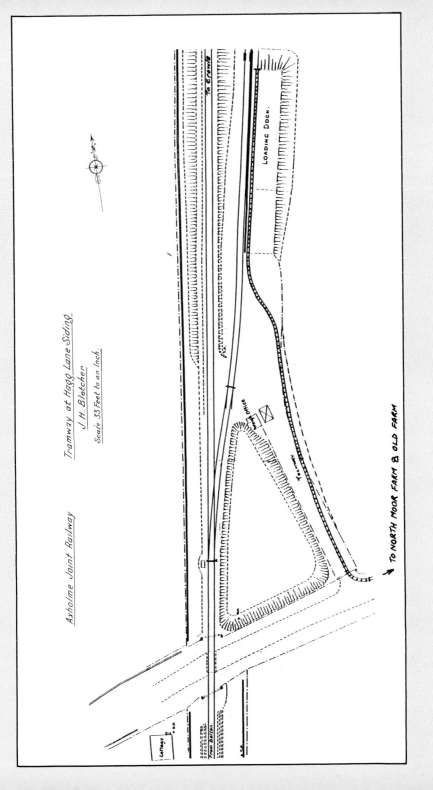

Axholme Joint Railway

Tramway at Hagg Lane Siding

J. H. Bletcher

Scale 33 Feet to an Inch.

To Crowle

LOADING DOCK.

Tramway

Weigh Office

Cottage

From Belton

TO NORTH MOOR FARM & OLD FARM

The 12-arch 'Crowle arches' pictured here in August 1981 just prior to being blown up by demolition contractors, after 76 years in existence. Only 15 ft 3 in. (clearance) in height, this was the site of many road accidents, however due to an important petroleum pipeline running on the eastern face of the viaduct, it was not until this pipeline was put under the road that the bridge could be demolished. *Courtesy Stan Teanby*

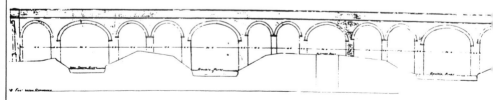

The official drawing by the NER (signed by Cudworth in 1913) of the 12-arch viaduct seen above.

into, and out of, railway wagons. Crops of potatoes, peas and carrots were sent out, and fertiliser and seed potatoes were received.

After World War II, the line's use decreased with each passing year and in about 1953 was closed completely.

In 1937, Charlie Arrand and Walter Powell used to work loading potatoes into trucks which were nickamed 'Jubilee' trucks. The horses would then be harnessed to them by roping across the length of the wagon to the back of the truck and not the fronts, this avoided them being pulled sideways off the uneven trackwork. Only two trucks were pulled at any one time and the horses uncannily knew which side of the track to walk so as to avoid walking over the points. The main line siding usually had five 8 ton open wagons and these normally were filled during the day. A porter from Belton station used to attend when the wagons were ready to be picked up and, in 1937, this was Ernest Addlesee.

From this point the line ran virtually on the level to the next station at Belton.

Belton

The large village of Belton (the name *Belinus* or *Bel:* one of the names under which the Druids worshipped the sun, was used to designate places remarkable for the fruitfulness of the soil or the beauty of the situation, is a straggling place composed of several hamlets; Beltoft, Westgate, Bractor, Grey Green and Churchtown. In the centre (situated on a small eminence) stands a church which in the old days received its revenue from the thriving flax industry which surrounded the village. The flax was offered for sale at the annual fair held within the village on the 25th September. Also in the parish once stood Temple Belwood, a large mansion with its own park, being the seat of the ancient Knight Templars.

Belton had a good-sized station for its population and provided the next passing loop* on the line although this was not brought into use for passenger trains until 1907. The main platform (once again built at the low level) was situated on the east side and accommodated the booking office, waiting room and toilets. The station master's house stood adjacent and opposite to the weighbridge and office. There were three long sidings and a short spur on the west side plus a large loading dock. All these sidings were protected by a catch point before entering the main line and were used extensively for the loading of sugar beet.

In the 1920s one regular visitor was the photographer J. Bottomley, who came from Goole on the train with his photographic caravan loaded onto a flat truck. This Mr Arrand used to unload at Belton and the photographer

*BOT MT/6 1559/1 dated 12th February,1907. The inspecting officer reported that 'at this station the existing up loop, which has hitherto been used only as a goods line is now to be brought into passenger use and signalled accordingly. The new line is now provided with a platform, but no station buildings, as these are situated on the down side!' The cost was £200, being approved by the Directors in March,1906. *Public Record Office, Kew*

The regular Pick-up goods seen at Belton.
Stan Teanby

N E R & L&Y R. AXHOLME JOINT RLY.
BELTON STATION.

The official track plan of Belton station showing the three sidings and small spur to the loading dock, giving 612 yards of sidings with just 384 yards of standage for wagons. Note the coal office which has a weigh office opposite the station master's house.
Courtesy T. Kay

toured the area capturing many wonderful rural scenes and events, many used in this book, (he later settled permanently at Epworth). The Arrands lived in the Porter/Signalman's house at Belton and raised nine children in this small dwelling including Charlie (who worked at Hagg Lane Sidings).

Leaving Belton the railway crossed two roads on the level in quick succession (both having crossing gates and gate houses) and continued in a straight line southwards. After a mile the track curved right and at this point another siding was situated. This was installed as late as 1936 and subject to an agreement dated 28th August, 1936 between the LMS/LNER and Richard Thomas & Co. Ltd (later Richard Thomas & Baldwins Ltd). There were in fact two 10-wagon length sidings again protected by a catch point which served a brickworks and claypits situated nearby. They remained in use until the end of the AJR's existence.

An interesting early view of Belton station with the station staff and locomotive crew posing for the photographer, after their arrival from Goole in 1905. The L&Y Barton Wright 0-6-0 goods locomotive was the standard class used at the time on the AJR and is seen hauling the 'hired' L&Y passenger stock. Note the large paraffin lamps with the station name in the upper part of the glass pane, these were supplied to all stations, yards and approaches. The man leaning on the engine is driver Jack Thurston, with station master W. Taylor next and then porter/signalman John Arrand with hands on hips.
Lens of Sutton

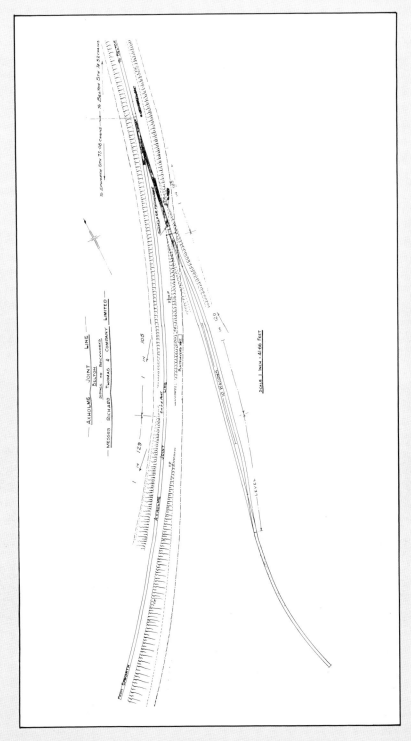

Official plan of the brickworks sidings just south of Belton

The driver of the RCTS Brake Special which toured the AJR on September, 1963, leans well out of cab of D2611 to exchange single tokens with the crossing keeper Belton. This crossing was the site serious accident in October 1 when a taxi belonging to Scunthorpe Co-operative Society t to 'rush' a goods train and v crushed to pieces between the t and the gate posts. Nobody v killed, but all four occupants w seriously injured. The taxi be worth £400, the matter subsequer went to court. *T.J. Edging*

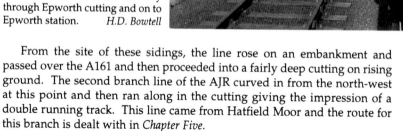

A view from the RCTS Brakevan Special on 14th September, 1963 of the Hatfield Moor Branch curving in from the left and running alongside the main line all the way through Epworth cutting and on to Epworth station. *H.D. Bowtell*

From the site of these sidings, the line rose on an embankment and passed over the A161 and then proceeded into a fairly deep cutting on rising ground. The second branch line of the AJR curved in from the north-west at this point and then ran along in the cutting giving the impression of a double running track. This line came from Hatfield Moor and the route for this branch is dealt with in *Chapter Five*.

The cutting is now filled in (almost!). Apparently when British Railways came to filling the cutting, Mr Brook who lived nearby pointed out that they would need to use the rubble from three field lengths of the embankment south of the Epworth station. They were adamant they knew best even though he had worked on the site as a 15 year old lad and witnessed the construction. So today the filled-in cutting has a large dip and parts are not restored to the original form of the hill.

The two lines passed under a high wooden trestle bridge (*see plate 110*) which carried a farm track to a nearby windmill, this being a familiar landmark near to Epworth station. As the two tracks neared Epworth station the cutting gave way to an embankment whereupon the branch joined the main line (which ran alongside for 11 chains) and then into Epworth station itself. This whole area is today a nature reserve and walks, with the A161 running through the central picnic area; the bridge having been removed, the cutting nearly filled and the embankments landscaped (*see Appendix Eight*).

Epworth

The Manor of Epworth and Westwood was conferred upon Geoffrey de Wirce follower of William the Conqueror. The entry in the Domesday book was '*Epeurde*', meaning hill farm or farm on rising ground. In the reign of Henry I, the Manor of Epworth was bestowed upon Nigel D'Albini (a bow-bearer to William Rufus). The family name was later changed to Mowbray and their mansion was situated near to the church at Epworth, at a site called Vine Garths (vines were common in early England and the Garth at Epworth had particularly good soil for their growth). In the late 1880s, remains of the mansion could still have been seen and the tiles bearing the Mowbray coat of arms were being dug up in the surrounding fields belonging to a farmer called Dawson.

The parish of St Andrew, on the north side of the town commands marvellous views of the Yorkshire Wolds to the north; Kirton-on-Lindsey to the east and the Derbyshire hills to the west. William de Noot was the first recorded Rector of Epworth and that was in the year 1319. Being situated 6 miles south of Crowle; 17 miles east of Doncaster; 11 miles north-west of Gainsborough and 3½ miles west of the River Trent, the town was heralded the 'metropolis' of the Isle of Axholme. Primarily a market town it consisted of a busy market place, approached by four roads and in the early 1880s the chief trade embraced the dressing of flax and hemp (all locally grown); sacking, canvas wool sheets and heavy linen goods were all being made locally. This was all greatly superseded by the agricultural industry in the late 19th century. In 1711 a school was established and in 1837 a Mechanics' Institute was formed followed soon after in 1848 by the opening of the police station.

Many visitors travel to Epworth to see the Wesley Memorial Church, situated in the High Street, which was erected in 1889 at a cost of £6,500, being dedicated to John Wesley, who was born in Epworth in 1703.*

The town is nearly two miles long and the station was sited over to the

*John Wesley (1703-1791) - A clergyman of the Church of England who was the founder of Methodism and leader of the Church with his brother Charles. Reportedly travelled over 200,000 miles in 50 years and preached over 40,00 sermons (as many as five in one day). Born the 15th of 19 children to parents who came from non-conformist families. Educated at Oxford's Christ Church College and ordained priest in 1728.

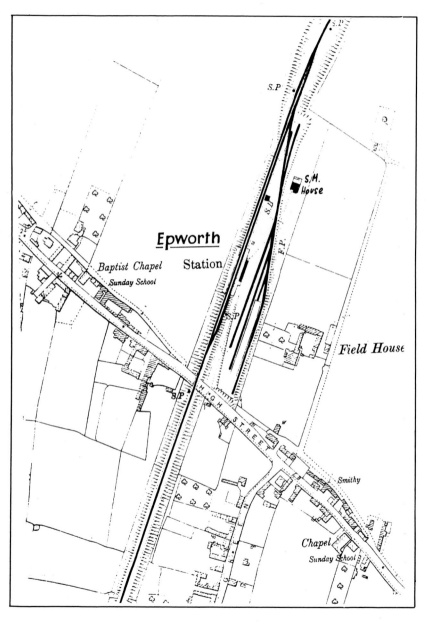

Epworth Station.   *Reproduced from the 25 in. Ordnance Survey map*

The Market Cross, Epworth (*middle distance*) can be seen in this pre-1900 view of the town, with many of the inhabitants 'out' for the camera.   *Courtesy Ian Snell*

western side of the town on the Sandtoft Road, situated high on an embankment with a fairly steep station approach (1 in 20) and a solid brick bridge spanning the road. The station buildings (*see next two pages*) were of timber construction (unlike most of the other stations which were built of brick) and situated on the east side of the track. The station master's house, (*see pages 108 and 109*) again brick built, was a little distance from the station area situated in an unusual position at the end of the goods yard. This house is now a private residence and has been substantially altered and enlarged, but still portrays a railway flavour. The accompanying plans show that extensive sidings and facilities were provided (five and a headshunt) doubtfully meeting the needs of the 'Capital'. Two windmills on a nearby hill could be seen from Epworth station, serving as a reminder that the character of the countryside had been changing since Crowle was left behind. The whole route traversed by the railway was rich in agriculture, but the flatness of the marshland had now given way to the gentle undulating hills scattered with pretty straggling villages. In this district the open-field system of agriculture was used with strip farming still apparent, being revealed in a colourful way during the height of summer. Epworth was unfortunate enough to have had a V1 flying bomb crash and explode nearby during World War II, and this event is recorded in *Lincolnshire Air War 1939-1945* by S. Finn.

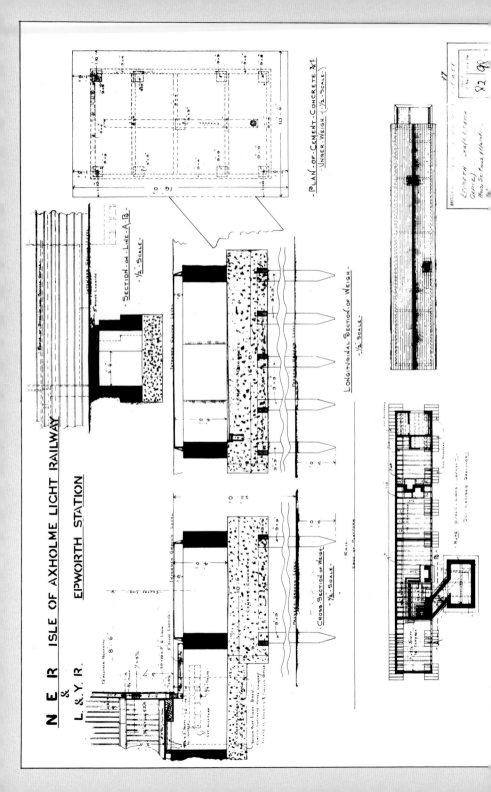

N E R ISLE OF AXHOLME LICHT RAILWAY
&
L. & Y. R.
EPWORTH STATION

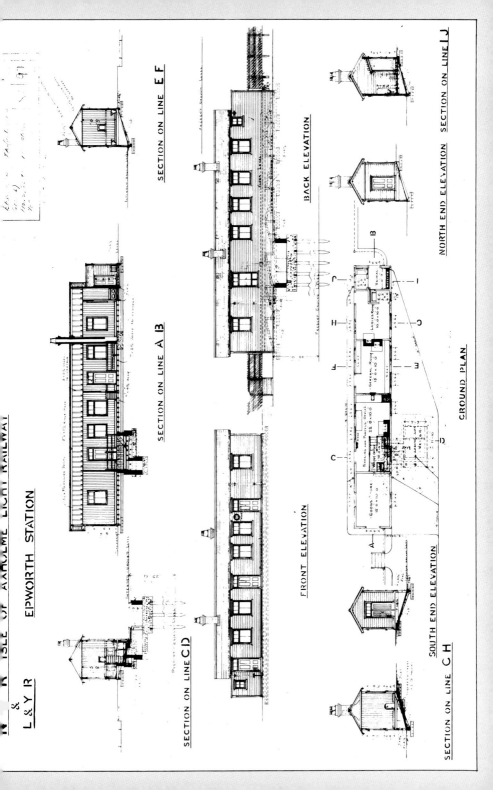

ISLE OF AXHOLME LIGHT RAILWAY

L & Y R

EPWORTH STATION

SECTION ON LINE E F

BACK ELEVATION

NORTH END ELEVATION   SECTION ON LINE I J

SECTION ON LINE A B

SECTION ON LINE C D

FRONT ELEVATION

GROUND PLAN

SOUTH END ELEVATION

SECTION ON LINE G H

N-E-R —— Isle-Of-Axholme-Light- Railway

Station-Masters- Houses —at—Belton

Epworth— Haxey—&

Haxey—Junction

FRONT ELEVATION —   **— BACK ELEVATION —**

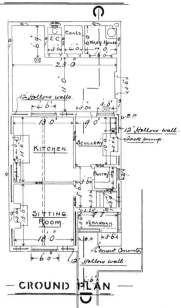

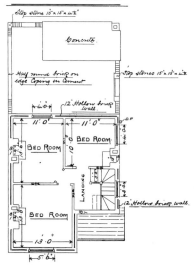

— GROUND PLAN —   **— FIRST FLOOR PLAN—**

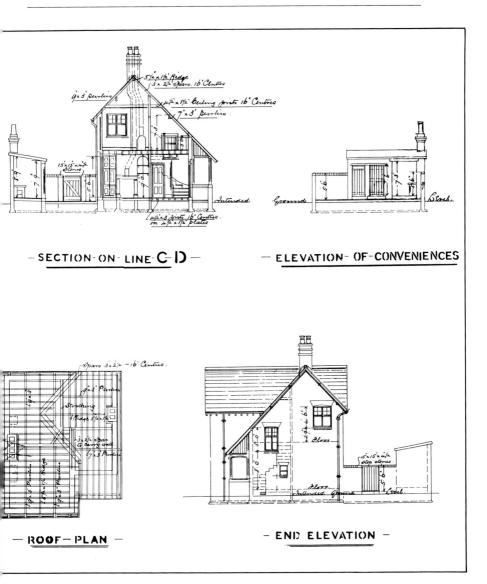

— SECTION·ON·LINE·C·D —

— ELEVATION·OF·CONVENIENCES

— ROOF—PLAN —

— END ELEVATION —

A good view of the station building at Epworth. The first door in the end of the build-ing led to a goods store, whilst doors along the platform were: (a) Booking and Parcels Office, (b) General Waiting Room, (c) Ladies room and on the end the gentle-men's toilet. The small shed was the lamp room and in the distance is the ground frame controlling the goods yard entrance, which is just beyond.   *Geoffrey Oates*

An undated view of a special train at Epworth station, with three six-wheeled coaches behind the locomotive and the bogie brake at the rear; the complement of coaches suggest a date after 1906.   *Edwin Harrison*

Epworth station seen here before the official opening with many contractor's tip-wag-ons waiting on the main line. Note the sails of the windmill which can be seen above the gable of the station buildings. One wonders who are the lady and child and why they are on the platform. The wagons appear to be of Manchester Ship Canal Co. type.

Lens of Sutton

The postman from Haxey seen here at Epworth station in the early 1900s. Note the sacks of mail, labelled Westwoodside. *Courtesy Ian Snell*

Epworth station before the official opening showing the cutting and wooden trestle-bridge in the distance (*north*). The signal has a cross of

The old blacksmith's shop, Epworth, *c.* 1930, used to shoe the coal merchants horses; the original 'Harris of Epworth'. On the left, Frank Harris with George Chant (*centre*) and Johnson Coggan, farmer, on the right.   *Courtesy John Harris*

Leaving the station area and proceeding southwards the line ran on a high embankment to cross the main Sandtoft road; this particular spot was lucky not to have been the site of a serious accident when, in June 1931, the following incident occurred:

What might have proved a very serious accident took place at Epworth Railway Station on Wednesday afternoon. When the passenger train due at Epworth from Haxey at 1.43 pm, was within a few yards of the platform, the engine and the first carriage left the metals, smashing up the sleepers and some of the chairs and doing damage to the springs of the engine. The accident happened at the point where the single line runs into a double line for the station. Luckily there were no passengers on at the time and those waiting on the platform to proceed towards Crowle and Goole had to be conveyed in the Guard's van of a goods train, which happened to be at the station at the time. The line at the point where the accident happened is on a very high embankment, but although the engine and one carriage were leaning sideways, fortunately, they did not fall down the embankment. The metals were badly twisted, and a breakdown party were sent for and were at work some hours before the engine and coaches could be lifted. We understand that the signal was in its proper position, and it is suggested that the points could not have been in their proper position. When the engine was brought to a standstill it was, along with the first coach, on the wrong line, but the second coach was on the proper one. The accident caused considerable excitement. The line was not cleared until 2.30 on Thursday morning.

Burnham Low gatehouse and weigh-bridge *c*. 1932. Mr Charlie Elvidge (plate-layer), his wife Beatrice (gate keeper) and family lived here from 1923-1949, and previously Mr Emmerson from 1905-1923.   *Len Elvidge*

This photograph shows Len Elvidge (sitting on the water tender). His mother Beatrice (with two young friends) was gate keeper at Low Burnham (1923-1949). The tender was based at Reedness Junction and used to supply water to various houses, when it was needed.

Len Elvidge

After crossing the road the line dropped gradually down off the embankment, crossing two brick-built overbridges before running along a flat section. Just over 1 mile from Epworth (at 3 miles 30 chains) and near to the village of Low Burnham, a further agricultural siding was encountered, named Burnham Lane. This was a single trailing siding protected by a catch point. Immediately after this the line climbed up onto a very high embankment, over two farm tracks and drains (the brick-built bridges for these being very substantial and constructed for double track). Entering a very deep cutting, the route ran under two high timber trestle bridges carrying farm tracks (these were later replaced by steel girder bridges that are still *in situ*). Today, the cutting is a very pleasant walk and nature reserve (*see Appendix Eight*).

Just before the end of the cutting a road bridge went over the track, however this has been filled in and the walker has to climb up and over the road before walking the final section to the level crossing on the B1396. The station master's house still stands on the right and over the road a bungalow has been built on the station site.

The official drawing by the Eastern Region at Doncaster of the bridges No. 21 and 22 in Haxey cutting in 1955. Both bridges still exist over the 'Nature reserve' as this photograph, taken in March 1993, shows.

Author

Haxey

This small straggling town, situated on the side of a hillock, reaches the highest point of the 'Isle' just beyond the church of St Nicholas. Lying in the midst of fertile fields of sandy loam, Haxey was known (in the 1920s) as the celery capital of England, with 80 per cent of the nations celery being grown in the area. The name '*Haxa*' is from the old German word for a Druidess and most probably some area near to the town was dedicated, by aboriginal Britons, to early 'blood rites'. The entry in the Domesday Book for *Haxa* is as follows;

In *Acheseia* (Haxa), Siward Barn had three carucates of land to be taxed. Land to six ploughs. Wazelin:, a vassal of Geoffrey's, has there two ploughs and a half, and sixteen villanes, and eight bordars with three ploughs and a half, and nine fisheries of seven shillings, and three acres of meadow. Wood, pasture here and there, five quarentens long and one quarenten broad. Value in King Edward's time and now, one hundred shillings. Tallaged at twenty shillings. Norman Crassus claims seven oxgangs of land of Geoffrey de Wirce in Haxey. The valuation of the ninth sheaf, the ninth fleece, and the ninth lamb in this parish, made in the reign of Edward III, was £xxi. xvis. viiid. (£21 16s. 8d.) This return was made on the oaths of William Cok, John Peacock, John the son of Henry, and Richard Bill.

Haxey* had a notable fire during the night of the 28th/29th February, 1744: '. . . there happened a sudden and most dreadful fire'. It was believed that the fire started near to the church in a house that was used for 'flax' manufacturing and torched by a disgruntled ex-employee! Within 3 hours the fire had completely burnt down 62 dwellings; people were driven 'naked' into the fields. The so-called arsonist was caught, but never punished.

There are few ancient games surviving in England today, but one played annually (6th January, the old Christmas) is believed to be a survival of an old 'rite of sun worship', a similar game being played in the Celtic province of France. However the game, called the 'Haxey Hood' is also credited to the whim of Lady de Mowbray, wife of Sir John de Mowbray, owner of most of the parish of Haxey in 1300. The name Hood is supposedly derived from the hood belonging to Lady de Mowbray who was out riding in the Parish of Haxey on 6th January. The hood was blown away by the wind and men (possibly farm hands) fought to recover it. Amongst their numbers was the village fool who 'lacked courage' to return it. The whole affair was said to have greatly amused her ladyship who promptly promised every man a 'broad piece of land' if they re-acted the game each year. An account from the Haxey and Westwoodside Heritage Society booklet entitled 'Historic Haxey Parish' describes the day's activities in more detail and should be read by those interested.

An Inn called the Railway Tavern (later called the Railway Inn and now a nursery) was built for the convenience of the Irish Navvies engaged in the

*The 1873 census states 572 inhabitants (300 female, 272 males).

Greenhill, Haxey, photographed around 1920. The Mowbray stone on the green was said to have been erected when Lord Mowbray went on his first crusade. On the right the Doctor's house, where at night the prescriptions were dispensed through the upper windows, when patients came by horse and cart. The station was at the far end of the road on the right. *Courtesy Ian Snell*

Old Butter Cross Main Street, Haxey. Not dated but note the railway crossing gates are just visible above the head of the child in the road, so the photograph is after 1903. Note the Kings Arms Hotel on the left. *Courtesy Ian Snell*

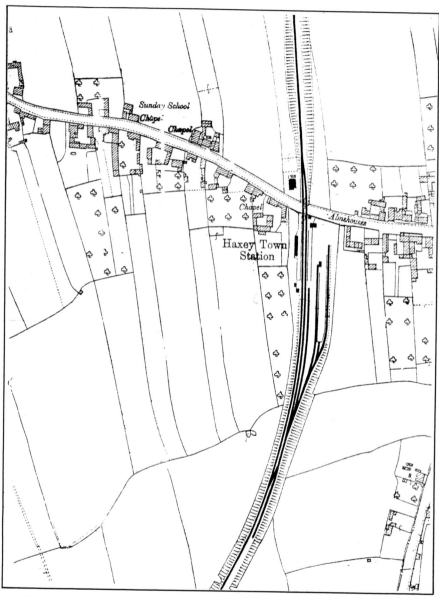

Haxey Town station showing the cutting north of the station.
Reproduced from the 1906, 25 in. Ordnance Survey map

Two very early views of the level crossing at Haxey Town. The top view is looking west with the station master's house on the right whilst the lower view looks east, out of town. Note the crude high footpaths either side of the road; the white gabled single-storey building in the lower view is the Almshouses. *Courtesy Ian Snell*

H·J·F·67·HAXEY·

Early days at Haxey Town station with a L&Y tank coasting in over the level crossing from Epworth, hauling the bogie brake and one six-wheeled coach. The station master's house stands in the middle of the photograph. *Courtesy Ian Snell*

A view of the brick-built Haxey Town station looking north towards Epworth. The station master's house is on the far side of the road and in the distance a wooden trestle bridge carries the bridle-path which meanders its way between Haxey and East Lound. Further on, in the far distance, a brick bridge carries a further road from Haxey to the A161 main road. The building on the right (with the fire buckets) is the weigh office. *Courtesy T. Kay*

An early view of a 'very new' Haxey Town AJR station with the station staff and two onlookers posing for the picture. The brick-built buildings are almost identical in size and layout to the wooden building at Epworth. *Lens of Sutton*

construction of the IOALR. To attract other passing customers the landlord placed a large tub beside the road filled with local fish caught in the warping drains nearby. The traveller could then choose his own dinner.

The railway ran through the middle of the town in a north/south direction. A long passing loop commenced prior to the road level crossing, with the station master's house situated alongside. The two platforms, with the brick-built station buildings on the west platform, were sited south of the level crossing. The goods yard was approached from the south and contained four sidings and a head shunt. During the first seven months of the railway's existence the station was known as Haxey Central but was then renamed Haxey Town AJR, later the 'AJR' was dropped from the nameboard.

An account of life at Haxey Town station is related by Mr Rowland of Doncaster:

Seventy years ago, the little Haxey Town Station was a hive of activity. There were three passenger trains a day and one goods train; often containing six or more trucks of manure, which had been sent from A. Coate of Hull (manure suppliers). These were 20 ton wagons and in the days before the war it was not unusual to be moving 'muck' for a week! During World War II it would be quite common to fill 20 or so wagons with celery and potatoes during the week and in the sidings stood a carrot washing shed of J.W. Burrell and another belonging to W.W. Whitehead. During the year thousands of tons of washed carrots left Haxey for Leeds Bradford,

Wakefield, Manchester, Liverpool etc. Whilst Charlie Johnson was station master, I remember that Whiteheads sent 400 bundles of celery to Jersey. The little station would be crowded with people waiting for the 9.30 am service to arrive from Goole. Then it was 'down' to the junction where Tom Newbitt (wearing his station master's hat) would shepherd the passengers out of the station yard, past the Great Northern Hotel and on to the platform of the main line GNR/GE station to catch the 10.10 am to Gainsborough. Another character on the line was the guard, Harry Sharp who lived in Crowle and a member of the Crowle Brass Band. When his goods train arrived at Haxey he could often been seen hurrying to the King's Arms for a pint or two before returning for duty. Among others employed on the line were Arthur Robert Curtis (platelayer), George 'Jud' Johnson (junior porter) and Bob Wilson who was once the 'Fool of Haxey Hood'. Bill Lockwood resigned from the 'Lanky' line and became the owner of Green Hill Stores in Haxey. I recollect that the fare to Doncaster was a shilling return and that a son of a local farmer told of his father being paid in gold sovereigns for the land he sold to the railway; not many people had 'the new fangled bank things'.

The railway continued southwards high up on an embankment, constructed with massive earthworks (for a so-called light railway), then dropping down all the way to the end of the line. The single track crossed Ferry Drain and Warping Drain on a substantial brick arched bridge before curving into the final station and terminus on the line, Haxey Junction.

Haxey Junction
   A double-reverse connecting line gave access to the adjacent Haxey & Epworth station on the GN & GE Joint Line. The AJR station master's house

This platform and brick-built station comprised the Haxey terminus of the AJR. The station Master's house is at the end of the buffer stops, and to the right are the three exchange sidings.   *M.A. King*

was situated right across the end of the line, and the station had a single platform and associated brick buildings constructed on a slightly curving track. Three sidings plus a loading dock allowed ample transfer-sidings; together with a head shunt. A proposal was made in 1906 by the Joint Committee for a turntable to be installed here (*see page 126*) but there is no evidence of this ever having been carried out. The line from Haxey Junction sidings crossed over the main line by a series of single and double slips right into the sidings on the Tickhill Light Railway. However a train wishing to use the Tickhill Light Railway would have had to reverse back into the Tickhill sidings before being able to proceed down the line. The two AJR branches are dealt with in the following chapters.

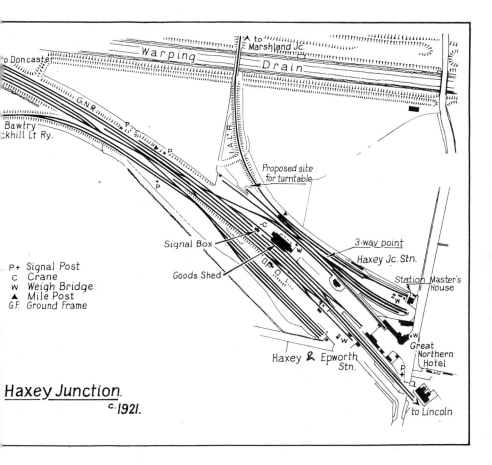

P+ Signal Post
c   Crane
w   Weigh Bridge
▲   Mile Post
G.F. Ground Frame

Haxey Junction.
c.1921.

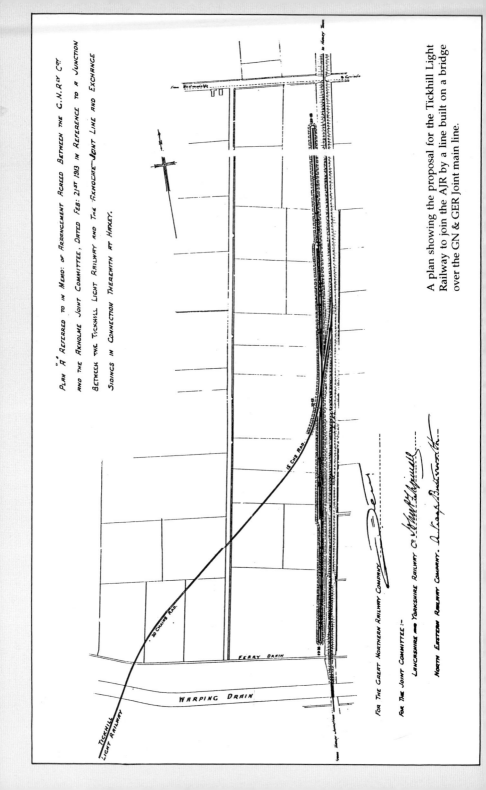

PLAN "A" REFERRED TO IN MEMO: OF ARRANGEMENT AGREED BETWEEN THE G.N.R.ᵞ Cᵒⁱ AND THE AXHOLME JOINT COMMITTEE, DATED FEB: 21ˢᵗ 1913 IN REFERENCE TO A JUNCTION BETWEEN THE TICKHILL LIGHT RAILWAY AND THE AXHOLME JOINT LINE AND EXCHANGE SIDINGS IN CONNECTION THEREWITH AT HAXEY.

FOR THE GREAT NORTHERN RAILWAY COMPANY

FOR THE JOINT COMMITTEE:-
LANCASHIRE AND YORKSHIRE RAILWAY Cᵒ
NORTH EASTERN RAILWAY COMPANY.

A plan showing the proposal for the Tickhill Light Railway to join the AJR by a line built on a bridge over the GN & GER Joint main line.

...e report on the *Epworth Bells* for Saturday 1st February, 1902 regarding a locomotive crossing from ...e AJR over to the GN & GE sidings:

...hat might have proved a fatal railway accident occurred just outside Haxey station on Tuesday night, about 7.30. ...appears that a Great Northern engine was taking some trucks out of the siding near the station. This necessitated ...crossing the main line of the GN and GE Joint Railway running from Doncaster to Gainsborough, in which direc- ...n a Great Eastern fast luggage was coming at, it is thought, the rate of twenty-five miles an hour. A thick fog had ...thered in the vicinity, and it is surmised that the driver of the GE fast luggage train was unable to see the signals, ...th the result that an awful collision took place, the engine of the fast goods striking the engine which was crossing ...e line on the side. The last named engine was broken from the tender and thrown sideways across the main line, ...d the force of the collision was so great as to throw the other engine off the rails, ploughing the embankment up ... several feet, and in the meantime causing serious damage to the waggons. The driver of the Great Northern ...gine was very much shaken and scalded, and it is considered to be almost a miracle how the driver and stoker of ...e engine escaped being killed, as it was stated that the last named jumped from his engine when he saw the colli- ...n was inevitable, and, fortunately, alighted on a heap of manure several yards away. A breakdown gang was ...spatched from Doncaster, but it was 10.30 before the train due at Haxey from Doncaster at 8.10 arrived. The efforts ...the breakdown gang resulted in traffic being worked early on Wednesday through the yard at Haxey, and by noon ...ingle line of the permanent way was in working order, whole being completed by nightfall. The damage done can- ...t at present be estimated, and it is doubtful whether it is possible to repair either of the engines, and should this be ..., the loss will be enormous. An inquiry into the circumstances will shortly be held, when no doubt the cause of the ...llision will be forthcoming. Had it been a passenger train it is almost certain that many people would have been ...riously injured or killed, as both engines presented an awful wreck.

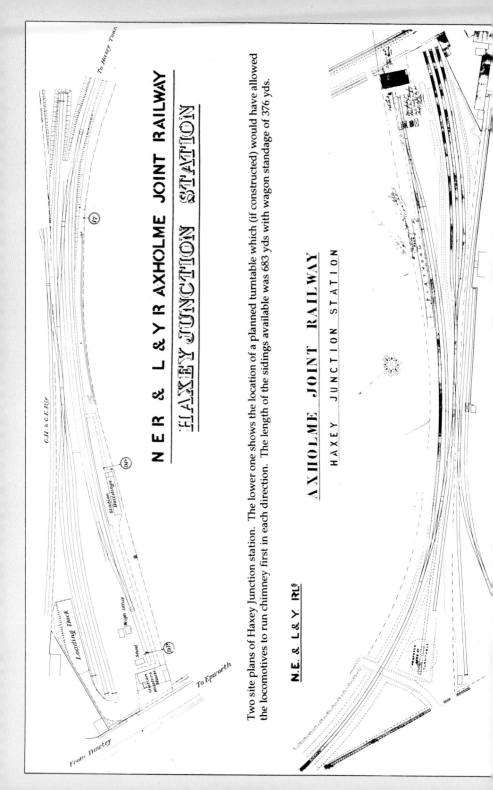

N E R & L & Y R AXHOLME JOINT RAILWAY

HAXEY JUNCTION STATION

Two site plans of Haxey Junction station. The upper one shows the location of a planned turntable which (if constructed) would have allowed the locomotives to run chimney first in each direction. The length of the sidings available was 683 yds with wagon standage of 376 yds.

AXHOLME JOINT RAILWAY

HAXEY JUNCTION STATION

N.E. & L. & Y. Rlys

A general view (looking west) of Haxey & Epworth, the 'other' Haxey station on the Great Northern Great Eastern Joint line. The AJR terminus is over on the right behind the water tower, while beyond the station buildings on the left the Tickhill Light Railway branched away quite sharply. *Courtesy Douglas Thompson*

A further view of the Great Northern & Great Eastern Joint station at Haxe & Epworth, this time looking east. To catch the AJR train, passengers left this station, walked past the Great Northern Hotel (extreme left of this picture) and then on down the road to Haxey Junction station. *Lens of Sutton*

This rather special photograph taken from the top of a signal post at Haxey Junction shows clearly the AJR (*on the left*) with the connecting line to the GNR which continued to the Tickhill Light Railway (*on the right*). The four sidings on this railway are full of wagons. This was a very busy junction and the signalman, Mr Magee from Haxey, used to operate the box (*middle*) which controlled the main line and exchange sidings. When locomotives arrived at Haxey on the AJR, they would (during calmer moments) be allowed onto the main line and into the station

Chapter Four

The Fockerby Branch

The line to the town of Fockerby, 5 miles 56 chains in length, branched away from Reedness Junction eastwards past the entrance to the sidings at the junction, sweeping in a curve northwards and then curving again eastwards, passing over two minor roads (one leading to Reedness Grange). Blackers Siding,* serving the local farms, was 110 yards long a trailing siding on the north side of the running line and was reached 1 mile 24 chains after the junction. After a further 31 chains, another farm siding was encountered, this time with a facing point, 150 yards long and situated on the south side of the main line and called Whitgift Siding.

A novel agreement, reached in 1906 between Mr Clegg, the farmer of Whitgift Common, was recorded in the Board minutes

> Mr Clegg stores potatoes on his land on the up side of the line at Whitgift Siding, and has on several occasions pulled down the length of the rail fence to enable him to obtain direct access with carts to wagons standing in the siding. It has now been arranged that removable fence rails should be provided at Mr Clegg's expense, and that an acknowledgement of 1s. per annum should be paid by the gentleman, who has also given an undertaking to replace the rails after the work is finished. Mr Clegg will also take every precaution to prevent animals obtaining access on to the line through the opening, and will indemnify the Company against any mishap which might arise from neglect on his part, or on the part of his men.
>
> An agreement has been entered into accordingly, terminable on one month's notice.

A level run of 1 mile 22 chains past Folly Plantation brought the line into Eastoft station.

Eastoft

Although called Eastoft, the village it served (situated on the site of the old river Don) was well over 1½ miles to the south, on the A161 road. The station also served Adlingfleet Grange, Sand and Pasture Farms and had two sidings with a total length of 425 yards, enclosing a loading dock between them to handle the considerable farm produce from the area. A weighbridge was provided just inside the yard entrance, with the station master's house south of the line close to the main buildings; these being of wooden construction sited on a low platform.

---

*Tonnage dealt with at Blackers Sidings: *1908*, 2289 tons; *1909*, 2298; *1910*, 4935; *1911*, 5774 tons.

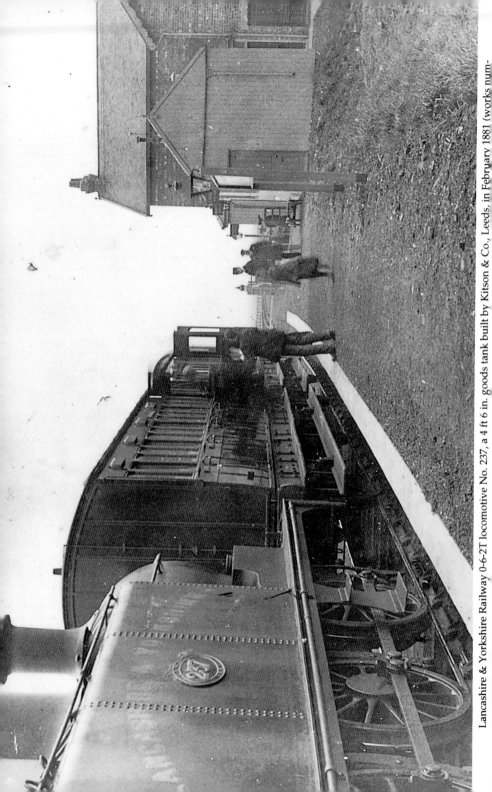

Lancashire & Yorkshire Railway 0-6-2T locomotive No. 237, a 4 ft 6 in. goods tank built by Kitson & Co., Leeds, in February 1881 (works num-

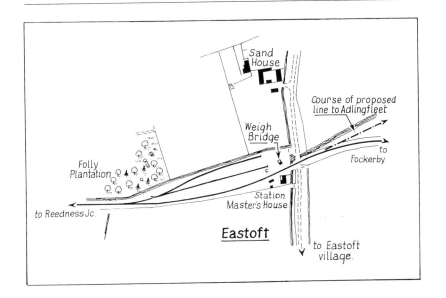

A view of Eastoft station looking towards Reedness Junction on 10th June, 1958. The station buildings were already in private hands by this date; the old station master's house is on the left. *John Edgington*

The line left the station over a culvert, then a level crossing, before curving sharply round to the right and striking south-eastwards for Luddington. Before reaching this station another siding was encountered on Haldenby Common (46 chains from Eastoft). Named Boltgate Siding (but often referred to as Bramhill Siding), this was 100 yards long with a facing point, laid on the south side of the line. It was operated by John and David Stubley (under an agreement dated 22nd December, 1903). This stated that 'agricultural produce, manure, machinery and implements only were allowed to be unloaded', at rates applicable to Fockerby.

In an essay written by Horace Shipley, entitled 'The day I best remember', he relates to a day in 1910, when he was 11 years old and found a job potato picking at Eastoft for six shillings a week. Having collected his horse and cart he continued . . .

> The farm had a railway running through the middle of the land, and at one point the cart track crossed the line by an unmanned level crossing. Naturally, it being October, a fog was becoming thicker with every hour, making visibility bad; unfortunately I had forgotten there was the eight o'clock train for Goole.
>
> The horse plodded on, the cart rattling and bumping behind. On to the railway, and horrified, I saw the train appear, a looming monster, black and ugly with pistons making the steam hiss and snort as it drew near then just as the horse had made the other side with me on its back, smash. The cart was ripped from the horse like a matchbox, part of it being taken up the line; and in the general commotion I found myself gathering my senses beside the railway, still sitting on the saddle which had slithered from the horse's back before the poor creature had bolted across the field.
>
> Before I had fully 'come to' and still sitting on the ground, the horse, for some curious reason, suddenly returned still with a piece of cart shaft hanging from a shoulder chain. He had been unyoked in seconds, while it had taken me some time to fix him up.
>
> I got up, went to him and stroked him and tried to calm him. The train had by now stopped, obviously to see if anyone was killed or injured and to dislodge part of the cart wheel which was wedged in the driving wheels of the locomotive.
>
> On being asked if I was all right I answered with a rather vague 'Yes'. The potato pickers, having heard the train stopped abruptly and heard voices carrying through the fog, came running to see what had happened. They were somewhat curious and unsettled, but when they realised I was not hurt and willing to carry on, I was helped back on to the horse and sent back for another cart.

The line continued, swinging left, to run eastwards and after 49 chains reached Luddington, the second station on the branch.

Luddington

The village of Luddington lay ¾ mile to the south of the station, along a small track which *en route*, passed a corn windmill; the station also had a windmill alongside the track. Haldenby Grange Farm and Park Farm used

Two views of the diminutive Luddington station. The top view is looking towards Fockerby and shows the low platform and station building, whilst the lower view, taken from the lane running to Haldenby Grange shows (*left*) station master's house and the goods office with weighbridge. *Both Douglas Thompson*

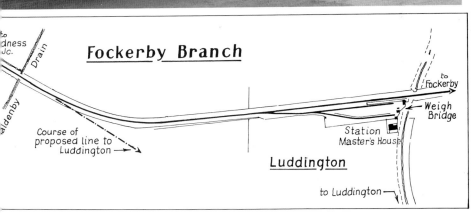

the station facilities which comprised two sidings totalling 379 yards with the customary loading dock between them.

A weighbridge and shed were situated in the station yard near the level crossing, whilst the station master's house* lay to the south of the yard. The usual low platform had a small wooden waiting shelter positioned near the level crossing.

Leaving Luddington and going on towards Fockerby, the last private siding was reached after 29 chains. This had a facing point and the line was laid on the north of the running line with provision to hold 'more than four wagons'. It was named Pindar's Siding, but often spelt 'Pinder's' on many maps and documents. Under an agreement (3rd May, 1902) between the G&MLR and John Pindar, the company was to provide a level crossing over the railway with proper gates and posts with openings of not less than 10 feet. This was so that John Pindar could use the private road from the Luddington to Garthorpe highway, up to Haldenby Hall. In October 1928, a further agreement with the LNER provided a new facility: 'to replace the existing fence in order to improve facilities for the loading or unloading of wagons with a moveable fence in sockets'. After travelling a further mile and 5 chains in a north-easterly direction from this siding, the branch terminus was reached at Fockerby.

Fockerby

The small township of Fockerby, situated on the west side of the River Don which separates it from Lincolnshire (now South Humberside), was a

*Station master George I. Field asked (29th July, 1904) to build a pig stye at the end of his garden; this was declined by the Board as 'un-railway like'.

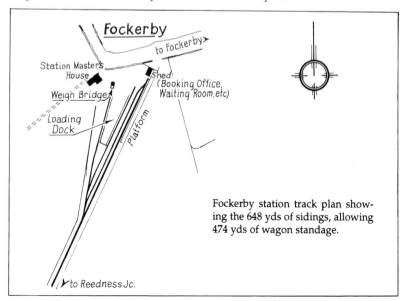

Fockerby station track plan showing the 648 yds of sidings, allowing 474 yds of wagon standage.

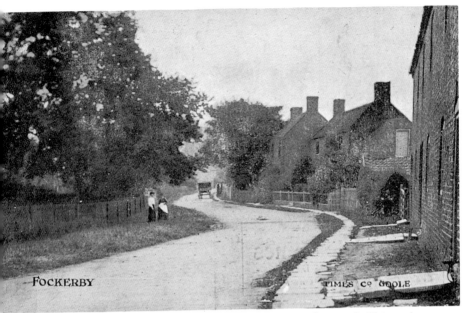

A view taken at the turn of the century, showing Fockerby village road. Note again the crude slab footpaths that seemed prevalent in the area. *Courtesy Mrs S.J. Bradwell*

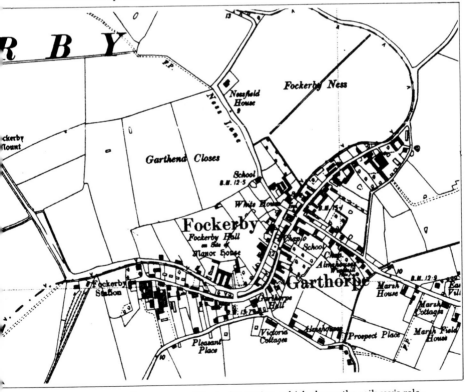

The 6 inch Ordnance Survey map of Fockerby station, which shows the railway's relationship (*west*) with the town. *Reproduced courtesy Ordnance Survey*

Lancashire & Yorkshire Railway Barton Wright 0-6-0 goods locomotive No. 954, built in August 1887 by Beyer, Peacock & Co., Manchester (works number 2837) is seen here at the branch terminus of Fockerby. It would seem that the locomotive crew and station staff are posing for the photographer whilst one young passenger in the train looks on.
Courtesy T. Kay

Ivatt class '2MT' 2-6-0 No. 46408 (built at Crewe Works in December 1946) on a pick-up goods at Fockerby station in the 1950s. With 16 in. by 24 in. cylinders and 5 ft 0 in. driving wheels, it was a new lightweight LMS design for branch line use. The weight of the locomotive (47 tons 2 cwt.) was just over 19 tons less than the admittedly much more powerful Hughes 2-6-0s introduced by the LMS in 1926.
Geoffrey Oates

mile south of Adlingfleet. In 1837 the parish of 1410 acres had only 103 inhabitants, however this was the terminus of the branch. The town consisted of two hamlets of Fockerby and Garthorpe, and the station (on the western edge of the village) also served the village of Adlingfleet to the north. Once again the station consisted of a low platform with a passing loop (256 yds long) running alongside. Two further storage sidings, 392 yds in length, served by a loading dock, occupied the station yard. A small wooden shed at the end of the platform, beyond the buffer stop, served as a booking office and supported a clock which faced up the platform. A weighbridge, with a brick built weigh-house stood in the yard near to the station master's house.

It is of interest to note that there were plans for the Fockerby branch to be extended.* The following sketch map shows the various proposals and a detailed history of these can be found in *The Railways of the South Yorkshire Coalfield from 1880* by Dr. A.L.Barnett (published by the RCTS). If just one of these proposals had come to fruition, then the AJR may have enjoyed the increase in traffic it needed and possibly a longer life.

*In the Board meeting minutes for September 1912 the secretary reported that a communication had been received from the Swinefleet Parish Council asking that the question of an extension from the Fockerby Branch, near Reedness Junction, to King's Causeway at Swinefleet should be considered, for which powers were included in the original Goole and Marshland Light Railway Order, 1898.
The matter was fully investigated by the Joint Superintendent, who stated that he could not see any justification for the expenditure which would be involved, and, after consideration, the Officers agreed to recommend the Joint Committee to decline the application.

Fockerby station terminus showing the weigh house (*left*) and the small waiting room-cum-ticket office at the end of the track. Note the clock and the milepost.
Geoffrey Oates

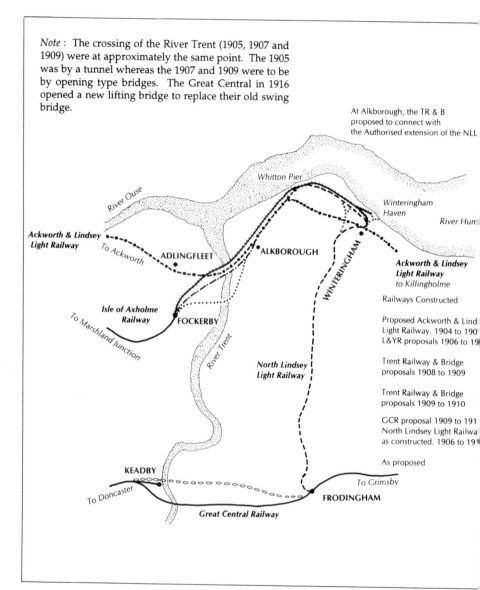

Note : The crossing of the River Trent (1905, 1907 and 1909) were at approximately the same point. The 1905 was by a tunnel whereas the 1907 and 1909 were to be by opening type bridges. The Great Central in 1916 opened a new lifting bridge to replace their old swing bridge.

At Alkborough, the TR & B proposed to connect with the Authorised extension of the NLL

Whitton Pier

Winteringham Haven

River Ouse

River Hum

Ackworth & Lindsey Light Railway

To Ackworth

ADLINGFLEET

ALKBOROUGH

Ackworth & Lindsey Light Railway to Killingholme

WINTERINGHAM

Railways Constructed

Isle of Axholme Railway

FOCKERBY

To Marshland Junction

River Trent

North Lindsey Light Railway

Proposed Ackworth & Lind Light Railway. 1904 to 190 L&YR proposals 1906 to 19

Trent Railway & Bridge proposals 1908 to 1909

Trent Railway & Bridge proposals 1909 to 1910

GCR proposal 1909 to 191 North Lindsey Light Railwa as constructed. 1906 to 19

As proposed

KEADBY

To Doncaster

Great Central Railway

To Grimsby

FRODINGHAM

Diagrammatic map showing the proposed railways from Fockerby, based on information by Dr A.L. Barnett from his book *The Railways of South Yorkshire Coalfield from 1880.*

... station master's house at ...erby, as seen in 1993. The ... now has farm buildings ...ructed on it.   *Author*

The enormous station master's house at Luddington, with the road track down the right hand side, seen in 1993.   The lower view shows the old goods office viewed from the position of the level crossing of the railway, the station having been to the right.   These were the only buildings around for at least a ¼ mile.
(Both) Author

Now part of a private residence, the weigh office stands in front of the station master's house at Fockerby in August 1989.   *Ken Smith*

POTATOES.

AXHOLME JOINT RAILWAY.

(N. E. and L. & Y. Joint).   (M 365)

Date_____

From FOCKERBY _____

To _____

Via _____

Owner and No. of Wagon_____

Owner and No. of Sheet_____

Owner and No. of Under Sheet_____

Consignee_____

Chapter Five

The Hatfield Moor Branch

The branch to Hatfield Moor was a further development to the AJR, an application for a Light Railway Order being made by the NER and L&Y (known as the Joint Companies) in November 1904. The original LRO, which contained the permission for the branch (dated 1899) had by this time expired. This new 1905 LRO included in its pages one significant difference to the original in that it proposed a branch with north and south facing curves to the main line, thus forming a useful triangular junction, just north of Epwcrth. However the northern connection was never built.

The inclusion of the complete 1905 LRO within this chapter allows the reader to see fully this official document relating to the branch.

The Joint Committee at its Board meeting held in October 1904 considered a report on their proposed branch to Hatfield Moor

Joint report signed by Messrs Hauxwell and Lake was submitted, stating that, after careful enquiry on the ground, they had ascertained that there are upwards of 40 farms with a total of 4,838 acres of arable land and 9,661 acres of grassland, or a gross total of 5,804½ acres of farm lands which might be served by the proposed railway. The traffic of the district is now conveyed by the Great Central Railway, by the Sheffield and South Yorkshire Navigation, and by the GN and GE Joint Line, and Messrs Hauxwell and Lake understand that the tonnage for which the proposed branch would be used or might compete is 25,940 tons per annum, made up as under:

	Tons
Agricultural produce and manure	13,890
Roadstone	1,250
Peat Moss Litter	10,800
	25,940

Assuming that the Joint Committee secured 60 per cent of the agricultural produce and manure and the whole of the other traffic, the present traffic to be obtained would amount to 20,384 tons per annum, and with the additional traffic which would be likely to arise if the railway were constructed, the total business would probably amount to about 34,000 tons per annum. The Directors of the Peat Moss Co. are unwilling to give any guarantee of traffic, but state that their business might be expected to be not less than 10,000 tons per annum, and after going into the matter the representatives of the Joint Companies consider that a total annual tonnage of 16,000 tons peat , moss traffic may be anticipated.

Having regard to all the circumstances, Messrs Hauxwell and Lake recommend that the Parliamentary Powers for making the branch railway be retained on the following grounds, viz.:

LIGHT RAILWAYS ACT, 1896.

AXHOLME JOINT RAILWAY (HATFIELD MOOR EXTENSION LIGHT RAILWAY) ORDER, 1905.

ORDER

MADE BY THE

LIGHT RAILWAY COMMISSIONERS,

AND MODIFIED AND CONFIRMED BY THE

BOARD OF TRADE,

AUTHORISING THE CONSTRUCTION OF

LIGHT RAILWAYS IN THE COUNTY OF LINCOLN AND THE WEST RIDING OF THE COUNTY OF YORK.

Presented to both Houses of Parliament by Command of His Majesty.

LONDON:
PRINTED FOR HIS MAJESTY'S STATIONERY OFFICE,
By DARLING & SON, Ltd., 34-40, Bacon Street, E.

And to be purchased, either directly or through any Bookseller, from
WYMAN AND SONS, Ltd., Fetter Lane, E.C.,
and 32, Abingdon Street, Westminster, S.W.;
or OLIVER & BOYD, Edinburgh;
or E. PONSONBY, 116, Grafton Street, Dublin.

1906.

[Cd. 2711.]   *Price 1½d.*

LIGHT RAILWAYS ACT 1896.

AXHOLME JOINT RAILWAY (HATFIELD MOOR EXTENSION LIGHT RAILWAY) ORDER, 1905.

ORDER authorising the construction of Light Railways in the County of Lincoln and the West Riding of the County of York.

Preamble.   WHEREAS an application was in November 1904 duly made to the Light Railway Commissioners jointly by the North Eastern Railway Company and by the Lancashire and Yorkshire Railway Company (hereinafter called "the Joint Companies") in pursuance of the Light Railways Act 1896 (hereinafter called "the principal Act") for an Order to authorise the construction of the light railways hereinafter described AND WHEREAS the said light railways will form extensions of and be worked in connection with the light railways authorised by the Isle of Axholme Light Railways Order 1898 (hereinafter called "the Order of 1898") AND WHEREAS by the North Eastern Railway Act 1902 the undertaking authorised by the Order of 1898 was vested in the Joint Companies as part of their joint undertaking and the Company incorporated by the Order of 1898 were dissolved such dissolution and vesting being an amalgamation within the meaning of Part V of the Railways Clauses Act 1863

NOW we the Light Railway Commissioners being satisfied after local inquiry of the expediency of granting the said application do in pursuance of the principal Act and by virtue and in exercise of the powers thereby vested in and of every other power enabling us in this behalf ORDER as follows:—

Short title.   1. This Order may be cited as "The Axholme Joint Railway (Hatfield Moor Extension Light Railway) Order 1905" and shall come into force on the date on which it is confirmed by the Board of Trade.

Interpretation.   2. Words and expressions (except the expressions to which meanings are by this section expressly assigned) to which by the principal Act or by the Order of 1898 or by any enactment incorporated therewith meanings are assigned have in this Order (unless the context otherwise requires) the same respective meanings and in this Order—

"The Joint Companies" means the North Eastern Railway Company and the Lancashire and Yorkshire Railway Company;

"The principal Act" means the Light Railways Act 1896;

"The Order of 1898" means the Isle of Axholme Light Railways Order 1898;

"The railway" means the railways and works by this Order authorised or (as the case may be) any part thereof;

"The undertaking" means the undertaking by this Order authorised;

"The whole undertaking" means the undertakings authorised by the Order of 1898 and by this Order;

"The railway of 1898" means the railway authorised by the Order of 1898;

"The Plan" "the Section" and "the Book of Reference" mean respectively the plan section and book of reference deposited in respect of the application for this Order with the Board of Trade and signed by an assistant-secretary of the Board of Trade;

The Interpretation Act 1889 applies for the purposes of this Order as if this Order were an Act of Parliament.

3. (*a*) Section 21 (As to crossing roads on level and gates) of the Order of 1898 shall be read and have effect as if the words "at all times" had been omitted from sub-section (2) thereof and as if the following provisions were inserted therein instead of sub-section (3) thereof which is hereby repealed; (that is to say)— *Amendment of Order of 1898.*

"The Board of Trade at any time after the completion and opening of the railway may if it appears to them necessary for the public safety require the Company to erect and maintain gates across the railway at each side of the road at any level crossing of a public carriage road and also may authorise the Company to remove subject to such conditions as the Board may prescribe any gates erected under this section and the Company shall observe such conditions";

(*b*) Sub-section 2 (A) of Section 21 of the Order of 1898 shall be read and have effect as if the public roads numbered respectively on the Plan 52 and 79 in the parish of Epworth had been inserted therein;

In construing the order of 1898 the expression "this Order" shall mean the said Order as amended by this section and the expression "the Company" shall mean the "Joint Companies."

4. (1) Except as otherwise expressly provided the provisions of the Order of 1898 as amended by this Order and of the Schedule thereto and of the enactments incorporated therewith shall so far as they may be applicable to the railway apply thereto and to the Joint Companies: Provided that the sections of the Order of 1898 and the part of the Schedule thereto hereinafter set out shall not apply to the railway; (namely)— *Application to railway of Order of 1898.*

Section 1 (Short title);

Section 2 (Interpretation);

So much of Section 3 (Incorporation of Acts) as incorporates provisions of the Companies Clauses Consolidation Act 1845 and of the Companies Clauses Act 1863;

Sections 4 to 9 (relating to incorporation of Company);

Section 10 (Power to make railways);

So much of Section 11 (Gauge of railways and motive power) as relates to motive power;

Setion 12 (Power to take lands);

Section 13 (Period for compulsory purchase of lands);

Section 17 (Restriction on taking houses of labouring class);

Section 19 (Period for completion of works);

Section 23 (Power to divert roads as shown on plan);

Section 27 (For the protection of the Great Northern and Great Eastern Joint Committee);

Section 28 (For the protection of the Great Central Railway Company);

Section 29 (For the protection of the Sheffield and South Yorkshire Navigation Company);

Section 35 (Power to enter into agreements with the Great Central Company the Great Northern and Great Eastern Joint Committee and the North Eastern Railway Company);

Section 36 (Saving for Postmaster-General);

Sub-section (2) of Section 37 (Provisions as to motive power other than steam);

Section 38 (Special provisions as to use of electric power as motive power);

Section 39 (For protection of the Postmaster-General);

Sections 41 to 47 (relating to tolls etc.);

Sections 48 to 58 (relating to capital);

Sections 59 to 62 (relating to deposit of money etc.);

Section 67 (Costs of Order);

So much of the Schedule as relates to the opening or swing bridge over the navigation of the Sheffield and South Yorkshire Navigation Company;

(2) Subject to the provisions of this Order and except where the context otherwise requires the railway shall in all respects and for all purposes be deemed to be part of the railway of 1898 and the undertaking to be part of the undertaking authorised by the Order of 1898.

Power to make new railways.
5. Subject to the provisions of this Order the Joint Companies may make form lay down and maintain in the lines and according to the levels shown on the Plan and Section the Railways hereinafter described with all proper and sufficient rails plates sidings junctions turntables bridges culverts drains viaducts stations approaches roads yards buildings and other works and conveniences connected therewith.

The said Railways are:—

A Railway (No. 1) 4 miles 6 furlongs 2 chains or thereabouts in length situate in the parishes of Belton and of Epworth in the County of Lincoln and in the parish of Hatfield in the West Riding of the County of York commencing by a junction with the Joint Companies' existing Axholme Joint Railway at a point about 540 yards north-east of Epworth Station proceeding thence in a north-westerly and westerly direction and terminating at a point about 20 yards south of where the lane known as Moor Lane crosses the Hatfield Waste Drain near the Peat Moss Litter Works.

A Railway (No. 2) 2 furlongs 9 chains or thereabouts in length situate in the said parishes of Belton and of Epworth commencing by a junction with the Joint Companies' existing Axholme Joint Railway at a point about 1,250 yards north-east of Epworth Station and terminating by a junction with Railway (No. 1) at a point about 620 yards from the commencement of the said Railway (No. 1).

Motive power.
6. The motive power on the railway shall be steam or such other motive power as the Board of Trade may approve: Provided that nothing in this Order shall authorise the Joint Companies to use electrical power as motive power on the railway.

Power to take lands.
7. Subject to the provisions of this Order the Joint Companies may purchase enter upon take and use such of the lands shown on the Plan and described in the Book of Reference as may be required for the purposes of this Order.

Period for compulsory purchase of lands.
8. The powers of the Joint Companies for the compulsory purchase of lands for the purposes of this Order shall cease after the expiration of two years from the commencement of this Order.

Power to take easements.
9. The Joint Companies instead of taking the properties specified in the Schedule to this Order may by agreement take an easement only or right of making and maintaining the railway over the said properties.

Period for completion of works.
10. If the railway is not completed within four years from the commencement of this Order or such extended time as the Board of Trade may approve then on the

expiration of that period the powers by this Order granted to the Joint Companies for making and completing the same or otherwise in relation thereto shall cease except as to so much thereof as is then completed.

11. (1) Notwithstanding anything contained in this Order any sanitary authority (in this section referred to as " the authority ") shall at all times have free access to and communication with any sewer or drain or any works in connection therewith under their control (in this section referred to as " sewers ") and may exercise any power which they may possess of laying drains to communicate therewith without the concurrence or consent of the Joint Companies: Provided that any works done by the authority so far as such works may affect the railway shall be carried out under the superintendence (if such superintendence shall be given) and to the reasonable satisfaction of the Joint Companies and if so required by the Joint Companies in accordance with plans sections and specifications to be previously submitted to and approved by them or in case of difference to be settled by arbitration under the Order of 1898 (such approval not being unreasonably withheld) and if the Joint Companies do not signify their disapproval within twenty-eight days after such submission they shall be taken to have approved; *For protection of sewers and drains of sanitary authorities.*

(2) Where any of the works authorised to be done by the Joint Companies under this Order pass over or under or interfere with any sewers or in any way affect the sewerage or drainage of the district under the control of the authority the Joint Companies shall give to the authority twenty-eight days' previous notice in writing of their intention to commence such works such notice being accompanied by plans and sections or other sufficient particulars thereof and the Joint Companies shall not commence the said works except with the approval of the authority and shall comply with all reasonable directions of the authority in the execution thereof: Provided that such approval shall not be unreasonably withheld and that if the authority do not signify their disapproval within twenty-eight days after receipt of such notice as aforesaid they shall be taken to have approved.

For the protection of the authority in respect of and for preventing injury or impediment to the sewers the Joint Companies shall either alter the existing sewers or substitute others for them in such manner as the authority may reasonably require and any such altered or substituted sewers as aforesaid shall thereafter be as fully under the control of the authority as were the said existing sewers before alteration or substitution as the case may be. The Joint Companies shall execute all works referred to in this sub-section at their own expense and under the superintendence of the authority (if such superintendence shall be given) and shall on demand repay to the authority any expenses which they may reasonably incur in accordance with this sub-section in respect of the said works;

(3) Instead of any such alterations or substitutions of sewers as are in the preceding sub-section referred to being executed by the Joint Companies they may be executed by the authority if they so require at the reasonable expense of the Joint Companies. If the authority intend to execute the same themselves they shall within twenty-eight days after receipt of such notice as aforesaid give to the Joint Companies notice (accompanied by sufficient particulars) of that intention and shall commence execute and complete the work with all reasonable despatch;

(4) If by reason of the execution of any of the powers of this Order the authority necessarily incur any expense in reconstructing lengthening altering or repairing any existing sewers or any additional expense in thereafter maintaining the same the Joint Companies shall repay to the authority such expense;

(5) If any difference arises under this section between the Joint Companies and the authority that difference shall be referred to arbitration under the Order of 1898.

12. If the Joint Companies fail within the period limited by or extended by the Board of Trade under this Order to complete the railway the Joint Companies shall be liable to a penalty of twenty pounds a day for every day after the expiration of the period so limited until the railway is completed and opened for the public conveyance of passengers or until the sum received in respect of such penalty amounts to five per centum on the estimated cost of the works and the said penalty may be *Penalty unless railway is opened within the time limited.*

Axholme Joint Railway (Hatfield Moor Extension Light Railway) Order, 1905.

applied for by any landowner or other person claiming to be compensated under this Order or interested in accordance with the provisions of the next following section of this Order and in the same manner as the penalty provided in Section 3 of the Railway and Canal Traffic Act 1854 and every sum of money recovered by way of such penalty as aforesaid shall be paid under the warrant or order of such Court or judge as is specified in that section to an account opened or to be opened in the name of the Paymaster-General for and on behalf of the Supreme Court in the bank and to the credit specified in such warrant or order and shall not be paid thereout except as hereinafter provided but no penalty shall accrue in respect of any time during which it shall appear by a certificate to be obtained from the Board of Trade that the Joint Companies were prevented from completing or opening the railway by unforeseen accident or circumstances beyond their control provided that the want of sufficient funds shall not be held to be a circumstance beyond their control.

Application of penalty.

13. Every sum of money so recovered by way of penalty as aforesaid shall be applicable and after due notice in the "London Gazette" shall be applied towards compensating any landowners or other persons whose property has been interfered with or otherwise rendered less valuable by the commencement construction or abandonment of the railway or who have been subjected to injury or loss in consequence of the compulsory powers of taking property conferred upon the Joint Companies by this Order and for which injury or loss no compensation or inadequate compensation has been paid and shall be distributed towards such compensation as aforesaid in such manner and in such proportions as to the High Court may seem fit and if no compensation is payable or if a portion of the sum or sums of money so recovered by way of penalty as aforesaid has been found sufficient to satisfy all just claims in respect of such compensation then the said sum or sums of money recovered by way of penalty or such portion thereof as may not be required as aforesaid shall if a receiver has been appointed or the Joint Companies are insolvent or the railway in respect of which the penalty has been incurred has been abandoned be paid or transferred to such receiver or be applied in the discretion of the Court as part of the assets of the Joint Companies for the benefit of the creditors thereof and subject to such application shall be repaid or re-transferred to the Joint Companies.

Rates etc.

14. For the purpose of demanding and recovering tolls fares rates and charges the railway shall be deemed to be included in the expression "joint undertaking" in Section 14 of the North Eastern Railway Act 1902 and the said section shall apply accordingly.

Power to apply funds.

15. The Joint Companies may apply for any of the purposes of this Order to which capital is properly applicable any moneys which they may have respectively raised under the authority of any Act or Acts of Parliament by shares stock debenture stock or borrowing and which are not by the Act or Acts under the authority of which they were raised made applicable to any special purposes or which being so made applicable are not required for such special purposes.

Costs of Order.

16. All costs charges and expenses of and incident to the preparing for obtaining making and confirmation of this Order or otherwise in relation thereto shall be paid by the Joint Companies.

Axholme Joint Railway (Hatfield Moor Extension Light Railway)
Order, 1905.

SCHEDULE

Describing properties over which the Joint Companies may take easements.

No. on Plan.	Parish.	Description of Property.
	RAILWAY (No. 1).	
46	Parish of Epworth	Folly Drain and Banks
48	Ditto	New Idle River and Banks
54	Ditto	New Torne River and Banks
80	Ditto	North Idle Drain and Banks
22	Parish of Belton	North Idle Drain and Banks
7a	Parish of Hatfield	Drain
9	Ditto	Hatfield Waste Drain

This Order made by the Light Railway Commissioners and modified by the Board of Trade is hereby confirmed in pursuance of the provisions of Section 10 of the Light Railways Act 1896.

Given under the Seal of the Board of Trade this Fifth day of August One thousand nine hundred and five.

SEAL OF
THE BOARD
OF
TRADE.

SALISBURY,
President.

HERBERT JEKYLL,
Assistant Secretary.

Wives of the peat cutters, stacking peat on the moors of Hatfield.   *Mrs S.J. Bradwell*

1. If the Branch be constructed at a cost not exceeding £22,500 (the present estimate), it might be expected to earn directly £1,700 per annum or £680 net, equivalent to a dividend of 3 per cent.
2. It would act as a feeder to the Axholme Joint Railway and to the lines of the parent companies.
3. It may be made the means of access to the undeveloped coal fields lying east and north east of Doncaster.

After due consideration the Board recommended that the branch construction should be proceeded with, as recorded in minute 33 of the meeting.

The first public meeting to discuss the branch was held on Tuesday 7th February, 1905 at the Station Hotel, Frodingham (an enquiry was also held there the same day into the proposed light railway from Blyton to Frodingham). The Commissioners for the enquiry were Colonel George F. Ottley Boughey, RE, CSI and Mr H.A. Steward, with Alan D. Erskine as secretary. Mr R.F. Dunnell (asst. solicitor with the NER, later chief legal adviser to the LNER) appeared for the NER and was questioned by a Mr Taylor, representing the Belton Parish Council as to the necessity for a level crossing over the Sandtoft road. Mr Dunnell said the five mile long railway would cross five roads and that gates would be provided although some of the crossings did not really warrant them. Mr Cudworth representing the engineering side of the NER stated that all the crossings would be of the 'common' type used elsewhere on the AJR and that the requested bridge over the Sandtoft road would cost at least £5,000 and be out of the question. As to North Ferry Lane, this was very narrow and not metalled and carried little traffic (only occasional horse and cart) and that cattle guards (grids) would stop any animals wandering on to the line.*

The LRO made by the Commissioners was confirmed (after modifications) by the BOT on 5th August, 1905. It will be seen that the concern expressed by the Belton Parish Council is catered for in *Section 3* of the Order. During September 1905, the officers of the AJR discussed the relevant sites for stations and sidings on the branch, but nothing positive was achieved. By March 1906, work on the building of the branch not having commenced, an approach was made by the British Moss Litter Co. Ltd that if the AJR would construct the branch, they would work the moors to a greater degree and use the line to transport their peat moss, thus increasing freight revenue over the AJR. Hatfield Moor Mill had been working since 1st November, 1905, but a more modern mill was being considered once the transport problems had been resolved. It is of interest that the British Moss Litter Company was unwilling to enter into a signed agreement with the AJR at this time, although they stated that the peat output would certainly exceed 10,000 tons per annum. An impasse was reached; the railway was not pre-

*The *Lindsey and Lincolnshire Star*, 11th February,1905.

pared to commence construction without a written guarantee and the British Moss Litter Co. would not sign a contract until the railway was built. Eventually, however the railway decided to approach all the landowners in anticipation of the building to acquire the necessary land 'on most favourable terms'.

In 1907, tenders were invited for the construction, this being awarded to John Moffatt of Manchester. The document is reproduced in full, however added to the printed stipulations was the following typescript:

> The contractor must take every precaution against engines emitting sparks and shall provide all engines with efficient spark arresters, both in the firebox and on top of the funnel. He will be held responsible for any damage by fire caused by his operation in connection with this contract and must settle all claims in connection therewith.

The Joint Committee was taking no risks!

A Bond to cover the successful completion of the contract was executed by Mr Moffatt on 24th December, 1907, his sureties being Charles Joseph Wills (a well-known contractor) and Samuel Isherwood, both of Manchester.

By March 1908 construction work had progressed sufficiently well to warrant the Board discussing the working arrangements for the line;

ARRANGEMENTS RECOMMENDED FOR ADOPTION ON OPENING OF HATFIELD MOOR BRANCH

1. *Names of Stations*
(a) Sandtoft - *Note.* Sandtoft is the name of the adjoining hamlet. There is only one farm at West Hale.
(b) Hatfield Moor Depot.

2. *Method of Working Branch Line*
Only one engine in steam to be allowed on the branch at one time. The connection between the branch and the main line will be made at a point within the control of Epworth Station.

3. *Houses for Gate Keepers at Crossings*
Under the Light Railway Order (Section 3), the Joint Committee are under obligation to provide level crossings and gates for the public roads at West Hale and Allen's Farm, near Hatfield Moor. Gatehouses should therefore be erected at:
(a) Sandtoft Crossing (otherwise West Hale), to be occupied by the Senior Porter in charge of the Station, whose wife shall attend to the gates and receive 2s. 6d. per week for the service.
(b) Allen's Farm Crossing This crossing is within a short distance of Hatfield Moor Depot. The Senior Porter in charge of that depot to occupy the gatehouse, and his wife attend to the gates, receiving 2s. 6d. per week for the service.

4. *Additional Staff Required*
Sandtoft - A Senior Porter at 20s. per week, less 2s. 6d. per week for rent of gatekeeper's cottage thereat.
Hatfield Moor Depot - A Senior Porter at 20s. per week, less 2s. 6d. per week for rent of gatekeeper's cottage at Allen's Farm Crossing (see above).
Epworth - A Clerk to perform all clerical work in connection with branch traffic.

Know all Men by these presents that John Moffat of Number 38 Arcade Chambers, Saint Mary's Gate, Manchester.

carrying on the business of Contractor for Public Works

(hereinafter called "the Contractor") Charles Joseph Willis of Number 28 Victoria Street, Westminster, Railway Contractor, and Samuel Lakewood of Number 10, Corporation Street, Manchester aforesaid, Cement Merchant

(hereinafter called "the Sureties") are bound to the NORTH EASTERN Railway Company and the Lancashire and Yorkshire RAILWAY COMPANY (hereinafter called "the Company") in the penal sum of one thousand four hundred and sixty-four pounds seventeen shillings and threepence

to be paid to the Company or to their certain attorney successors or assigns For which payment we bind ourselves and each of us our and each of our heirs executors and administrators jointly and severally by these presents Sealed with our Seals Dated this twenty-first day of December one thousand nine hundred and seven WHEREAS by a Contract bearing even date herewith and made between the Contractor of the one part and the Company of the other part the Contractor contracted with the Company to make execute and complete the whole of the works in connection with the construction of the Hatfield Moor Branch of the Axholme Joint Railway according to the Specification Detailed List of Quantities Plans

Sections and Drawings referred to in the said Contract and subject and in manner as therein mentioned for the sum of fourteen thousand six hundred and forty-eight pounds twelve shillings and sixpence

---

the Contractor together with two sureties to be approved of by the Companies should execute a Bond in the penal sum of one thousand four hundred and sixty four pounds seventeen shillings and threepence conditioned for the due performance of the said Contract AND WHEREAS the Companies have approved of the Sureties as the sureties for the Contractor NOW THE CONDITION of the before written Bond is such that if the Contractor shall well and completely make execute and complete the said works according to the said Specification Detailed List of Quantities Plans

Sections and Drawings and in all other respects faithfully perform the covenants agreements clauses conditions stipulations and provisions of the said Contract And so that any alteration which either in pursuance of the written instructions of the Companies Engineer or by agreement between the Contractor and the Company may be made in the terms of the said Contract or in the nature or quantity of the work to be done thereunder or the giving by the Company of any extension of time for the performance of the said Contract or any part thereof (whether altered as aforesaid or not) or any other forgiveness or forbearness on the part of the Company to the Contractor his executors or administrators shall not in any way release the Sureties or either of them their or his heirs executors or administrators from their or his liability under the before written Bond Then the before written Bond shall be void otherwise the same shall remain in full force

Signed sealed and delivered by the said
John Moffat
in the presence of

John Moffat

Count Pribble
13 Scarr Terrace
York
Ripier.

Contract for the Construction of the Hatfield Moor Extension Light Railway, Axholme Joint Railway, and Works in Connection therewith.

To the Axholme Joint Railway Committee.

I, *Wm Wilson* of *Manchester* in the County of *Manchester* do hereby propose to make and complete the whole of the Works in connection with the construction of the Hatfield Moor Extension Light Railway, Axholme Joint Railway, including the Excavations, Embankments, Bridges, Retaining Walls, Road Diversions, Drains, Fencing, Ballasting, Laying the Permanent Way, Sidings, &c.; Removal of the Materials excavated to the Embankments, and keeping the whole of the Works hereby contracted for in Repair for nine Calendar Months after completion, and to find and provide all requisite materials (except the Rails, Chairs, Sleepers, Fishing Plates, and Bolts), according to the Specification, Plans, Sections, and Drawings on *me* and on the terms and conditions mentioned and contained in the Draft of Contract exhibited to *me* or before for the sum of £146 4 8 : 12 6 and descriptions of Work at which the Aggregate Amount of this Tender is computed.

I have hereinafter set forth the Price of the different descriptions of Work at which the Aggregate Amount of this Tender is computed.

AND I further propose that any alterations, reductions, or omissions in, or additions to, the Works hereby contracted for shall be paid for to *me* or deducted for by *me* as the case may require, according to the List of Prices also hereinafter set opposite to each description of Work.

AND in case this Tender shall be accepted, I hereby undertake to execute a Contract to be prepared by the said Company, according to the Draft before referred to, within a month from this date.

AND propose Securities for the due performance of such Contract.

as

AND I do hereby undertake that they shall, within a month from this date, execute a bond to be prepared by the said Company, conditioned for that purpose in a penal sum equal in amount to 10 per cent. on the said sum of £

AND lastly, I do hereby undertake and agree that in case the said Contract and Bond shall not be executed by and the said two sureties, within the time above-mentioned, the said Company shall not [unless they think fit] be bound by this Tender and Contract, but the same shall be absolutely void in case the said Company shall so think fit.

Witness *my* Hand this 27. day of *September* 1907

NORTH EASTERN & LANCASHIRE & YORKSHIRE RAILWAYS.

Contract for the construction of the Hatfield Moor Extension Light Railway (Axholme Joint Railway), and Works in connection therewith.

SPECIFICATION.

This Contract comprises the whole of the Earthwork, Concretework, Brickwork, Masonry, Steelwork, Ironwork, Woodwork, &c., necessary to complete the Engineering works in connection with the construction of the North Eastern and Lancashire and Yorkshire Companies' Hatfield Moor Extension Light Railway (Axholme Joint Railway), and Works in connection therewith. It also includes the excavation of the foundations for the above works to the depths shown on the several Plans, or to such other depths as may be found necessary, and the removal of the surplus materials excavated to embankment or to spoil; also it includes all pumping, coffer dams, piling, shoring, draining, fencing, painting, labour, and materials, whether temporary or permanent, which may be necessary; and also the taking down and removal to some place of deposit, to be provided by the Engineer, of all trees, buildings, bridges, walls, fences, and other materials and things now upon the land to be occupied or required by the works. This contract also includes the laying of the Permanent Way, or any portion or portions of it which the Engineer may determine, as shown on the Contract Plans or upon any other Plan or Plans which the Engineer may from time to time issue. The whole of the work is to be done in accordance with the

PARTICULAR STIPULATIONS.

The cuttings and embankments are for a single line of railway throughout. As the cuttings do not provide sufficient material for the embankments by about 9,500 c. yards, this deficiency must be obtained by side cutting from the land which has been provided at the commencement of the railway, and which is coloured green on Plan No. 1. The side cutting is to be excavated to a depth of not less than 6 feet, unless ordered otherwise by the Engineer, with slopes of 1½ feet horizontal to 1 foot vertical.

The Railway is to be fenced with the standard 5 rail post and rail fence, but in the case of accommodation works 4 rail fencing is to be used. The specification for this fencing is the same as for five rail, with the exception that the posts are to be only 6 feet long.

The Contractor will be required to cut down, &c., the thicket shown upon Plan No. 1 for the whole width between the Companies' fences, and if the Engineer should consider it necessary to lay the brushwood, &c., upon any boggy or soft places, this must be done before the earthwork in the embankment is tipped. The Contractor's prices under the heading of Sundries must be inclusive of this requirement.

Before the lengths of the piles required for the timber bridges are determined upon, the Contractor will be required to drive a trial pile until the set given by a ram weighing one ton and having a fall of ±0 feet is satisfactory to the Engineer.   6.

The Engineer will then decide upon the length of pile to be used, and the Contractor will be paid for the net length of pile at the schedule rates.

The piles must be driven as closely in the positions and to the inclinations shown upon the drawings as is possible. The heads of all piles must, after driving, be cut to the inclination shown upon the drawings, and tenoned into the crowns with tenons 4 in. by 3 in.

Where sleepers or other materials are specified to be provided by the Company, these will be delivered in the "Contractor's Siding" at Epworth Station, and the Contractor's prices for laying and fixing, &c., must be inclusive of the labour required for unloading the material and conveying to the site where it may be required to be fixed.

Where concrete is specified to be in the proportion of 4 to 1 it is to be composed of 2½ parts of hard stone, brick, or slag, broken to pass through a ¾ inch diameter ring, 1½ parts of sand and 1 part of Portland Cement. The Contractor's price for concrete in culvert covers, &c., is to include the building in of rails, expanded metal, &c., as shown upon the detailed drawings. The rails which will be supplied by the Company will be delivered in the "Contractor's Siding" at Epworth Station. The Company will lay the Permanent Way from the commencement of the new line, and also slew the existing Main Line as far as 0 m. 8 chs. The Contractor will be required to execute the necessary earthwork in the cuttings, &c., and also to provide and spread the necessary ballast for the same. The Contractor will lay the Permanent Way from 0 m. 8 chs. to the termination of the new line.

Although the total amount of the Contractor's tender must cover the cost of laying the Permanent Way upon gravel ballast only, the Contractor is required to furnish in the Schedule of Prices alternative prices for slag and cinder ballast.

North Eastern and Lancashire and Yorkshire Railways.

Contract for

THE

Construction

OF THE

Hatfield Moor Extension Light Railway

(AXHOLME JOINT RAILWAY).

AND

Works in Connection Therewith.

SPECIFICATION

AND

DETAILED LIST OF QUANTITIES.

Engineer's Office,

York.

September, 1907.

HATFIELD MOOR EXTENSION LIGHT RAILWAY.

AXHOLME JOINT RAILWAY.

SUMMARY.

	£	s.	d.
EARTHWORK	1,125	7	.
BRIDGE NO. 1 AT 1 m. 49½ chs. Plans Nos. 8 and 11	237	7	.
BRIDGE NO. 2 AT 1 m. 51 chs. do.	597	13	6
BRIDGE NO. 3 AT 1 m. 67 chs. Plans Nos. 10 and 11	759	7	3
BRIDGE NO. 4 AT 2 m. 66½ chs. do.	844	1	.
BRIDGE NO. 5 AT 3 m. 57 chs. Plans Nos. 8 and 9	505	14	9
CULVERT AT 0 m. 42 chs. Plan No. 13	34	16	.
CULVERT AT 0 m. 51 chs. do.	16	11	.
CULVERT AT 1 m. 42 chs. do.	15	18	.
CULVERT AT 1 m. 08 chs. do.	17	19	.
CULVERT AT 3 m. 21 chs. do.	19	15	.
CULVERT AT 3 m. 44 chs. do.	16	15	.
CULVERT AT 4 m. 7 chs. do.	18	7	.
CULVERTS AND DRAINS do.	442	1	.
FENCING, GATES, &c. Plan No. 12	4,015	18	7
PERMANENT WAY, &c. Plans Nos. 1, 4, 5, 19, 20, 21, 22, 23, 24, 25	5,509	11	4
WEIGH OFFICES AND FOUNDATIONS FOR WEIGHBRIDGES. Plan No. 26	120	4	11
	81	11	11
SUNDRIES	700	0	.
PROVISION MONEY	1,000	0	0

Total Amount of Contract ... £14,648 17 6

5. *Accounts*
All clerical work to be done at Epworth by additional Clerk recommended above. Clerk to visit Sandtoft and Hatfield Moor Depot daily to enter inward invoices in delivery books, see to signatures being obtained, supervise labelling of outward wagons, and collect consignment notes, &c. Separate invoices and abstracts to be made out for traffic dealt with at each Station. Debits and credits to be included in Epworth balance sheet.

6. *Rate Books*
Separate rate books to be kept at Sandtoft and Hatfield Moor Depot. Similar information to be kept at Epworth as an appendix to the rate book at that Station.

7. *Cash for Bank*
All cash to be accounted for at Epworth and remitted to bank with the cash for that Station.

8 *Train Service*
The question of train service to be considered when the branch is approaching completion.

On 20th October,1908 the Joint Board visited the new branch and decided upon the following names;

a) The crossing at 1 mile 60 chains from Epworth South Junction, 'Torne Crossing'
b) The siding at 2 miles 60 chains from Epworth South Junction 'Sandtoft'
c) The siding near Allen's Farm, 4 miles 10 chains from Epworth South Junction 'Allerton's Siding'
d) The sidings at the end of the branch, 4 miles 60 chains from Epworth South Junction, 'Hatfield Moor Depot'

They also discussed the staffing arrangements and decided that at:

a) Torne Crossing: A platelayer to occupy the cottage whose wife shall attend to the gates
b) Sandtoft: A senior porter to be in charge of the station at 20s. per week, less 2s. 6d. per week for rent of gate-keeper's cottage thereat, whose wife shall attend to the gates
c) Hatfield Moor Depot: A senior porter at 20s. per week who was to also attend to traffic loaded at Allerton's Siding. A cottage would not be required at present.
Epworth: A clerk to perform all clerical work in connection with the branch

A siding for seven wagons was proposed at Torne Crossing, but after considerable discussion it was decided that this was too close to Epworth where ample siding accommodation was available.

The joint superintendent reported that Sandoft and Allerton's Siding were opened for traffic on 5th January, 1909 and that 11,052 tons of forwarded and received traffic had been dealt with up to 28th February,1909. The depot at Hatfield Moor was opened for traffic on 1st March, 1909 and it transpired that in order to encourage more traffic to the depot, a loading dock was necessary. After discussion, it was agreed that the Engineer prepare a plan and estimate. This was approved on 24th September, 1909 at an estimated cost of £871, but by 1911 had not been built.

The Route

Epworth

The branch was single line throughout, starting at Epworth station with a trailing point just north of the goods yard entry point. It ran parallel to the main line in a north-easterly direction for 11 chains, through Epworth cutting before peeling off to the left in a north-westerly direction. On the 1909 NER siding diagram, a siding* of 261 yards was situated to the left and alongside the running line, with a 45 yard headshunt, allowing traffic to be held awaiting clearance for the main line. The only gradient on the branch was a slight fall occurring on the initial 90° curve near Epworth cutting, however from that point to the end of the 4 miles 78 chains-long branch the track was virtually level. All the underbridges were constructed of timber and the first was encountered after about a mile, when the track crossed Folly Drain and South Engine Drain (New Idle River) before continuing to the Sandtoft to Epworth road which it crossed by a gated level crossing. Soon after the line crossed the River Torne and the direction changed about 10° towards the west. For about a further mile the track was again straight before arriving at the Doncaster to Sandtoft road (the subject of the public enquiry).

Sandtoft

The only intermediate goods station of Sandtoft (2 miles 71 chains) was situated here on the east side of the level crossing and had a siding for 10 wagons. The NER placed a water column (No.151) at Sandtoft, which incidentally was the only water available on the branch. In September 1909, the AJR authorised a borehole to be sunk at the branch junction near Epworth at a cost of £220, but no water was found. A further borehole sunk at Sandtoft in the following year did however produce the required flow of 5,000 gallons per hour, from a depth of 230 feet. Nearby was sited a World War II airfield (which was only 10 ft above mean sea level). After a survey was made in January 1942, construction commenced in October 1942. The base was opened in December 1943 as a satellite for No. 11 Base at Lindholme, in No. 1 Group (Bomber Command). Halifax Bombers of the 1667 Heavy Conversion Unit were the first arrivals, moving in from Faldingworth (near Market Rasen) on 20th February, 1944. These were gradually replaced by Avro Lancasters from November onwards, but on 10th November, 1945, 1667 Unit was disbanded and the station closed down. The airfield was placed in the hands of the USA in 1953, but they never commissioned it and returned control back to the MOD in 1955, which some time later sold off the 700 acres to private individuals. The site now houses the Sandtoft Transport Museum (in the old T2 hangar) and various local companies. In 1982, a new

*Reference: MT6/1688/5. New siding inspected 3rd March, 1908 and points remodelled. (Public Record Office, Kew)

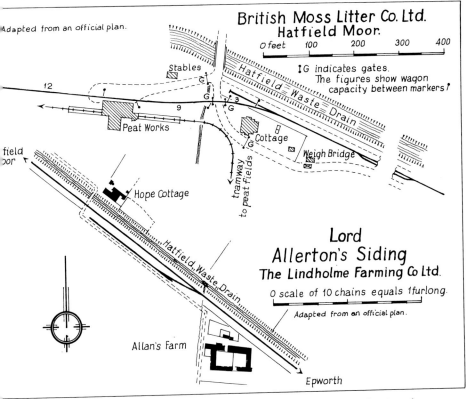

British Moss Litter Co. Ltd.
Hatfield Moor.

0 feet 100 200 300 400

Adapted from an official plan.

Stables

G indicates gates.
The figures show wagon
capacity between markers!

Hatfield Waste Drain

12

Peat Works

9

Cottage

Weigh Bridge

field
oor

Hope Cottage

tramway to peat fields

Lord
Allerton's Siding
The Lindholme Farming Co Ltd.

0 scale of 10 chains equals 1 furlong.

Adapted from an official plan.

Hatfield Waste Drain

Allan's Farm

Epworth

hangar was added and a part of the airfield reopened for use by light aircraft and flying clubs, and it is still very active today. During its wartime service the airfield recorded the following accidents:

28th February, 1941	Anson of 14 OTU crashed at Haxey
3rd April, 1942	Spitfires P8438 & P8595 of 133 Squadron collided over Epworth
7th March, 1944	Halifax Mk V EB184 of 1667 HCU crashed at Graiselound, near Haxey after colliding in mid-air with HR657 whilst on bombing practice
18th April, 1944	Halifax Mk V DG386 of 1667 HCU crashed at Epworth
24th May, 1944	Halifax Mk V DG403 of 1667 HCU crashed at Butterwick
26th June, 1944	Halifax Mk V DG395 of 1667 HCU crashed two miles east of Thorne
25th July, 1944	Halifax Mk V EB190 of 1667 HCU crashed at Hatfield Moor
6th September, 1944	Halifax Mk V DK133 of 1667 HCU crashed at Crowle
10th October, 1944	Halifax Mk V LL501 of 1667 HCU crashed into a mudbank at the mouth of the River Trent
5th April, 1945	Lancaster Mk 3 ND639 of 1667 HCU crashed at Crowle at 2.58 am whilst on an exercise
15th April, 1945	Lancaster Mk 3 PB565 of 1667 HCU broke up in mid-air and crashed at Owston Ferry

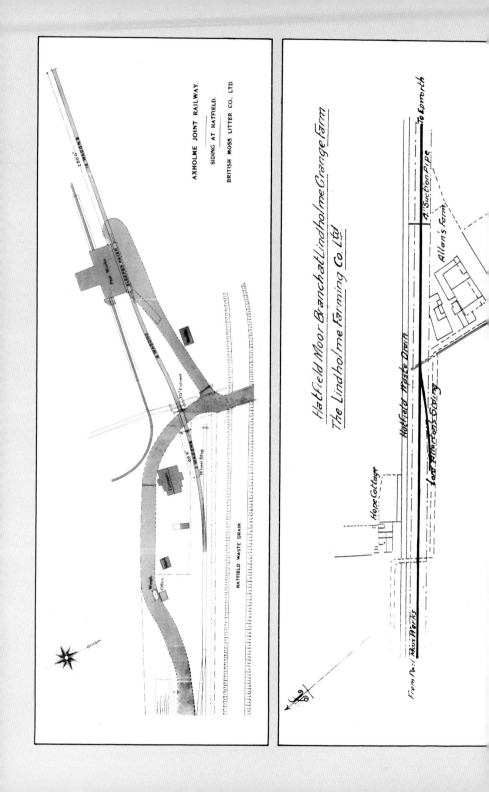

AXHOLME JOINT RAILWAY.

SIDING AT HATFIELD.

BRITISH MOSS LITTER CO. LTD.

Hatfield Moor Branch at Lindholme Grange Farm

The Lindholme Farming Co. Ltd.

Class '2MT' 2-6-0 No. 46436 built at Crewe Works in January 1950, and originally allocated to Fleetwood shed, seen here on the Hatfield Moor branch at Sandtoft. The sidings are full of wagons, which can be seen behind the brake van. *Geoffrey Oates*

A further view of No. 46436 this time at the Hatfield Moor terminus with 'the cottage' on the left. *Geoffrey Oates*

For another two miles the line wended its way on the level alongside the Hatfield Waste Drain before reaching the branch terminus at Hatfield Moor (originally Lindholme Moor). Here was the peat works of the British Moss Litter Company which provided the main source of traffic for the line.

About ¾ mile from this terminus (just opposite Hope Cottage), a single siding holding just three wagons was situated at Allen's Farm (now Lindholme Grange) for the use of the Lindholme Farming Co. Ltd. It was known as Allerton's Siding and subject to an agreement in relation to pockets of land sold for £250 by Lord Allerton in previous dealings with the Joint Committee.

Hatfield Moor

The terminus had a run round loop of 202 yards, but no platforms and no other facilities.

As early as 24th September, 1909 the British Moss Litter Company (BMLC) discussed the question of constructing a siding into their peat works, but six months later they were unable to give the AJR any estimate of the amount of traffic that might be forwarded. Despite the increased AJR rates quoted, compared with the freight charges the GCR levied to the BMLC for the railhead at Mauds Bridge, the BMLC was still very interested in being linked to the AJR. In September 1911 the AJR decided that, to attract the peat traffic, they would build (at their expense) a loading dock at Hatfield Moor, even though BMLC was still unable to supply any estimated tonnage. The estimated cost was £1,823 (including land charges) but the Engineer hoped to build for £1,700, if suitable earth was available. The loading dock had been built by December 1911 and still the BMLC continued to cart its traffic to the GCR. This continued until eventually an agreement was reached in April 1913 with the AJR who agreed to provide (at its own cost) a siding between Hatfield Moor terminus and the peat works, in return for receiving all BMLC's traffic. On 27th June, a formal agreement with Lord Allerton was executed and the L&Y agreed to construct the spur on behalf of the AJR.

Hatfield Moor Further Extension Railway

The Joint Committee of the L&Y and NER applied, in June 1908, to the Light Railway Commissioners for the Hatfield Moor Further Extension Railway Order. This line, with two intermediate stations was to run from the Hatfield Moor Terminus to the GN&GE Joint Railway near Black Carr. Included in the proposal was a connection to a new colliery nearby but this was strongly opposed by the GCR. This being the case, the Order was refused by the Light Railway Commissioners. Undaunted, the Joint Committee lodged a Bill for the railway before Parliament in November 1908. The Select Committee of the House of Lords, in March 1909, called Sebastian Meyer as a witness and he stated that this 'new' railway would improve the transportation of freight in the area. This statement was strongly supported by local farmers, but Lord Allerton (Chairman of the GNR)

HATFIELD MOOR LIGHT RAILWAY.

A view of Hatfield Mill Peat Works show the standard gauge wagons on the siding the mill. The building on the right was the horse stables and the tramway from the m entered the main building through the doc the end. *Stan Mar*

A wagon specially prepared for dignitar passengers and even shooting part (Sundays) which ran on the peat m tramways. *Stan Mars*

Two early views of the old horse drawn peat tramways working the moors near Low Medge Hall. These tramways brought the peat into the Mills which was subsequently loaded into standard gauge wagons and then transported over the AJR to all parts of the country. The upper view shows Jack Stringer of Crowle, with daughter Pearl in the wagon. Whilst the lower photograph, *c.* 1946, has 'Blossom' (white Horse) and 'Prince' (black horse) being handled by M. Kempen of Low Medge Hall, riding a well-filled wagon. *Courtesy Stan Marshall*

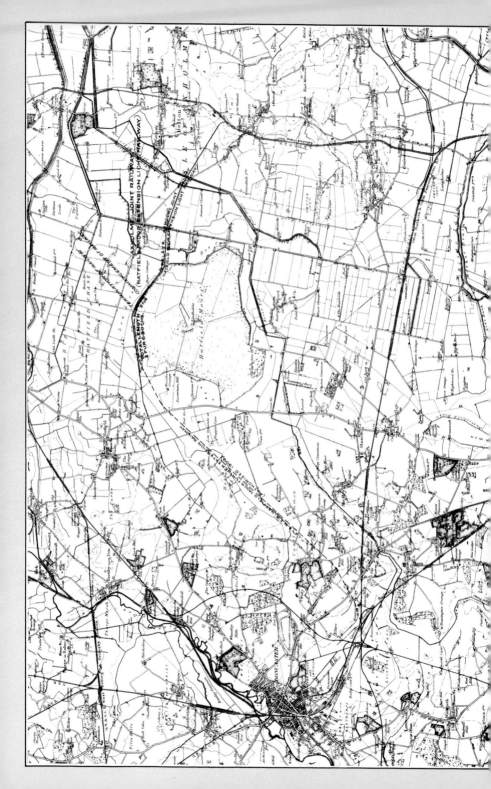

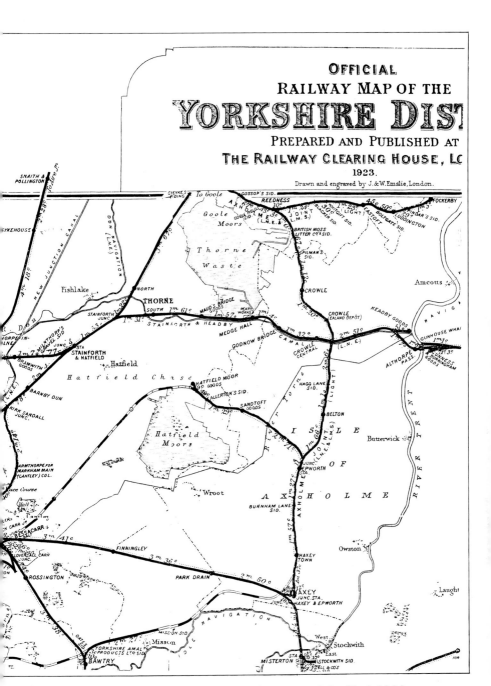

A 1923 RCH map of the area showing the proposed the Hatfield Moor Extension Railway from Hatfield to Black Carr Junction and also the Tickhill Light Railway from Bawtry to Haxey Town (proposed to cross the Doncaster line). Neither of these materialised.

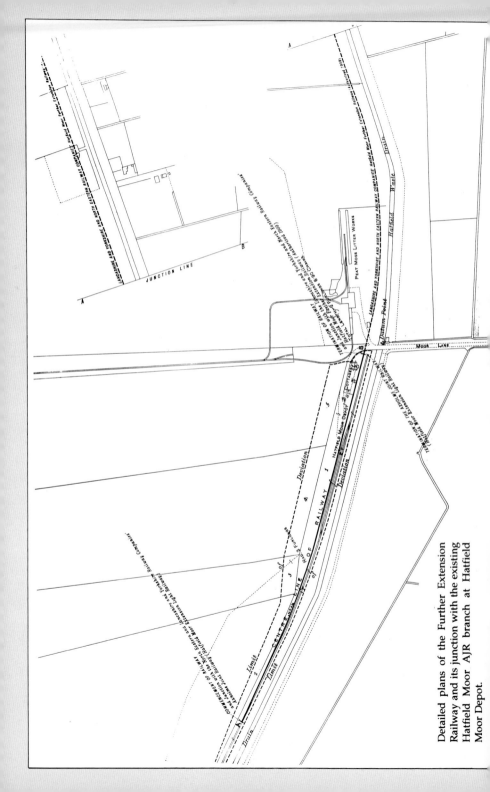

Detailed plans of the Further Extension Railway and its junction with the existing Hatfield Moor AJR branch at Hatfield Moor Depot.

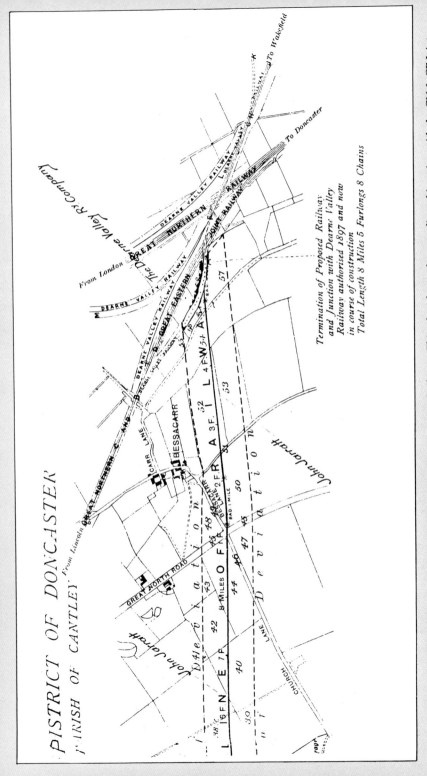

The other end of the proposed Hatfield Moor Further Extension Railway. This plan shows the complicated junction with the GN & GE Joint Railway, the GNR and the Dearne Valley Railway.

strongly opposed the railway due to 'undeclared' interest in a new local coal mine, and also traffic on the Stainforth & Keadby Canal, again in which he had interests.

After all the opposition, a private agreement (dated 31st March, 1909) was made between the L&Y/NER Joint Committee and Earl Fitzwilliam, who owned large portions of the parishes of Armthorpe and Cantley, through which about 3 miles of railway would have passed. He made the agreement to protect his interests and listed over ten pages of amendments in striking a hard bargain! Several are of interest

1. The Earl would have the right to hunt game over the embankments and take hounds on to the railway
2. Several roads being severed by the railway would become redundant and the Earl would claim the redundant sections.
3. If and when the railway was constructed, a suitable station with a goods yard would be built for the convenience of the Earl and his tenants at Common or Gate Lane. This station was to provide reasonable conveyance of farm produce, cattle and general goods to Doncaster.
4. To provide conveyance between this railway and the new sidings (connected to the proposed new colliery to be sunk by the Earl) by providing (at the Joint Committee's expense) a branch railway, not exceeding two miles in length from a point near to the said station and along a course to a point on the east side of the railway of the South Yorkshire Joint Line, with all proper junction signals and equipment. The Earl would pay Railway rates and charges in accordance with the NER Order Act of 1892.
5. He would not ask for any bridges to be constructed and would settle for normal level crossings, about 10 in all.
6. A further 13 items were listed, mainly comprising the supplying of proper culverts, drainage and metalled access to fields etc.

The Bill was finally approved by Parliament and received the Royal Assent on 16th August, 1909.

On 29th July, 1912, the Joint Committee served a notice on George Dunston and Lord Allerton that they intended to acquire from them land on the northern edge of Hatfield Moor. Dunston conveyed his land, plus 8½ acres of the remaining plot of which it formed part, on 16th February, 1917, nearly five years later however no reference to Lord Allerton's conveyance can be found.

The line was never constructed although the Joint Committee and their successors kept their options open until 1932. If the line had been built, a useful and shorter route for the South Yorkshire coal traffic to Immingham port would have been created.

Termination of the agreement relating to traffic at Hatfield Moor was served by British Railways on Fisons PLC by a letter dated 28th August, 1963. It stated that freight facilities would be withdrawn when the line ceased to operate on 29th February, 1964. Some of the land from the lifted branch, offered to Fisons PLC on 28th October, 1966 was declined, but later sold to the Lyon family of Lindholme Hall on 28th September, 1967.

Chapter Six

Locomotives, Railcars and Carriages

The Construction Period Locomotives

No less than seven standard gauge saddle tank locomotives were used during the construction period of the Axholme Railways, all being built at the Boyne Engine Works in Leeds of Manning, Wardle & Company. Locomotives from this builder were considered to be first class products, better than most and highly favoured by the major contractors of the day. Much of the information which follows derives from the entries in Manning, Wardle's surviving records. In the table below, the entries in the last three columns are as stated in their *Engine Book* (but with the owner's name not abbreviated in the original)

Name	Works No.	Class	Sent Away	Owner	Destination
Margaret*	1381	E	17th April, 1899	G&MR†	
Elgie	1456	L	24th November, 1899	IofALR§	
Halkon	1448	Q	1st June, 1900	G&MLR	Marshland Jn
Epworth	1468	K	4th December, 1900	IofALR	Haxey
Bletcher	318	M	(second-hand)	IofALR	
Haxey	1507	K	13th February, 1901	IofALR	Haxey
Cawood	1360	L	(second-hand)	G&MLR	Rawcliffe Br.+

Notes:

* *Margaret* was an outside cylindered 0-4-0 saddle tank, the others being inside cylinder 0-6-0 saddle tanks

† Later entry: Isle of Axholme Light Railway, Haxey.

§ Later entry; Goole & Marshland Light Rly Co., Marshland Junction.

+ With the Goole & Marshland already opened for goods traffic, *Cawood* may have been obtained to work this traffic, rather than for construction work. The significance of 'Rawcliffe Bridge' is not known: this is a village half a mile south-east of Rawcliffe station on the Selby to Goole line over which *Cawood* may have travelled *en route* to Axholme. It would be unwise to speculate further!

Name		Elgie		Epworth	
	Margaret	Cawood	Halkon	Haxey	Bletcher
Type/(Class)	0-4-0ST (E)	0-6-0ST (L)	0-6-0ST (Q)	0-6-0ST (K)	0-6-0ST (M)
Cylinder size	9″ x 14″	12″ x 18″	14″ x 20″	12″ x 17″	12″ x 18″
Wheel Diameter	2′ 9″	3′ 6″	3′ 6″	3′ 0″	3′ 0′
Coupled Wheelbase	4′9″	5′ 5″+ 5′ 4″	5′ 11″+ 6′ 1″	5′ 5″+ 5′ 4″	5′ 10″+ 5′ 8″
Heating Surface (Tubes)	217.5 sq.ft.	402 sq.ft.	600 sq.ft.	326sq.ft.	500 sq.ft.
Heating Surface (Firebox)	30.5 sq.ft.	46 sq.ft.	60 sq.ft.	40 sq.ft.	50 sq.ft.
Grate Area	5 sq.ft.	7 sq.ft.	8.8 sq.ft.	7 sq.ft.	8 sq.ft
Boiler Diameter/Length	2′ 3″/7′ 3″	3′ 1″/7′ 9″	3 6″/8′ 8″	2′ 9″/7′ 9″	3′ 4″/8′ 4″
Water Capacity (Gallons)	250	450	600	450	550
Weight empty/Loaded (Tons)	10¾/12¾	15¾/19½	23¾/27¾	15½/19	17½/22½

It would appear that none of the locomotives listed previously was owned by either the Goole & Marshland or Isle of Axholme companies. The inference is that ownership vested in one of Sebastian Meyer's companies, the most likely candidate being the Yorkshire District Light Railway Syndicate Limited. An advertisement which appeared in the *Contract Journal* for 5th October, 1904 gave notice of an auction sale of contractors' plant to be held at Crowle Wharf on 19th and 20th October, 1904 by the celebrated auctioneers, A.T. and E.A. Crow the plant included five standard gauge Manning, Wardle locomotives, four- and six-coupled, with either 10 in., 12 in., 13 in., or 14 in. cylinders, which were to be sold on behalf of the Yorkshire District Light Railway Syndicate Limited on completion of their Axholme Joint Railway contract.

The first locomotive to be used was *Margaret* and was by far the smallest of the locomotives, an 0-4-0 saddle tank, with just 9½ in. diameter cylinders. Manning, Wardle's class 'E' dates back to 1860 when works number 14 was supplied to E.M. Bainbidge's, West Staveley Colliery, near Beighton, Sheffield. The type rapidly found favour with contractors as well as industrial concerns. Ordered on 6th March, 1899 (Works No. 1381) *Margaret* was

The first locomotive to work on the Goole & Marshland Light Railway was *Margaret*, built by Manning, Wardle & Co. at the Boyne Engine Works, Leeds, in 1899 (works number 1381). She is pictured after being sold to James & Fredk. Howard, Britannia Ironworks, Bedford, and renamed *Howard Bedford*. This firm, established in 1811, manufactured steam ploughing engines and other agricultural machinery In 1926 they began building internal combustion locomotives, one (their number 957 built in 1929) being their works shunter and posing here with the diminutive Manning, Wardle.
                                                                    F. Jones Collection

MANNING WARDLE & C°
BOYNE ENGINE WORKS

Plans of the class 'E' 0-4-0 locomotive, the class which included *Margaret*.

steam tested on 15th April, 1899 and when dispatched to Axholme two days later, just made the six weeks delivery date quoted. As new she was equipped with ¾ in. thick steel plate buffer beams and block buffers for use with contractors' type wooden wagons. Railwashing gear and an Evers direct acting steam pump were fitted, although the pump is recorded as removed in March 1900. As with the other locomotives, it is not known precisely when *Margaret* left Axholme, but by 28th January, 1909 she was working (nameless) at Britannia Ironworks in Bedford of James & Fredk. Howard, agricultural engineer. She was renamed later *Howard Bedford* before the company ran into financial difficulties and the works were closed down (at thirty minutes notice!) on 15th February, 1932. Shortly afterwards this little Manning moved to the Goldington Depot of Bedford Corporation, where she ended her days in 1943.

Elgie was named after Sebastian Meyer's daughter Ellen Grace, the brass nameplates having letters 3¾ in. high. She worked on the construction of both the Goole & Marshland and Isle of Axholme railways; and was one of a trio of Manning, Wardle class 'L' locomotives supplied at this time to light railways with which Sebastian Meyer had an association, (the others were *Cawood* on the Cawood, Wistow & Selby Light Railway - *see later* - and *Bamburgh*, Manning, Wardle works number 1394 of 1898 on the North Sunderland Railway in Northumberland. All three had full cabs, whereas the standard contractor's style class 'L's' had weatherboards only. *Elgie* had some other modifications - special cast iron wheels and buffer beams; Wallace's patent drawgear with hook and screw coupling; and an Evers steam pump and an 8 ft delivery pipe. With 20 feet of 4-ply India rubber suction piping and an 8 ft delivery pipe, the pump enabled *Elgie* to take water from the drainage channels or rivers.

When the order was placed on 23rd August, 1899, Manning, Wardle undertook to deliver within three months. In the event they were a day late as *Elgie* was not dispatched to Axholme until 24th November, 1899. This locomotive was involved in a serious collision with *Halkon* on the evening of Friday 4th January, 1901 (*see page 31*).

Elgie was later recorded as with Gates & Hogg, Barmbro' in Manning, Wardle's *Engine Book*. This indicates that she was worked on the Thurnscoe to Cadeby section of the Dearne Valley Railway in South Yorkshire, which was built by Gates & Hogg between 1902, and 1906 (Barmbro' is an alternative spelling for Barburgh which is on the line of the route.) *Elgie* later worked for S. Pearson & Son Ltd who built the Hull Joint Dock between 1906 and 1914. During World War I many contractors' locomotives went to Scotland to assist with the construction of the vast munitions factory at Gretna, near Carlisle, where the Ministry of Munitions appointed Pearson's as construction managers in October 1915. *Elgie* is said to have worked at Gretna; afterwards she passed into industrial ownership as number 15 at

A fine view of *Elgie* 0-6-0 seen here standing on the Swinefleet Warping Drain bridge during construction of the G&MLR.   *J.H. Bottomley*

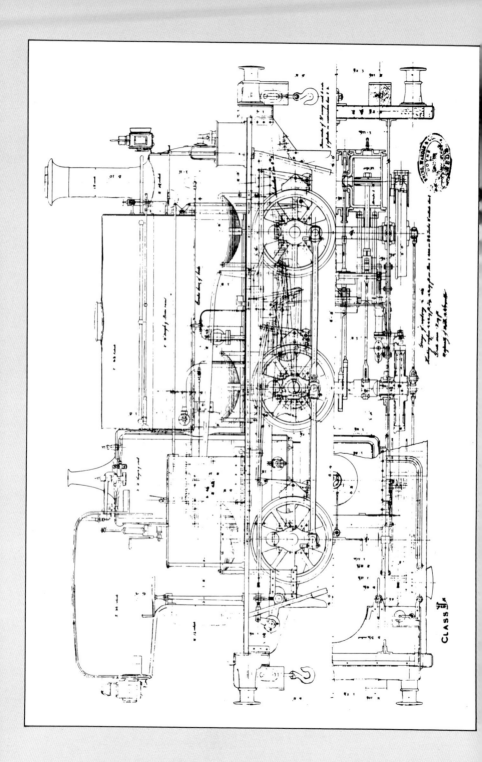

CLASS II

Frodingham Ironstone Mines Ltd in Scunthorpe, from where she disappeared at an unknown date.

Locomotive *Halkon* was a 'Q' class and by far the largest of the seven construction locomotives and amongst standard Manning, Wardles, was eclipsed only by the class 'O' which had 15 in. x 22 in. cylinders. Works number 547 (built in 1875 for the Manston Coal Company, near Leeds) was the first class 'Q' but the design was not produced in quantity. Only 23 more were built over the years up to 1905, the most famous one possibly being works number 1154 of 1890, which was delivered to Ashford as South Eastern Railway No. 353.

Locomotives Nos. 1448 and 1449 were built for stock under internal order number 43800 dated (by extrapolation), about the end of November 1898. At this time all British locomotive builders had full order books and in some instances long delivery dates were being quoted, such that three main line railways (the Great Central, the Great Northern and the Midland) had to buy from America to satisfy their needs. It is not known how quickly construction proceeded, but significantly 1449's works plates were dated 1900 and it was not dispatched until 29th October that year! No.1448 (*Halkon*) was probably more advanced than No. 1449 as its works plates were dated 1899. Seemingly, however, it could have been by no means complete, for when ordered on 15th February, 1900, Manning's were not prepared to quote a delivery date of less than three months. Even that was not met as *Halkon* was

Locomotive *Halkon*, built by Manning, Wardle & Co. Ltd Leeds, to works No. 1448 in 1899. This photograph was taken after it had been sold into colliery ownership.

F. Jones

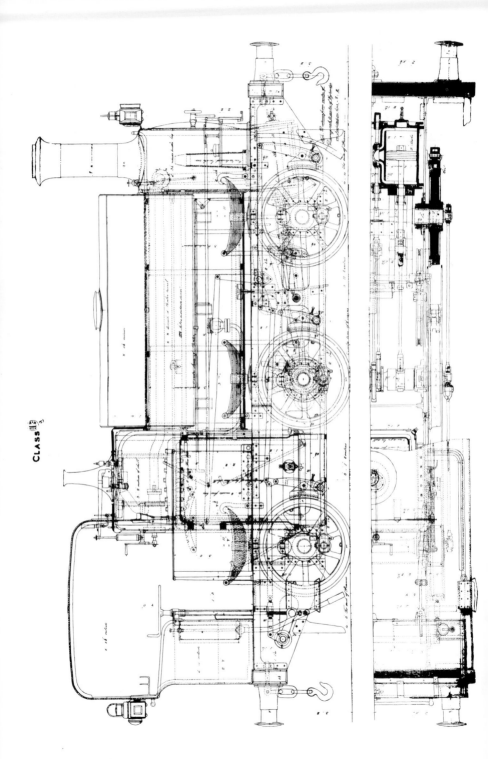

CLASS $\left(\frac{4}{4}\right)$

not tested in steam until 1st June, 1900, leaving Leeds for Axholme later the same day. She was named after the Chairman of the Goole & Marshland Light Railway Company, the letters on its brass nameplate being 3¾ in. high. It was standard 'Q', but fitted with a drawbar and hook, complete with Wallace's India rubber rings and washers and screw couplings. All the latest developments were introduced and the design was thoroughly updated. After the railway construction work had been completed, *Halkon* was sold to the Glass Houghton & Castleford Collieries Ltd, Glass Houghton Colliery, but moved to the Prince of Wales Colliery at Pontefract before the National Coal Board took over in January 1947. Although rebuilt at the Colliery in 1951, *Halkon* was eventually scrapped in 1961.

Epworth was a class 'L' 0-6-0 saddle tank, probably Manning's most successful design. It was ordered on 3rd December, 1900 and having been built for stock earlier in the year, it was available for immediate delivery. A steam test was carried out speedily and *Epworth* was on its way to Axholme the following day. A handrail 5 ft long, for fitting to the rear of the bunker, was sent out shortly afterwards. Brass nameplates were fitted with standard size letters 3¾in. high. It had block buffers for earth spoil wagons and railwashing gear. Manning's record a spares order from the Leeds Contract Co. Ltd at Winteringham, and this indicates that *Epworth* worked on the construction of the North Lindsey Light Railway, north of Scunthorpe - another of Sebastian Meyer's lines - which was built between 1905 and 1907. *Epworth* acquired the number 4 when sold to Logan & Hemingway, a large company of public works contractors, for whom it worked on several contracts - the Cranwell Railway in Lincolnshire for the Admiralty (built between 1916 and 1919); widening of the LMS Birmingham to Bristol line between Longbridge and Barnt Green (about 1925-26); removal of the Hattersley Tunnels and widening work for the LNER at Mottram, near Manchester (*Epworth* was here from at least July 1928 to July 1929); and widening of the East Coast Main Line between Skelton Bridge (just north of York) and Beningborough (spares being ordered from Kitson & Co. Ltd, Manning, Wardle's successors, for delivery to Beningborough in August and November 1931). Detail of *Epworth*'s ultimate demise is regrettably not known

Bletcher, a standard class 'M' with no modifications, was the oldest Manning, Wardle locomotive to work on the Axholme. It was tried in steam on 28th September, 1870 and dispatched new on 11th October, 1870 to Benton & Woodiwiss at Warrington as their No. 14, presumably for work on their Cheshire Lines Committee contracts. These included the building of the main line between Manchester (Cornbrook East Junction) and Garston (Cressington Junction) as well as some short branches at Warrington. Manning's *Engine Book* records a subsequent owner as J. Brier Son & Wilson at Dewsbury. This firm secured a contract from the Great Northern Railway on 5th August, 1885 for building parts of the Beeston to Batley railway

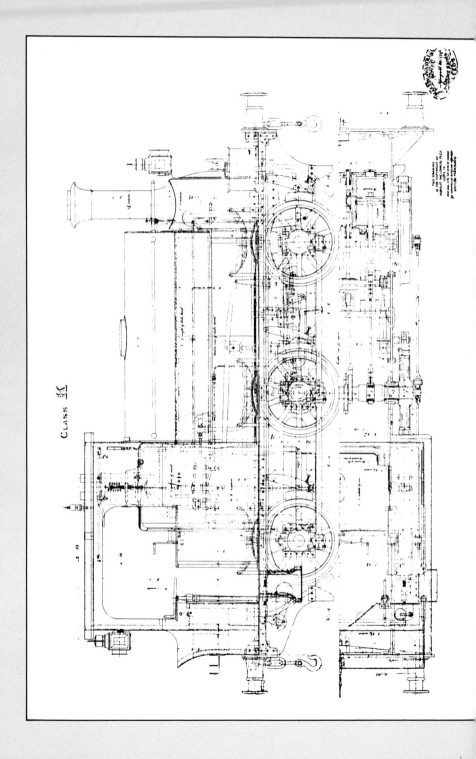

CLASS K

Locomotive *Epworth* (seen here as Logan & Hemingway No. 4) built by Manning, Wardle & Co. in 1900 to works No. 1468 and went new to the Axholme Light Railway in December 1900.

Oakwood Collection

(Batley West Junction to Soothill Colliery) and also the Dewsbury branch (Dewsbury Junction GNR to Headfield Junction L&YR). By 17th July, 1896, this class 'M' locomotive had passed to another firm of contractors, Holme & King by whom it was named *Alicie*. At that time Holme & King were carrying out considerable work for the L&YR, but it is not known on which contract she worked. *Alicie* was brought back by Manning, Wardle and extensively overhauled in November 1899, being fitted with a new Best Yorkshire Iron boiler, new smokebox and a new brake arrangement with cast steel hangers and cast steel brake blocks. This preceded her despatch to Axholme where she was renamed *Bletcher* after the Isle of Axholme Railway Chairman. A full cab to replace the paltry weatherboard was ordered on 11th July, 1900 and this may well have been fitted immediately before its move.

With its work on the Axholme completed, *Bletcher* found employment with the Leeds Contract Co. Ltd on the North Lindsey Light Railway construction during the 1905-1907 period, being photographed at the NLLR station in Scunthorpe at the head of two splendid 6-wheel Great Central Railway coaches. Some time later it passed into the hands of Logan & Hemingway, becoming No. 7 in their fleet and was used on various contracts. The first recorded was the construction of the Cranwell Railway at Sleaford for the Admiralty, about 1916-1919, where it rejoined *Epworth!* Manning, Wardle & Co. Ltd went into receivership in September 1927 and the Boyne Engine Works were closed down. However the goodwill was acquired by near neighbours, Kitson & Co. Ltd and it was at their works (the Airedale Foundry in Leeds) that No. 7 was extensively rebuilt in the early part of 1928. New frames 3 in. longer were fitted, together with a new Best Mild Steel boiler and a copper firebox at a cost of £1,124. It was turned out in a coach green livery with yellow lining, embellished with three coats of varnish. Logan & Hemingway were proud of their fleet, and introduced several special features and modifications on their locomotives which gave them a unique 'Logan's' appearance. So much so that in this instance, Kitson's saw fit to record in their order book: 'This engine has been very much altered by the owners'. No. 7 met up with *Epworth* once again on Logan & Hemingway's Hattersley Tunnels contract for the LNER at Mottram, spares being ordered from there in May 1929 and April 1930. Construction of the Westbury and Frome avoiding lines for the GWR in the next year or so was *Bletcher*'s last known contract for Logan & Hemingway. By May 1935 it had gone into industrial service at the North Lincoln Slag Works, Frodingham, of Sandwith & Clugston. A new cab was ordered from the Yorkshire Engine Co. Ltd, Sheffield on 16th November, 1942 and it was subsequently overhauled there in May 1946. Noted derelict at the Slag works in August 1955, lettered *Clugston & Cawood* No. 2 and still carrying its 1928 Kitson rebuild plate, it was eventually scrapped about 1961.

An official photograph of Manning, Wardle 1360 of 1897, before it was named *Cawood*.
Hunslet Engine Co. Ltd

Cawood was built by Manning, Wardle & Co. at the Boyne Engine Works, Leeds, in 1897 (works number 1360). It is seen here at work on the Cawood, Wistow & Selby Light Railway before being sold to work as a contractor's locomotive on the construction of the Goole & Marshland Light Railway. *F. Jones*

Locomotive *Haxey* was a standard class 'K' 0-6-0 saddle tank fitted with just one extra item, a contractor's speciality - railwashing gear. It was another of Manning's popular designs and, like *Epworth*, had been built for stock. When ordered on 6th February, 1901, it was almost complete and left for Axholme a week later on 13th February. Standard brass nameplates were fitted with the letters 3¾ in. high. Manning's *Engine Book* shows that *Haxey* was later with Gates & Hogg at Barmbro', their No. 6, in company with *Elgie* on the construction of the Thurnscoe to Cadeby section of the Dearne Valley Railway which was built between 1902 and 1906. A new copper firebox was ordered on 22nd November, 1907, and new cylinders complete with pistons on 13th March, 1917; and whilst Manning's History Sheet is silent as to the identity of the customer, in fact they may be those recorded in the *Engine Book* (i.e. Gates & Hogg and Henry Lovatt Ltd). The latter is shown as a later owner and the address quoted (nr Bramley, Rotherham) identifies Lovatt's contract as that for the Great Central & Midland Joint Committee - the line between Thrybergh (GCR)/Roundwood(MR) and Anston Junction (South Yorkshire Joint Railway) which was built between 1907 and 1909. *Haxey* was No. 22 in Lovatts's fleet and is said to have worked on another contract, the Ealing & Shepherd's Bush Railway which was the only line built for the GWR during World War I and opened for goods traffic on 16th April, 1917.

Haxey's next known move took it to Dolgarrog Aluminium Works in Caernarvonshire of the Aluminium Corporation Ltd, where it was renamed *Dolgarrog*. It had certainly arrived by August 1928 (when spares were ordered from Kitson & Co.), and it could have been there as early as 1916 when the works was connected to the LNWR's Blaenau Festiniog branch. It is perhaps significant datewise that Manning's History Sheet, whilst showing the change of name to *Dolgarrog*, records no spares order after the one placed on 10th August, 1920 for a new mild steel axle and some 2¼ in. thick tyres. When replaced by a new locomotive in 1943, *Dolgarrog* was sold to Cudworth & Johnson Ltd, dealers at Wrexham. After working on hire to shunting contractor W.J. Lee in Birkenhead Docks for some years, it stood idle until scrapped there, early in 1951.

The last locomotive to arrive at Axholme was *Cawood* a class 'L' 0-6-0 saddle tank similar to *Elgie*, but with several alterations from standard. These comprised a special cab with the handbrake column on the left-hand side; Westinghouse air brake; special injector and pump arrangement; new style frames with special frame ends; steel buffer beams; class 'K' style wheel splashers; screw couplings; new style boiler with circular firehole and sliding door to suit; Ramsbottom type safety valves inside the cab with steam escape tubes through the roof; railguards; and a new sandbox control system with the levers and rods underneath the footplate. The overall length was 22 ft 4 in. width 7 ft 3 in. and height 10 ft 9½ in. Whilst the builders did not weigh this particular locomotive, some class 'Ls' built earlier tared about 15¾ tons empty and 19½ tons in working order; others built later were about 1½ tons heavier. *Cawood* had brass nameplates with the usual standard size letters 3¾ in. high.

It was ordered on 2nd October, 1896, steam tested on 30th March, 1897 and dispatched new the following day to Brayton Gates, Selby for the Cawood, Wistow & Selby Light Railway. Its purchase was financed by a hire purchase agreement entered into on 7th April, 1897 with the Yorkshire Railway Waggon Co Ltd, Wakefield, which provided for a 7 year hire period and an annual rental payment of £203 5s. [£203.25p]. The Light Railway was taken over by the NER on 1st January, 1900, but the agreement was not determined until 6th July, 1901 when *Cawood* was assigned to the Yorkshire District Light Railway Syndicate Ltd of Central Bank Chambers, Leeds.

In the same year, *Cawood* moved east to Axholme for construction work on the Goole & Marshland Light Railway. Although there is no confirmation in Manning, Wardle's records, *Cawood* is said to have later worked for the Leeds Contract Co. Ltd on the building of the Winteringham to Whitton section of the North Lindsey Light Railway, which was undertaken between 1907 and 1910. About 1911, *Cawood* was purchased by Logan & Hemingway, numbered 6, and used on a contract awarded in February 1911 by the Great Central Railway for the deviation of the Doncaster to Scunthorpe line between Keadby Junction and Frodingham; this was in connection with the installation of a swing bridge across the River Trent at Keadby by Sir William Arrol & Co. Ltd, which was completed in October 1914.

Logan & Hemingway had a contract during World War I at the Gretna Munitions Factory where construction work was supervised by S. Pearson & Son Ltd. Several of their locomotives went to Gretna including *Cawood*. Manning, Wardle's records in fact quote 'Ministry of Munitions, Gretna' as an owner and this suggests that they may well have commandeered *Cawood* for the duration of the War as they did with other contractors' plant and equipment. About 1918 she went to work in the Scunthorpe Ironstone quarries of Frodingham Ironstone Mines Ltd as plain number 13, together with her former Axholme stablemate *Elgie*. Spares were ordered from Kitson's & Co. Ltd in February 1928, but the date of her ultimate end does not appear to have been recorded.

Sentinel Railcars

As early as March 1907, moves were afoot to introduce 'Autocars' on to the line and a Board minute No. 171 is relevant:

LMS Sentinel steam railcar No. 2232 (built in 1925 to works No. 6177), seen here at Perth in 1932, is the one which may have worked on the AJR during 1926. In the 1933 renumbering scheme this vehicle was allotted No. 29900 but this number is thought to have been carried as withdrawal took place in July 1935. *Photomatic Ltd*

AJR steam railcar No. 44 stands at Haxey Junction waiting to depart for Goole in the 1930s. *Real Photographs*

171. Proposal to Work Goole and Haxey Junction Passenger Train Service by Autocar. Reported that this matter had been fully considered by Messrs Nicholson and Watson who state that there will be no saving if the service were worked by autocar and that on Wednesdays and Saturdays ordinary trains would be required on account of the number of passengers then travelling.

In July 1926, the following paragraph appeared in *The Railway Gazette*:

Sentinel-Cammell coach on Axholme Joint Line - By arrangement with the LMS Company, which provides engine power on the Axholme joint line and in conjunction with tests carried out by the LNER on various sections, a Sentinel-Cammell steam coach has been running experimental trips between Goole and Haxey Junction in place of the ordinary steam trains, except at busy periods. For some time past the LNER has been conducting experiments with cars of this type in East Anglia.

The AJR Board minutes infer that this experiment was carried out for one month's duration in July 1926. The LMS (as successor to the L&YR) purchased 13 Sentinel steam railcars in 1926/27 (LMS Nos. 2232, 4143 to 4154) and put one of them (based at Goole shed) to work on the AJR. The only possible car available was LMS No. 2232 (Sentinel No. 6177). Careful research by John Edgington found that the number of this railcar has always previously been quoted as 2233, but this is incorrect as No. 2233 was a former MR steam railcar, which was not withdrawn until late 1926.

The specification for this vehicle was as follows; boiler pressure, 275lb per sq. in. with 100 hp chain-driven two cylinder steam engine with 6¾ in. x 9 in. cylinders. Bogie wheels were diameter of 2 ft 6 in. with a front bogie wheelbase of 7 ft 0 in. and rear bogie wheelbase of 5 ft 6 in. Length over buffer was 57 ft 5 in. and the body was 8 ft. wide. The overall height was lower than a conventional coach at 11 ft, and the weight empty (without coal and water) was 17 tons. There were seats for 52 third class passengers in the saloon, 28 in the forward section and 24 in the rear, as well as six tip-up seats in the rear luggage compartment. The saloon seats were reversible for 'both-ways' travel as on most street tramcars of the period.

In the order book for June 1928 is a reference to a further order placed for a Sentinel double-engined steam railcar for the AJR. It was works No. 7565, with two power units to be built by Sentinel at Shrewsbury. The carriage portion (as usual) was to be constructed by Cammel Laird & Co. Ltd, Nottingham and the whole assembled at the same place. It was a bogie railcar with 3 ft 1 in. wheels on a 7 ft wheelbase, geared to attain 38 mph at 500 rpm. It was ordered on 27th June, 1928 (by LMS Derby) for the AJR (for trial purposes only); then on 2nd August, 1928, the reference to 'Axholme Joint Railway' was deleted and the project was to be known as the double-engined

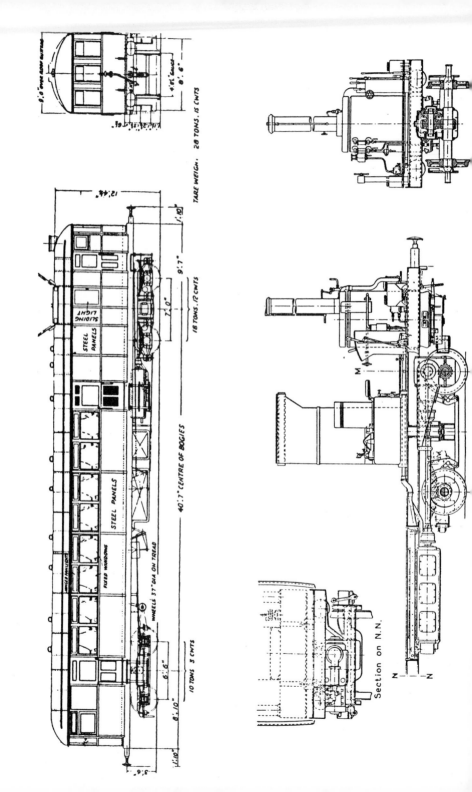

Section on N.N.

A works view of No. 44, new before delivery to the AJR. Note the route board 'Goole & Haxey'

Two views of No. 44, the Axholme Joint Railway steam railcar, a useful vehicle for the line. The top view was taken at Crowle and the lower view at Haxey Junction station.

Author's Collection

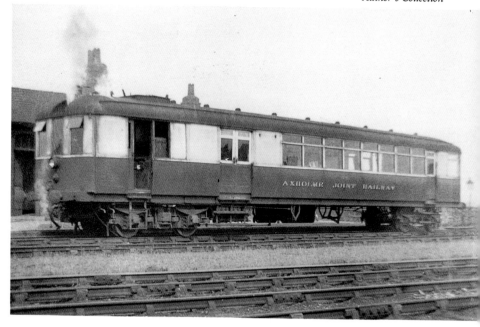

200 hp 'Trial Car'. Later, on 22nd April, 1929, the materials for this project were transferred to Sentinel job No. 7822, which became LNER No. 2281* delivered in June 1930, and Job No. 7565 was declared 'defunct'. So No. 7565 never existed as a railcar!

The Axholme Joint Railway's own steam railcar was Sentinel No. 8228. This was ordered by the LMS on 28th February, 1930 and put into service in December 1930. As usual the coach body was built and fitted at Nottingham, although there had been an amalgamation and Cammell's works were now part of Metropolitan-Cammell Carriage, Wagon and Finance Co. Ltd.

The steam railcar was a single six cylinder-engined car of reputed 100 hp, with 3 ft 1 in. wheels, 7 ft 0 in. engine bogie wheelbase and a 6 ft 6 in. trailing bogie wheelbase and geared to run at 38 mph at 500 rpm. The boiler pressure was 300 1b. per sq. in. The overall length was 61 ft 6 in. with a width of 9 ft (overall buffers 65 ft 8 in.). It seated 64 passengers and a further 10 could be accommodated in the luggage compartment on tip-up seats. The weight empty was 29 tons 5 cwt.; coal and water would add another four tons, plus about six tons if there was a full load of passengers and their luggage.

This car was lettered 'AXHOLME JOINT RAILWAY' on each side and the livery was, surprisingly, green and cream. It is one of the rare instances in which a joint line possessed its own motive power. Bearing the number 44 ,[†] under the 1933 renumbering scheme, it became LMS No. 29987, but this was never used or carried. This proved a very useful vehicle for the small amount of traffic on the line and worked two return daily services between Goole and Haxey Junction (with an extra trip on Goole Market day, Wednesday). On Saturdays, it ran five return journeys. Up to the cessation of passenger services in 1933, this railcar ran 53,786 miles. It was then sold to the LNER in November 1933, becoming No. 51915 (but nameless) in their coaching stock list (Diagram 209). After being reconditioned at Gorton Works, it entered service in January 1934 and lasted until July 1944.

Main Line Locomotives

On 1st July, 1903 the contractor ceased to work the traffic and the L&YR took over the task, the motive power being supplied by Goole shed. Main line locomotives may have ventured on to the Axholme railways prior to this date, but if so do not appear to have been recorded. In the early years passenger trains were generally hauled by Barton Wright 0-6-2 side tanks, with Barton Wright 4 ft 6 in. 0-6-0 goods tender engines used on both goods and

---

*No.7822 became LNER No.2281 *Old John Bull*
[†]The number 44 in the LMS list was a former MR six-wheeled passenger brake van and LNER No. 44 was a Clayton railcar, so what '44' meant on the AJR railcar is something of a mystery.

L&YR 0-6-0 No. 555 (constructed by Sharp, Stewart & Co. Ltd, Manchester in 1877, works No. 2697 with 17½ in. x 26 in. cylinders and 4 ft 6 in. diameter wheels) was one of 280 goods engines of this type, introduced by William Barton Wright in 1876 and built at several works until 1887. The first 230 were rebuilt to 0-6-0 saddle tanks, between 1891 and 1900, but the last 50 built in 1887 by the Vulcan Foundry Ltd, Newton-le-Willows (L&YR 928-947) and Beyer, Peacock & Co. Ltd, Manchester (L&YR 948-977), had long lives. All of them survived to be taken over by British Railways in 1948 and examples based at Goole shed continued to work on the AJR until replaced by modern 2-6-0s about 1960.

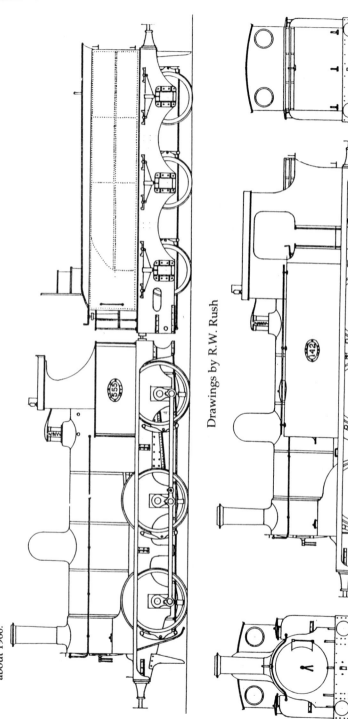

Drawings by R.W. Rush

L&YR 0-6-2 radial tank No. 142 (constructed by Kitson & Co. Leeds in 1880 to works No. 2313). This was a small class of 10, all built be

passenger traffic*. Aspinall's 2-4-2 side tanks were subsequently drafted in to work passenger trains when the 0-6-2s were withdrawn from service - eight of the ten had been withdrawn by 1914 - and prior to the introduction of the Sentinel railcar.

In L&YR days, although the engines were painted plain black, they looked extremely smart with red and white lining and the company's name in gold lettering completed by the embellishment of the coat of arms. This comprised the shields of Lancaster and York, surmounted by a crown, with a red and white rose entwined below, the whole surrounded by an Oxford blue garter inscribed 'Lancashire & Yorkshire Railway' in gilt serif lettering, shaded black.

The old Barton Wright 0-6-0 goods tender engines worked the AJR goods traffic for long after the passenger service was withdrawn in 1933. It was not until after World War II that they were gradually displaced by a new type, the lightweight taper-boilered class 2, 2-6-0 locomotive designed by H.A. Ivatt. The first to be built (LMS No. 6400) was initially allocated to Derby shed (17A). Nos. 6405 and 6406, although allocated new to Goole shed (25C)

*Both these types were designed and built by Kitson & Co. of Leeds, William Barton Wright being the L&YR chief mechanical engineer at the time they were introduced. Further information on these classes can be found in the photograph captions. The following locomotives have been recorded running on the AJR: 0-6-2 tanks: Nos. 145, 229 and 237. 0-6-0's: 934, 947, 950, 954, 956, 957, 959, 960, 962, and 969. Aspinall 0-6-0 : 1064.

Lancashire & Yorkshire Railway 0-6-0 tender locomotive No. 954 (built in August 1887 by Beyer, Peacock & Co., Manchester, to works No. 2837) is seen here at Reedness Junction. It was withdrawn from service in October 1950 from Newton Heath shed, Manchester, as British Railways No. 52041.   *Real Photographs*

when turned out of Crewe Works in December 1946, may never have actually reached Goole. In that month No. 6405 was working around Mirfield and Wakefield and to Stockport and Bradford Exchange in February 1947. No. 6406 was noted at Southport and Preston in December and appears to have been based at Newton Heath, Manchester (26A) in January. Both were officially transferred to Farnley Junction, Leeds (25G) in April 1947. No. 6407, allocated to Goole, did eventually arrive there in 1947 as did No. 6408, both of which had worked the Mirfield and Wakefield areas first, when new.

These 2-6-0's were used initially by Goole on passenger turns to and from Wakefield, but before long they were rostered more and more on the Axholme line where they became instantly popular with the crews. The tender cab provided a more comfortable working environment in the exposed conditions of the flat landscape, especially when working tender first back to Goole. Crews had a good view of the track in this direction, as the tender sides were cut-back for this purpose. At the beginning of 1950, Nos. 46405 and 6409 (not renumbered then) arrived at Goole, followed shortly before the year end by Nos. 46436 and 46437. Two of the 1887-built Barton Wright 0-6-0s - BR Nos. 52037 and 52056 (formerly L&YR Nos. 950 and 969) - were still on the Goole allocation, but it is doubtful if they were ever

Lancashire & Yorkshire Railway 4 ft 6 in. 0-6-2 Goods Tank No. 229 (built by Kitson & Co., Leeds, in February 1881, works No. 2317, and finally withdrawn in December 1912) is seen at Haxey Junction with the 1.35 pm service to Goole. Note the number 10 on the rear of the cab back sheet which was the L&YR code for Goole shed. The first carriage is an L&YR 3rd brake with five compartments, on 6 ft 6 in. narrow bearing bogies, on hire from the L&YR.   *Real Photographs*

required to work on the AJR. In December 1950, they were transferred away to Wakefield where they ended their days in August 1952 and August 1951 respectively. One further class '2' 2-6-0 (No. 46487) was transferred to Goole in October 1953, and it is presumed that all seven of this class worked at sometime or another on the joint line.

On 17th September, 1956, at the time of the motive power crisis, Goole shed was transferred from the London Midland Region of British Railways to the North Eastern Region and recoded 53E. Its new parent shed, Hull Diarycoates (53A), loaned seven locomotives which included three class 'J25's' (Nos. 65693, 65695 and 65726) sent out on 22nd September. On 4th February, 1957, two more 'J25s' - Nos. 65655 and 65677 - made the same journey, and it was said that Axholme trips formed part of their duties at Goole. Built by the NER between 1898 and 1902, these 0-6-0 tender locomotives had 18½ in. x 26 in. inside cylinders and 4 ft 7¼ in. coupled wheels. The weight in working order was 78 tons and the maximum axle load 15 tons 16 cwt. substantially more than the 55¼ ton Barton Wright 0-6-0s. It is unlikely that the 'J25s' were on loan for any great length of time, and those which worked on the AJR appear to have escaped record.

In July 1957, four even heavier and older 0-6-0 tender engines were transferred from Liverpool (Brunswick) Cheshire Lines shed to Goole specifically for Axholme duties. These were former Great Central Railway class '9H' (LNER class 'J10') Nos. 65142, 65145 and 65147 (built by Beyer, Peacock in 1896) and No. 65196 (Gorton 1902), having 18 in. x 26 in. inside cylinders and 5 ft 1 in. coupled wheels. The weight in working order was just over 84 tons, and the maximum axle load 15½ tons. British Railways placed them in the power classification '3F' as against '2F' for the 'J25s'. No. 65147 was soon a casualty, being withdrawn in March 1958; the others went later the same year in October, December and June respectively.

During 1960 various small diesel shunters were delivered new to Goole shed for use in the docks, but they soon ventured out on to the AJR. In December 1961, Ivatt 2-6-0 No. 46407 became the first of its class to be withdrawn, and within six months all but one of those allocated to Goole had gone. A Branch Line Society brakevan tour on 10th March, 1962, was worked by Hunslet 0-6-0 diesel No. D2610 and No. D2611 worked another special on 14th September, 1963. These had a Gardiner eight-cylinder type 8L3 engine, developing 204 bhp at 1200 rpm. With diminishing traffic and a need for economy, it was an ideal type to see out the final years of the Axholme Joint Railway.

Passenger Carriages

When the line was eventually opened for passenger traffic, the Axholme Joint Railway hired three carriages from the Lancashire & Yorkshire Railway

Class '2MT' 2-6-0 No. 46408, shedded at Goole (25C shed-plate) shunting at Haxey Town in the early 1950s. This class worked most trains on the AJR in BR days before the introduction of 0-6-0 diesel shunters.   *Geoffrey Oates*

A weed killing train being hauled by a class 14 diesel at Crowle in the late 1960s, at which time the line was being worked as a 'long siding' by British Railways.
T. Kay Collection

these being: (a) a third class 52 ft bogie brake with one luggage and six passenger compartments; (b) a six-wheeled, third class carriage, 32 ft long with
six passenger compartments and (c) a six-wheeled brake third class carriage,
32 ft long with one luggage and two passenger compartments.

The first vehicle was hired (on a 3 month basis) at a rate of £90 per annum
and the other two at £100 per annum each.

At an AJR Committee Meeting held on 17th February, 1904, it was
agreed that the following rates be paid to the Lancashire & Yorkshire
Railway: 5s. 3d. [26p] per hour for passenger engines and 5s. 8d. [28p] for
goods engines; 6d. [2½p] per hour for guards; and £240 per annum for the
hire of coaching stock 'on regular service'.

A fourth carriage was added in 1906, because of the increase in traffic,
this being a six-wheeled L&Y third class carriage. The numbers of the carriages running on the AJR have been recorded as 1537 (3rd class), 2646 and
1234. All would have featured the L&Y third class 'horsehair seats' which, by
all reports, would not have been appreciated by the passengers using them.

Cranes

An agreement was made between the L&Y and the NER that all mobile
crane power required by the AJR was to be supplied by each company in
alternate years.

Courtesy H. Hackney, Belton

(115).

AXHOLME JOINT RAILWAY

(N. E. and L. & Y. JOINT).

On **SATURDAYS :**	*Attractions at the Grand Theatre, Hull Matinees commence at 2-0 p.m,*
January 20th.	" Jack and Jill."
Feb 10th Pantom " Dick Whittington, Alex. Theatre	" Perplexed Husband."
March 2..	Denhof Operatic Festival.
March 23rd	George Edwardes' " Peggy."
April 13th	Carl Rosa Opera.
May 4th	" Bunty Pulls the Strings."
May 25th	

DAY and HALF-DAY EXCURSION TICKETS to

Leeds AND Hull

And EVENING EXCURSION TICKETS to

 # GOOLE,

Will be issued as under :

FROM	Day to Hull		Day to Leeds and Hull	Half Day to Leeds and Hull	Evening to Goole		Fares there and back (third class).				Evening to Goole
							DAY.		**HALF-DAY.**		
							To Leeds	To Hull	To Leeds	To Hull	
	a.m.	a.m.	a.m.	p.m.	p.m.	p.m.					
Crowle dep	8 39	11 15		2 2	4 52	7 23					1s. 0d.
Fockerby „			10 5	1 40		*7 5					1s. 1d.
Luddington „			10 9	1 44		7 9					1s. 1d.
Eastoft „			10 13	1 48		7 13	2/9	2/6	2/6	2/3	1s 0d.
Reedness Junc „	8 52	11 24	10 23	2 12	5 1	7 32					9d.
Goole arr.	9 5	11 36	10 35	2 24	5 13	7 45					
„ (To Leeds) dep			11 5	2 27							
(To Hull) „	9 23	11 53	11 10	2 58							

On above dates the 6-23 p.m. Ordinary Train Fockerby to Reedness Junction will leave at 7-5 p.m.

Leeds (Well'ita-up)	...	...	...	dep.	7 50 p.m.
Hull (Paragon)	...	...	...	dep.	5 5 p.m. or 9 20 „
Goole	...	...	...	„	10 15 „

Passengers must change at Goole both going and returning.

ORDINARY and MARKET TICKETS will be available by the late train from Goole.

Children no exceeding 3 years of age, free ; above 3 and under 12 years of age, half-fare.

Excursion Tickets are not transferable, and are available only to and from the Stations named upon them and by the Trains advertised in the Bills &c., and if used to or from a Station beyond or short of the Stations named on the Tickets. or by Trains not advertised in the Bills, &c., they will be forfeited. and the holders thereof will be charged the full Ordinary Fare for the whole distance travelled.

For further information apply to MR. M. WOODHOUSE Joint Superintendent

January, 1912. Crowle.

The Isle of Axholme Printing Company, Limited Crowle.

Chapter Seven

Traffic and Operation

Passenger Services

For 30 years the Axholme Joint Railway enjoyed a weekdays-only passenger service, but during that time the timetables showed many changes. Although of interest to the railway historian, no doubt passengers would have had 'other' feelings about the sparse services on offer. On 10th August, 1903, passenger services were introduced between Goole and Crowle (also the Fockerby branch), with a train at 7.45 am from Goole, arriving at Crowle at 8.51 am (*see timetable, Chapter Two, page 54*). The return service left Crowle at 8.55 am and arrived at Goole at 9.18 am. On the outward journey there was a trip up the branch to Fockerby station and back. In the evening a train left Goole at 6.15 pm and went straight though to Crowle arriving at 6.38 pm; it ran back immediately at 6.42 pm and, after a return trip to Fockerby arrived back at Goole at 7.48 pm.

There was also a mid-day service on Wednesdays and Saturdays which enabled the people of the area to enjoy the delights of Goole market which was held on Wednesdays. By 1905, when the line had been opened throughout for passenger traffic, there were three trains in each direction between Goole and Haxey (*see* Working Timetable), and the Fockerby branch was operated independently from Reedness Junction.

It was possible for the whole system to be worked by just three locomotives each day. The engine on the 6.30 am goods (based at Reedness Junction) worked passenger and freight traffic as required to Fockerby (the branch) and also collected traffic from the Peat Moss Works sidings (just south of Reedness Junction). The engine on the 7.18 am passenger service from Goole worked the three 'main line' passenger return trips to Haxey each day whilst the other engine on the 8.50 am goods (based at Haxey) performed a freight trip working to Belton, and all the other shunting and siding work on the line, as requested. It appears that the whole line closed down between 7.30 pm and 6.30 am every day and completely on Sunday, the staff presumably working every day on a single shift basis. The service from Goole took almost an hour to cover the 19 miles to Haxey Junction with stops at the five intermediate stations. By November 1905 the mid-day service ran on Wednesdays only. In April 1906 a further early afternoon train was introduced in each direction which ran daily, except Wednesdays, and also an additional morning train on Saturdays only, but this service did not traverse the Fockerby branch. It is of interest to note that the Fockerby branch was served by the return train from Haxey to Goole, rather than the

Axholme Joint Railway (N. E. and L. & Y.).

Distance from Potters Grainge Junction	WEEK DAYS	1 6·20 a.m. Goods Goole to Fockerby A	2 Passenger Goole to Haxey Junction	3 8·50 a.m. Goods Goole to Haxey Junction A	4	5 Goods—Reedness Junc. to Peat Works Siding C	6 Passenger Goole to Haxey Junction WO	7 Passenger Reedness Jn. to Fockerby WO	8 Passenger Goole to Haxey Junction W	9 Passenger Reedness Jn. to Fockerby W	10	11	12 2·10 p.m. Goods Reedness Jn. to Fockerby	13 3·20 p.m. Goods Belton to Haxey Junction	14 Passenger Goole to Haxey Junction	15 Passenger Reedness Jn. to Fockerby
Mls. Yds.		a.m.	a.m.	a.m.		a.m.	a.m.	p.m.	p.m.	p.m.		p.m.	p.m.	p.m.	p.m.
· · ·	Goole (N.E.) .... dep		7 18				11 50		12 17					5 25	
· · ·	Goole (L.&Y.)	6 30		8 50											
· · ·	Goole Junction ...... { arr	6 35		8 55											
	...... { dep	6 40		8 58											
· · ·	Potters Grainge Junc. { arr	6 42		9 2											
	{ dep	6 45		9 5											
1 1691	Marshland Junction	6 55		9 15											
5 220	Reedness Junction { arr	7 10	7 31	9 23			12 3		12 30					5 38	
	{ dep	7 30	7 32	9 38		11 30	12 5	12 7	12 32	12 35		2 10		5 40	5 43
6 968	Blackers Siding														
8 371	Eastoft	7 50					12 16		12 44		2 20				5 52
9 704	Luddington	8 5					12 20		12 48		2 30				5 56
10 1452	Fockerby ...... arr	8 15					12 24		12 52		2 35				6 0
6 242	Peat Works Siding "					11 35									
8 261	Crowle { "		7 40	9 18			12 13		12 40					5 48	
	{ dep		7 41	10 8			12 14		12 41					5 49	
· · ·	Hagg Lane Siding														
12 801	Belton		7 54	11 0			12 27		12 54				3 20	6 2	
14 584	Epworth		8 1	11 40			12 34		1 1				3 30	6 9	
· · ·	Burnham Siding														
17 661	Haxey Town		8 10	12 20			12 43		1 10				3 40	6 18	
18 1544	Haxey Junction ...... arr		8 14	12 25			12 47		1 14				3 45	6 22	

Distance from Potters Grainge Junction	WEEK DAYS	1 Passenger Fockerby to Reedness Jn.	2 Passenger Haxey Junction to Goole	3 Goods—Peat Works Siding to Reedness Junc.	4 Passenger Haxey Junction to Goole	5 Passenger Fockerby to Reedness Jn. WO	6 Passenger Fockerby to Reedness Jn. WO	7 Passenger Haxey Junction to Goole W	8 1·35 p.m. Goods Haxey Junction to Goole W	9 3·0 p.m. Goods Haxey Junction to Goole E	10 4·0 p.m. Goods Haxey Junction to Goole	11 Passenger Fockerby to Reedness Jn.	12 6·40 p.m. Goods Reedness Jn. to Goole B	13 Passenger Haxey Junction to Goole	14	15
Mls. Yds.		a.m.	a.m.	a.m.	p.m.	p.m.	p.m.	p.m.	p.m.	p.m.	p.m.	p.m.	p.m.	p.m.		
· · ·	Haxey Junction .... dep		8 20		12 55			1 20	1 35		4 0			6 29	
· · ·	Haxey Town		8 25		1 0			1 25	2 0		4 15			6 31	
· · ·	Burnham Siding														
· · ·	Epworth		8 34		1 9			1 34	2 40		4 40			6 43	
· · ·	Belton		8 42		1 16			1 42	2 50		5 5			6 51	
· · ·	Hagg Lane Siding														
· · ·	Crowle { arr		8 54		1 28			1 51			5 20			7 3	
	{ dep		8 55		1 29			1 55			6 0			7 4	
· · ·	Peat Works Siding			11 45											
· · ·	Fockerby	8 42				1 17	1 40			3 0		6 5			
· · ·	Luddington	8 46				1 21	1 44			3 20		6 9			
· · ·	Eastoft	8 50				1 25	1 48			3 45		6 13			
· · ·	Blackers Siding														
· · ·	Reedness Junction { arr	8 59	9 3	11 50	1 37	1 34	1 57	2 3		4 0	6 10	6 22		7 12	
	{ dep		9 5		1 40			2 6			6 20		6 40	7 13	
· · ·	Marshland Junction										6 30		6 52		
· · ·	Potters Grainge Junc. { arr										6 40		7 0		
	{ dep										6 43		7 20		
0 1386	Goole Junction { arr												7 25		
2 792	Goole (L.&Y.) ...... arr										6 55		7 30		
0 814	Goole (N.E.) .... arr		9 18		1 53			2 20					7 35		

NOTES—**A** Propels train from Goole Engine Shed Sidings to Potters Grainge Junction. **B** On arrival at Potters Grainge Junction leaves rear portion of train on the branch, runs to Goole (N. E. Station) with traffic for via Staddlethorpe or via Thorne, detaching same in down sidings; engine returns light to Potters Grainge Junction and works train to Goole (L. & Y.), propelling same from Potters Grainge Junction to Goole Engine Shed Sidings. **C** Makes a trip at 10·10 a.m. from Reedness Junction to Goole Fields, returning immediately. **E** Makes a trip Reedness Junction to Goole Fields and back 4·5 to 4·30 p.m.

The Single Line between Marshland Junction Signal Box and Reedness Junction Station is worked on the Electric Train Staff Block System, and the Single Line from Reedness Junction to Haxey Junction is worked on the Electric Train Tablet Block System. The Single Line between Reedness Junction and Fockerby is worked on the "One Engine only in Steam" System.

The October 1905 Working Timetable. 'WO' denotes Wednesdays only, and 'W' indicates Wednesdays excepted.

local newspaper, the *Epworth Bells*.

AXHOLME JOINT RAILWAY.

TIME TABLE OF PASSENGER TRAINS.

From		A a.m.	a.m.	B a.m.	C p.m.	p.m.
Goole	dep.	7.0	9.50	11.50	12.17	5.25
Reedness Jun.	arr.	7.13	10.3	12.3	12.30	5.38
Reedness Jun.	dep.	....	....	12.6	12.35	5.43
Eastoft ...	,,	....	....	12.15	12.44	5.52
Luddington ...	,,	....	....	12.19	12.48	5.56
Fockerby	arr.	7.14	10.4	12.23	12.52	6.0
Reedness Jun.	dep.	7.22	10.12	12.5	12.32	5.40
Crowle ...	arr.	7.23	10.13	12.13	12.40	5.48
,, ...	dep.	....	10.13	12.14	12.41	5.49
Belton ...	,,	7.36	10.26	12.27	12.54	6.2
Epworth ...	,,	7.43	10.33	12.34	1.1	6.9
Haxey Town	,,	7.52	10.42	12.43	1.10	6.18
Haxey Junction	arr.	7.56	10.46	12.47	1.14	6.22

From		a.m.	a.m.	p.m.	p.m.	p.m.
Haxey Junction	dep.	8.7	10.54	12.55	1.20	6.29
Haxey Town	,,	8.12	10.59	1.0	1.25	6.34
Epworth	,,	8.21	11.8	1.9	1.34	6.43
Belton	,,	8.29	11.16	1.16	1.42	6.51
Crowle	arr.	8.41	11.27	1.28	1.54	7.3
,,	dep.	8.42	11.28	1.29	1.55	7.4
Reedness Jun.	arr.	8.50	11.36	1.37	2.3	7.12
Fockerby	dep.	8.30	....	1.17	1.40	6.5
Luddington	,,	8.34	....	1.21	1.44	6.9
Eastoft	,,	8.38	....	1.25	1.48	6.13
Reedness Jun.	arr.	8.47	....	1.34	1.57	6.22
Reedness Jun.	dep.	8.52	11.37	1.40	2.6	7.13
Goole	arr.	9.5	11.50	1.53	2.20	7.26

A Saturdays only.   B Wednesdays only.
C Wednesdays excepted.   B Wednesdays excepted.

GOOLE, REEDNESS JUNCTION, FOCKERBY, CROWLE, and HAXEY JUNCTION (3rd class only).—Axholme Joint.

Secretary, H. Marriott, Hunt's Bank, Manchester.   Supt, M. Woodhouse.

Mls	Down	mrn	mrn	mrn	Wednesdays only	Sats. only.	aft	Except Wednesdays.	aft	Sats. only.	Except Saturdays.	aft
—	Goole ... ... dep.	7 0	8 9	9 25	11 50	12 18		3 5	30			5 45
5½	Reedness Junction ... arr.	7 13	8 9	9 37	12 2	12 30		3 17	42			5 57
—	Reedness Junction ... dep.			12 6	12 34		3 17	46			6 10
8½	Eastoft ...			12 15	12 43		3 25	55			6 14
10	Luddington			12 19	12 47		3 29	59			6 18
11¼	Fockerby ... arr.			12 23	12 51		3 33	6 3			6 22
—	Reedness Junction ... dep.	7 19	8 38	12 13	12 41		3 13	5			6 8
8½	Crowle 648, 654 ... arr.	7 30	9 47	12 13	12 49		27	53			6 20
13	Belton ...	7 42	9 59	12 25	12 53		39	6 5			6 26
14¼	Epworth ...	7 48	10 5	12 31	12 59		45	6 11			6 34
17½	Haxey Town ...	7 56	10 13	12 39	1 7		53	6 19			6 38
19½	Haxey Junction 359 ... arr.	8 0	10 17	12 43	1 11		57	6 23			

Mls	Up	mrn	mrn	aft	Sats. only.	Wednesdays only.	aft	Sats. only.	aft	Except Wednesdays.	aft	aft	Sats. only.	Except Saturdays.	aft	aft
—	Haxey Junction ... dep.	8	10 43	12 57	2		30		4 20	6 36		6 51
1½	Haxey Town ...	8 13	10 81	2		35		4 25	6 41		6 56
4½	Epworth ...	8 21	10 66	11 10		43		4 33	6 49		7 4
6	Belton ...	8 29	11 31	17		50		4 40	6 56		7 11
10½	Crowle ... arr.	8 40	11 51	29	2 10		4 52	7		7 16
13½	Reedness Junction ... arr.	8 48	11 58	57	9		5 0	7 8		7 31
—	Fockerby ... dep.	8 30		34		44		6 13		6 27
1¼	Luddington ...	8 34		38		47		16 17		6 40
3	Eastoft ...	8 47				57		5 17 17		6 82
5½	Reedness Junction ... arr.	8 53	12 1		2 12	2 12		5 1	7 17		7 38
19½	Goole 721, 786 ... arr.	9 7	12 15	2 24	2 24		5 15	7 29		7 43

Bradshaw's January 1910 Timetable

Passenger timetable for October 1914

GOOLE, FOCKERBY, CROWLE, AND HAXEY JUNCTION.

(AXHOLME JOINT RAILWAY.)

One Class Only.

WEEKDAYS.

Newcastle
Darlington
York
Hull
GOOLE
Reedness Junction
Eastoft
Luddington
Fockerby
Reedness Junction
Crowle
Bolton
Epworth
Haxey Town
HAXEY JUNCTION

HAXEY JUNCTION
Haxey Town
Epworth
Belton
Crowle
Reedness Junction
Fockerby
Luddington
Eastoft
Reedness Junction
GOOLE
Hull
York
Darlington
Newcastle

A Saturdays only.   B Wednesdays only.   C Wednesdays excepted.   D Saturdays excepted.

GOOLE, FOCKERBY, CROWLE, AND HAXEY JUNCTION.

(AXHOLME JOINT RAILWAY.)

One Class Only.

WEEKDAYS.

Newcastle
Darlington
York
Hull
GOOLE
Reedness Junction
Eastoft
Luddington
Fockerby
Reedness Junction
Crowle
Bolton
Epworth
Haxey Town
HAXEY JUNCTION

HAXEY JUNCTION
Haxey Town
Epworth
Belton
Crowle
Reedness Junction
Fockerby
Luddington
Eastoft
Reedness Junction
GOOLE
Hull
York
Darlington
Newcastle

outward working from Goole in the morning. By January 1910 (*see Bradshaw's timetable page 199*) the service included a further late afternoon train in each direction on Saturdays only. For a period of about three weeks in April 1912 (during the coal strike) passenger services were withdrawn except for two return trips on Wednesdays and Saturdays.

Also in 1912, the Joint superintendent reported that, because firemen were no longer allowed to leave the footplate to work tablet points during shunting operations, it had become necessary to send out an additional man with the Fockerby and Haxey goods trains to carry out this duty, as from 6th March and 8th May, 1912 respectively.

During 1916, in order to reduce overcrowding on AJR trains, it was decided to rescind the instruction that passengers could not use the two compartments next to the locomotive, thus allowing more seats and standing room for the ever-complaining passengers. Apart from minor alterations, the timetable remained the same except that the Fockerby branch lost (except on Saturdays) its early afternoon train service. However, on 1st January, 1917, to assist the war effort the service was drastically cut back to the original morning and evening trains; although the mid-day Wednesday only service survived.*

After the cessation of hostilities, the first series of more complicated timetables were introduced, and in April 1919 the service returned to that pre-war, except that the evening train ran 40 minutes later on Mondays. By 1920 the timetable was quite substantially different, the whole volume of traffic being much heavier with increased goods service but a reduced passenger service (the freight increase was mainly due to the opening of the single branch line to Hatfield Moor Depot.) However, by October 1920, a meeting was arranged at Haxey to discuss the inadequacies of the AJR and the following *Epworth Bells* newspaper report summed up the local feelings:

*The Board minute of March 1917 reads.
RESTRICTION OF PASSENGER TRAIN TRAVEL - CURTAILMENT OF JOINT LINE SERVICE
Reported that, in view of the necessity, at the present time, for reducing engine mileage to a minimum, certain alterations had been made as from January 1st, 1917, in the goods and passenger train services running over the Joint Line, thus enabling one engine to be entirely withdrawn.
The alterations included the withdrawal of the mid-day passenger trains and this together with the increased scale of passenger fares, recently adopted in common with other Railway Companies, had resulted in 4,306 (or 45.73%) fewer passengers being booked at Joint Line Stations (including bookings at Goole to the Joint Line) during the months of January and February, 1917, than was the case in the corresponding months in 1916, whilst during the same period the passenger receipts had decreased by £36 18s. 7d. (or 11.75%). Approved.

HAXEY JUNCTION, CROWLE, FOCKERBY AND GOOLE
(Axholme Joint Railway).
One Class Only.

Page		SO	WO	C	SO	SX	SO
		a.m	a.m.	p.m.	p.m.	p.m.	p.m.
	HAXEY JUNCTION dep.	8 6	1050	....	1 30	4 20	6 15	6 49
	Haxey Town — — „	8 11	10 55	....	1 35	4 25	6 20	6 54
	Epworth „	8 20	11 4	....	1 43	4 33	6 28	7 2
	Belton — „	8 27	11 12	....	1 50	4 40	6 35	7 9
	Crowle { arr.	8 38	11 24	....	2 1	4 51	6 46	7 20
	{ dep.	8 39	11 25	....	2 2	4 59	6 47	7 21
	Reedness Junction ... arr.	8 47	11 33	....	2 10	5 7	6 55	7 29
	Fockerby — — dep.	8 25	—	1 48	—	—	5 54	6 25
	Luddington	8 29	—	1 52	—	—	5 58	6 29
	Eastoft — — „	8 33	—	1 56	—	—	6 2	6 33
	Reedness Jc. ...... arr.	8 42	—	2 5	—	—	6 11	6 42
	Reedness Junction — dep.	8 52	11 34	—	2 15	5 12	6 56	7 30
	GOOLE .... arr.	9 5	1147	....	2 28	5 25	7 9	7 43
331	Hull.................. arr.	1033	12 30	—	3 41	6 17	7 49	8 52
A 86 {	York .... arr.	1127	2 17	....	4 33	7 21	10 50	10 50
	Darlington — — „	1 39	3 52	—	5 40	9 10	2 3	2 3
	Newcastle .... „	2 49	5 15	....	6 39	10 9	12 57	3 7

Page				a.m	a.m.	a.m.	a.m.	p.m.
99 { B	Newcastle .... dep.			1 50	8 0	10 20	1 2
	Darlington — — „			2 37	8 55	11 21	1 56
	York .... „			7 40	1030	1135	3 17
332	Hull.— — — —dep.			5 58	8 55	10 45	12 0	4 13

				SO	C	SO	SX
				a.m.	p.m.	p.m.	p.m.
	GOOLE .... dep.			6 50	9 32	12 18	3 7	5 15
	Reedness Junction —arr.			7 2	9 44	12 30	3 19	5 27
	Reedness Jc. ...... dep.				12 34	—	5 31
	Eastoft — — „				12 43	—	5 40
	Luddington .... „				12 47	—	5 44
	Fockerby — — arr.				12 51	—	5 48
	Reedness Junction ...dep.			7 3	9 45	12 32	3 20	5 29
	Crowle — — { arr.			7 11	9 53	12 40	3 28	5 37
	{ dep.			7 12	9 54	12 41	3 29	5 38
	Belton — — — „			7 24	10 6	12 53	3 41	5 50
	Epworth .... „			7 30	10 12	12 59	3 47	5 56
	Haxey Town .... „			7 38	10 20	1 7	3 55	6 4
	HAXEY JUNCTION arr.			7 42	1024	1 11	3 59	6 8

A See pages 67, 331, 339, 340.   **SX** Saturdays excepted.
B See pages 78, 332, 326, 340.   **WO** Wednesdays only.
C Mondays, Wednesdays and Fridays only.   **X** Rail Motor Bus.
SO Saturdays only.

LNER passenger timetable for July 1925

Indignant protests were made at a well-attended meeting of merchants, farmers and others at Duke William Hotel, Haxey, on Wednesday evening, against the inadequate goods and passenger service on the Axholme Joint Railway. Major Molson, MP was present, and the meeting was presided over by Mr W.A. Ross, JP CC who spoke of the great inconvenience, loss and damage to produce caused by irregularity of the goods service, the shortage of trucks when trucks were lying idle elsewhere, the late opening and early closing of the goods yards, and the system allocation at Haxey. It was urged also that the goods train ought not to leave Haxey Junction earlier than 4 o'clock in the afternoon and Mr Belk suggested that there should be at Haxey Junction and GN stations a list of the main stations to which goods could be dispatched from each.

Mr G.H. Newborn and Mr J.H. Harrison (Chairman, Isle of Axholme Rural District Council), spoke of the inadequacy of the passenger service, which Mr Newborn said seemed to be arranged to miss connections and exasperate the travelling public. He gave details showing how the trains on the AJR arrived at Haxey Junction a few minutes after the departure of trains on the GN and GE Joint Line.

AXHOLME JOINT RAILWAY
L.N.E. and L.M.S. Joint

GOOLE, FOCKERBY, CROWLE, and HAXEY JUNCTION—Weekdays

	1	2	3	4	5	6	7	8	10	12	15	16	18	19	21	22	24	25	26	29	30	32	33	34
DOWN	D Goods	PASSENGER Steam Coach		D Goods	PASSENGER Steam Coach		D Goods	D Goods	Light Engine		PASSENGER Steam Coach	PASSENGER	Engine and Van	Engine and Van		PASSENGER Steam Coach	PASSENGER Steam Coach	PASSENGER Steam Coach	PASSENGER	PASSENGER Steam Coach	PASSENGER	Engine and Van	
											S O													
											TTh X	WO	WO	W X		S O		SX	SX		S O	S O		
	arr. dep.			arr. dep.			arr. dep.	arr. dep.																
		B Y						V																
	a.m. a.m.	a.m.		a.m. a.m.	a.m.		a.m. a.m. a.m.	p.m. a.m.			p.m.	p.m.	p.m. p.m.		p.m.		p.m. p.m.	p.m.		p.m.	p.m. p.m.		
le { L.N.E.		6 45					9 32		11 55		12 18	—	—			3 7		5 25	—		5 45	—	8 9	
{ L.M.S.	5 30			8 38			— 10 20															—	8 21	
r's Grange	5 40 5 45			8 48 8 50			10 30 10 32	12 5 12 8																
ahland	5 53			9			10 39	12 13					12 50											
ness Junct. ⊕ arr.	6 8	6 57		9 15	9 44		10 48				12 30		12 34 2 10	12 50		3 19		5 37			5 57			
,, dep.	7 20	6 58		9 55	9 48	10 5	11 3			12 32 12 34		2 10 1 0			3 20		5 39 5 41			5 59 6 1			
stoft	7 32 7 40			—	—		—				12 43					—	5 50			6 10			
ddington	7 45 8 0			—	—		—				12 47					—	5 54			6 14			
ckerby	8 5			—	—		—				12 51 2 30	1 20			—	5 58			6 18				
Works Siding	—			—	—		10 10																
wle ⊕ arr.	—	7 6		10 5	9 53		11 17				12 40					3 28	5 47			6 7			
,, dep.	—	7 7		—	9 54		— 11 42				12 41					3 29	5 48			6 8			
on ⊕	—	7 19		10 20 10 6			11 57				12 53					3 41	6 0			6 20			
oith ⊕	—	7 25		10 57 11 30 10 12			12 7 12 22				12 59					3 47	6 6			6 26			
adtoft	—			11 41 11 50			—																
tfield Moor Depot	—	7 33		12 0			—									3 55	6 14			6 34			
ey Town	—			10 20			12 42 12 52				1 7					3 59	6 16			6 38			
ey Junction ⊕	—	7 37		10 24			12 57				1 11													

ropels train from Goole Engine Shed Sidings to Potter's Grange Jct. and from Reedness Jct. to Fockerby. V—Burnham Sdgs. 12.27—12.33 p.m. Y—Steam train MO.

ONE Vehicle may be attached to the Steam Coach by arrangement with the Goole S.M.

Virtually the last Working Timetable to include passenger trains, showing the steam railcar working most of the passenger services, Summer 1931. Note that one vehicle could be attached to the steam railcar.

HAXEY JUNCTION, CROWLE, FOCKERBY, and GOOLE—Weekdays

	1	2	3	5	6	8	9	10	12	13	14	16	17	18	20	21	22	24	26	28	30	31	32	33	34
UP	PASSENGER	PASSENGER Steam Coach		D Goods		PASSENGER Steam Coach		Light Engine	D Goods	PASSENGER	PASSENGER Steam Coach	D Goods		D Goods	D Goods		D Goods	PASSENGER Steam Coach	PASSENGER	PASSENGER	PASSENGER Steam Coach	D Goods	PASSENGER Steam Coach		
												S O													
										WO	T Th X	WX		WO	S O		SX	S O		SX	S O	SX		S O	
										arr. dep.			arr. dep.		arr. dep.		arr. dep.								
	Y		B								V				J										
	a.m.	a.m.	a.m.							a.m. a.m.	p.m. p.m.	p.m. p.m.		p.m. p.m.	p.m. dep.		p.m. dep.	p.m. p.m.	p.m. p.m.	p.m.		p.m. p.m	p.m p.m	p.m	
Junction ⊕	8 0									10 50	1 30						2 45		3 15 4 22			6 50	7 19		
wn	8 5									10 55	1 35				2 53 3 20		3 20 4 10 4 27			6 55	7 24				
Moor Depot									12 20																
t		8 15						12 28 1 25																	
⊕		8 15						11 4 1 40 1 53		1 43				5 30	4 25 5 30 4 35			7 3	7 32					
⊕		8 22						11 12 2 1 2 35		1 50				5 40 5 50	5 40 5 53 4 42			7 10	7 39					
⊕ arr		8 33						11 24 3 5 3 45		2 1					4 53			7 21	7 50					
dep		8 34						11 26		2 2				6 10	6 10 5 1			7 22	7 51					
rks Siding				10 20					1 49		2 20														
oy	8 25								1 52	2 26 2 40			2 40 3 0			6 20 6 25			6 24 6 29					
gton	8 29								1 56	2 49 3 10			3 9 3 29			6 28 6 33								
t	8 33								2 5 2 10 3 48	2 15			3 59	6 20			6 37 6 42 7 30			7 59				
Junct. ⊕ arr.	8 42 8 42		10 25					11 33 3 55						6 20 6 40 5 14			7 31 7 41 8 7							
dep.	8 47								11 34 4 10					6 53			7 50								
d						12 25			12 28 4 25					6 59 7 1			8							
Grange						12 35 4 35 4 35								7 13										
L.M.S.						4 45									5 27			7 44 8 4 8 21						
L.N.E.	9 0					11 47			2 28																

Runs to Goole Fields Sidings and back, Reedness Junction arr. 10.40 a.m. J—Boltgate 3.5—3.6 p.m., Whitgift's Sidings 3.32—3.39 p.m., Blacker's Sidings 3.42—3.54 p.m. gate 2.45—2.46 p.m., Whitgift's Sidings 3.14—3.20 p.m., Blacker's Sidings 3.23—3.43 p.m. L—Ealand Depot 2.47—3.0 p.m. Y—Steam train MO.

ONE vehicle may be attached to the Steam Coach by arrangement with the Stationmaster at Goole.

No trains at all ran on the line during the 1926 General Strike. For a time, also in 1926, the mid-day service ran on Wednesdays only although it was later restored to Mondays and Fridays as well.

Passenger Services Withdrawn

When buses began to appear in the Isle of Axholme (about 1924), the sparse passenger potential from the under-populated area began to be eaten into. There is no doubt that the lack of a direct rail connection at Haxey Junction with the Lincoln-Doncaster line robbed the AJR of the importance that it might otherwise have had, and it remained a rural backwater.

One of the last Working Timetables to contain the passenger services (summer 1931) showed that the Sentinel steam railcar was rostered for most trains. However even the introduction of attractive cheap fares and the steam railcar did not stem the dwindling passenger traffic. Services on the Fockerby branch were rationalised and latterly there was just an evening train in each direction (except Saturdays) and a daily early morning train to Goole only. This meant that anyone travelling out on Saturday morning could not get back from Reedness Junction until Monday evening! No wonder the service collapsed! Thus in July 1933 came the following announcement:

L.N.E. & L.M.S. RAILWAYS

STILL AT YOUR SERVICE

WITHDRAWAL OF PASSENGER TRAINS

AXHOLME JOINT LINE

OWING to the decline in passenger traffic to and from Reedness Junction, Eastoft, Luddington, Fockerby, Crowle, Belton, Epworth, Haxey Town and Haxey Junction, the L.N.E. & L.M.S. Railways have reluctantly decided to withdraw the passenger trains at these stations on and after

MONDAY, 17th JULY, 1933

Alternative Services

So far as Crowle and Haxey Junction stations are concerned passengers and parcels traffic can be dealt with at Crowle (Central) station and Haxey & Epworth (L.N.E.) station.

¶ Road Services are available in the district.

Parcels, Perishable Traffic, Horses, etc.

The above-mentioned stations will be kept open for Parcels, Horses, Perishables, and other traffic hitherto conveyed by passenger train, for which a train service on the Branch will be available.

This service will provide good passenger train connexions at Goole for Parcels, Perishable Traffic, and Horses to all parts.

Goods Train Traffic.

Goods train traffic will continue to be dealt with at the stations concerned.

Passengers' Luggage in Advance.

Passengers travelling by bus to join passenger trains at a neighbouring station may, under the usual conditions, send their luggage in advance from the stations from which the passenger train service is being withdrawn on payment of the usual charges. Similarly luggage in advance may be forwarded to these stations.

Inquiries.

The Staff at the Stations mentioned will willingly furnish information regarding Passenger train services, fares, etc., from the neighbouring Railway Stations, and will answer inquiries relating to the conveyance of luggage in advance, parcels, perishable traffic, horses, cattle, and general merchandise traffic.

There was no Sunday service and the last passenger train therefore ran on Saturday 15th July, 1933. The passenger timetable consisted of one early morning and one evening train daily, supplemented by a train which ran at mid-day on Wednesdays and Saturday. On Saturdays there was a comparatively lavish service for traffic demanded also a train mid-morning and another mid-afternoon, making five trains in all.

Excursion Traffic

The line had its fair share of excursion traffic during its 30 years while open for passengers, for the Lancashire & Yorkshire Railway lost no time (right from the time the line opened) in arranging special trains to Epworth at Whitsuntide and on August Bank Holidays from places as far away as Liverpool, Wigan, Bolton, Manchester and the Yorkshire woollen towns; this was to allow 'pilgrims to visit the Mecca of Methodism'. In fact the *Epworth Bells* for June 1905 carried the following report;

The Axholme Joint Railway arranged excursions from Yorkshire and Lancashire towns to Epworth during Whitsuntide, and their efforts appear to be crowned with success. Undoubtedly, a large number of people have been awaiting a convenient train service to Epworth, as was proved on Monday and Tuesday last, and we believe the company intend making a special feature of these excursions during the summer. On Monday, the number of passengers who came by the new railway were 170, and 91 booked away. On Tuesday, the number of visitors was 323, and 51 tickets were issued. Many of the visitors expressed great delight at their visit, and on their return there were a large number of residents present to give them a send off. We believe that a still larger company is expected to-day, Saturday. Although the Railway Company certainly made a step in the right direction respecting excursions, they do not seem anxious to meet the wishes of the agriculturist, by reducing the rates for produce, or arranging a better service of ordinary passenger trains.

The AJR even had a guide published by the L&Y specially for Epworth and the following paragraph appeared in the *Railway Magazine* for July 1905;

The Lancashire and Yorkshire Railway has issued a very attractive programme of tourist arrangements for the current winter season, including cheap week-end and long date tickets by ordinary trains (with a few exceptions) from the principal stations on the line to Blackpool, the Lake District, the East Coast, etc. The programme draws attention to the fact that the opening of the Axholme Joint Railway (the property of the Lancashire & Yorkshire and North Eastern Railways) has made Epworth (Lincolnshire), the birthplace of the Rev. John Wesley, easily accessible, and removed the inconvenience hitherto experienced in driving from Haxey, on the south side, or from Crowle on the north. The direct route to Epworth from towns in Lancashire and the West Riding of Yorkshire is by the Lancashire and Yorkshire Railway to Goole, and thence per the new Axholme Joint Railway. An interesting illustrated booklet, entitled 'Epworth: What to See and How to Get There', can be obtained from the passenger superintendent, Lancashire and Yorkshire Railway, Manchester.

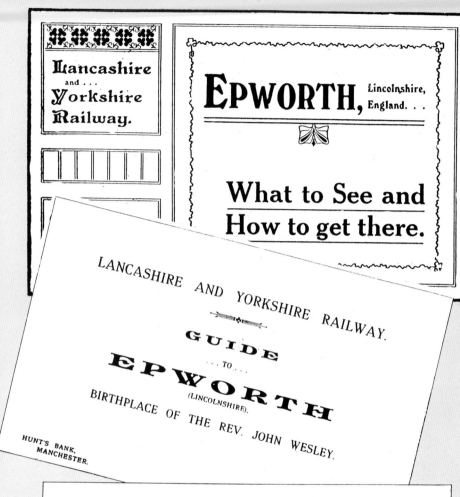

Lancashire and ... **Yorkshire Railway.**

EPWORTH, Lincolnshire, England. ...

What to See and How to get there.

LANCASHIRE AND YORKSHIRE RAILWAY.

GUIDE

... TO ...

EPWORTH

(LINCOLNSHIRE).

BIRTHPLACE OF THE REV. JOHN WESLEY.

HUNT'S BANK, MANCHESTER.

HINTS To American Tourists desirous of visiting Epworth. . . . . .

The Omnibuses of the Lancashire and Yorkshire Railway await the arrival of Passengers at the Prince's Landing Stage, Liverpool, to convey them to the EXCHANGE STATION, where Hotel accommodation of the most modern and complete character will be found, under the management of the Company (*vide* opposite page).

Thence proceed to EPWORTH by the Express Trains leaving Exchange Station at 9-0 a.m. and 2-10 p.m. for Goole, arriving at 12-10 p.m. and 4-34 p.m. respectively. Distance : 105 miles.

FARES FROM LIVERPOOL (Exchange Station).

	Single.	Return.		Single.	Return.
To Goole—1st class...	14s. 9d.	26s. 6d.	3rd class...8s.	od.	15s. 6d.
To Epworth	......	......	,, ,, 8s.	od.	15s. 6d.

At Goole there are several conveniently-situated Hotels for those who desire to break their journey at this the most inland port on the East Coast, with its quaint neighbouring villages of Airmyn and Hook. The journey to **Epworth** may be continued the following day.

(90).

AXHOLME JOINT RAILWAY

(N.E. and L. & Y. JOINT).

Trip to the Sea-Side.

A splendid opportunity for Choir, Schools, and Club Parties.

On THURSDAY, 4th August,

A THROUGH EXCURSION TRAIN

WILL BE RUN FROM

—— CROWLE, FOCKERBY, &c., to ——

BLACKPOOL

(WITH BOOKINGS FOR 4 DAYS),

AS UNDER :

Returning from Blackpool (Central) at 7-48 p.m. same day.
Holders of 4 Days' Tickets return on the following Friday, Saturday, or
Monday, by any train having a through connection.

From					Times of Starting A. M.	Return (Fare third class) DAY.	4 DAYS
CROWLE	...	...	...	dep.	6 20		
FOCKERBY	...	...	...	..	6 8		
LUDDINGTON	...	...	...	,,	6 12	3s. 9d.	6s. 6d.
EASTOFT	...	...	...	.,	6 16		
REEDNESS JUNCTION	...	...	..		6 32		

No Luggage allow-d to Passengers holding Day Tickets. Passengers holding 4 days' Tickets are allowed
60 lbs of Luggage Free, at their own risk.

Children not exceeding 3 years of age, free ; above 3 and under 12 years of age, half-fare.

A limited number of carriages will be provided, and in order as far as possible, to secure the comfort of the
passengers and to avoid delay, the issue of Excursion Tickets will be limited to the carriage accommodation
provided, and passengers who intend to travel should therefore apply early for such Tickets, which can now
be obtained at the above-mentioned stations.
Excursion Tickets are not transferable, and are available only to and from the Stations named upon
them and by the Trains advertised in the Bills, &c., and if used to or from a Station beyond or short of
the Stations named on the Tickets, or by Trains not advertised in the Bills, &c., they will be forfeited,
and the holders thereof will be charged the full Ordinary Fare for the whole distance travelled.

For further information apply to MR. M. WOODHOUSE, Joint Superintendent,
July, 1910. Crowle.

The Isle of Axholme Printing Company, Limited Crowle.

Market Fares were introduced on the 4th April, 1905 allowing travel to Goole by the afternoon train on Wednesdays and Saturdays; to Hull by the morning train on Tuesdays and Fridays and returning by an afternoon train on the day of issue. A 'long day' excursion to the seaside became very popular, Blackpool being the favourite destination (*see previous page*); surprisingly these excursions were continued even after the closure of the normal passenger service. In 1913, over 600 passengers travelled from the 'Isle' on one of these specials, whilst in 1922 (for the occasion of the Great Yorkshire show at Hull), over 750 passengers were booked from Joint Line stations. Cheap weekend and day excursion tickets were also a feature of the line, with the aim of encouraging people from this sparsely populated area, to use their railway.

In 1912 (one of the best years for passenger receipts) an analysis of ticket sales showed the Fockerby branch was responsible for nearly a third of the passenger traffic, whilst Crowle was the best revenue-earning station.

Main Line	%	Branch	%
Reedness Junction	6	Eastoft	9
Crowle	20	Luddington	11
Belton	9	Fockerby	12
Epworth	16		32%
Haxey Town	8		
Haxey Junction	9		
	68%		

Tickets

As the Lancashire & Yorkshire Railway was responsible for working the line it supplied the tickets which were headed 'Axholme Joint Railway'. It also provided ticket cases, dating presses, and cancelling nippers following L&YR practice. The 3rd singles were printed green, whilst ordinary returns had green outward and orange return halves. Child 3rd singles had about one-quarter left white on the left-hand side, and the ordinary returns had a similar white portion on each half. The centre lower part of the ticket was removed if issued to a child, and the snipped-out part attached to a sheet returned to the audit office as an accounting check for the reduced fare. These child snips carried number codes for audit purposes, the number being that of the issuing station.* After grouping in 1923, tickets were printed in the standard colours used by the LMS Railway; as first class accommodation was not provided on the Axholme Joint Line, no first class tickets were printed.

The Guard had to perform the ticket collection at Reedness Junction (the last stopping place) in the case of trains going in the direction of Goole. There appear to have been no goods or travel agents appointed in the area as ticket sellers.

---

*The L&YR issued numbers 323 to 331 for AJR stations as follows; 323, Reedness Junction; 324, Eastoft; 325, Luddington; 326, Fockerby; 327, Crowle; 328, Haxey Junction; 329, Haxey Town; 330, Epworth and 331, Belton.

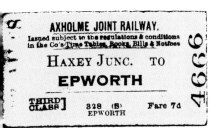

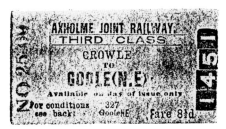

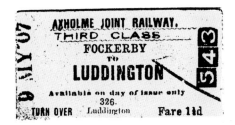

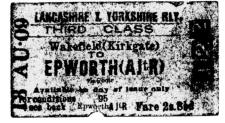

Freight Workings

The Joint Line (as previously stated) had been proposed in the first instance by the farmers of the area and therefore, in its heyday, the line had been kept in business by the transportation of the agricultural products such as potatoes, celery, peas, swedes, clover, carrots, sugar beet etc. and the inward consignments of manure! This was in addition to the large amounts of peat being moved out of the area to all parts of Britain. This industry in relation to the AJR was summed up by an article in the *North Eastern Railway Magazine* of 1912, entitled 'Peat Traffic from the Axholme Joint Railway' by J.H. Dobson, a goods clerk at Reedness Junction.

Many readers of the *North Eastern Railway Magazine* will have noticed at times consignments of peat which have been received at their stations from Goole or from points on the Axholme Joint Railway. To a station clerk a study of the traffics peculiar to his district is very interesting, and, although I cannot claim distinction as a sphagnologist, my short article on 'The Peat Traffic of the Axholme Joint Railway' may be of interest to many.

From the extensive moors which lie between the North Eastern, Great Central and Axholme Joint Railways, large quantities of peat are obtained and dispatched for various purposes to all parts of the country.

The peat, moss litter, or sphagnum, is decayed vegetable matter and is found on the moors underneath various other growths. After removing the herbage from the top, the peat is cut into blocks or turves with knives specially adapted for the purpose. These turves, as removed, are walled in pigeon-hole fashion in order to let the air dry them. Afterwards, they are built into small stacks or pyramids, and then when thoroughly dry, are made into large stacks, in which condition they remain until they are required at the peatworks. In due course, the turves are conveyed from the moors to the works, this being done by means of trucks drawn by horses along a tramway. At the works the turves are torn by machinery into small pieces which are then pressed, also by machinery, into the bales familiar to many readers of this magazine.

Previous to the general use of coal, peat was the most common article of domestic firing in the less wooded districts; nowadays, however, it is not much used as fuel in this country. It would be difficult to say at what period peat was first applied to domestic firing, but that it was used from a very early period of our history there can be no doubt. In all probability it was the accidental ignition of turf which first led to the general use of peat. I have read that in 1833 the heat of the ground in Switzerland was so great as to inflame it spontaneously, and that, in the middle of the 18th century, the inhabitants of a Siberian village accidentally kindled the ground, which is said to have burned for several months.

Although in cases of this kind we say, in common parlance, that 'the ground took fire', it is obvious that mere earth could not so burn; there must have been something of a more inflammable nature partaking more or less of the bituminous character of peat. Many readers will remember the fire which occurred on the moors here early in 1911 and which destroyed large quantities of peat, lighting up the district for many miles.

During the recent trouble in the coal world, several people in this neighbourhood obtained peat turves to burn when they had no coal. I may mention, also, that the engines at the peat works are regularly fired with this fuel.

The purpose for which peat is now chiefly used is to provide bedding for horses and cattle, and large quantities are sent from the Reedness district for the use of many large business firms, of the principal railway companies, of well-known racing stables and of private persons in all parts of the country. Peat turves are also used for making firelighters, and peat dust is used in making meal for cattle feeding. Peat is also used for making cardboard and various articles of that nature.

For bedding purposes, peat is cheaper than straw, and it is claimed that it makes much better manure than straw, as it absorbs more moisture. Owing to the prevalent high price of straw during last winter, the demand for peat was good, and the tonnage forwarded from the Axholme Joint Railway has been heavier than ever before in the history of the line. During 1911 10,060 tons were forwarded from the Reedness Junction alone. Eventually, of course, the supply of peat will be exhausted, but there will be peat traffic from this district for many years yet.

The land laid bare by the removal of the peat is 'warped' ('warping' is a method of fertilising the land by flooding it with water) and, by the rich alluvial covering gained from the specially constructed warping drains, is turned into fertile land on which crops are grown second to none in the country. As a striking example of the fertility of newly warped land, I may mention that last year there was near this station a crop of oats - the first crop the land had produced - the heads of which were over 6 ft, from the ground.

The loading of bales of peat on to wagons is a matter which requires no little skill and care, as, being of a shifty nature, the bales might be a menace to passing traffic if the loads were not well made and the ropes taut. Owing to the number of ropes used to secure a load of peat the traffic entails a considerable amount of clerical work, the task of keeping an account of ropes being, as many of my readers will know, one of the most troublesome of railway duties.

Until the motor lorry began to take over, there was always brisk business from the farms of the area and it was not uncommon for the superintendent of the line, M. Woodhouse to send memos to stations advising them to let Goole control know the number of wagons needed for the day for pea or potato traffic, or indeed if a special train would be required. During the 1926 season over 4,000 tons of green peas were carried and in 1927, 7,000 bundles of celery were dispatched from Epworth alone in a three day period, and incidentally Haxey claimed to be the centre of the celery industry! By 1929 the pea traffic was so vast that the AJR featured in the LMS Freight Train Arrangements for Working Fruit and Vegetables (*Section F*) and the appropriate section is included overleaf:

By the 1930's the freight service had decreased to just three workings a day (*see July 1937 Working Timetable page 215*), and these ran only if needed. Six wagons a day (on average) were collected from the Hatfield branch and this whole operation was co-ordinated by one porter, George Johnson, who was the son of the station master at Haxey (Charlie Johnson). A porter at Sandtoft, George Sowerby handled all the traffic for that siding.

John Whiting's reminiscences of the AJR in 1940-1941, during a 12 months stint at Epworth station 'as a general clerical factotum and assistant to the

LONDON MIDLAND AND SCOTTISH RAILWAY COMPANY.

FREIGHT TRAIN ARRANGEMENTS
FOR WORKING

FRUIT AND VEGETABLE TRAFFIC.

(A) POTATO AND VEGETABLE TRAFFIC from ORMSKIRK AND SOUTHPORT DISTRICTS,

(B) CONTINENTAL FRUIT AND VEGETABLES, via HULL,

(C) FRUIT FOR C.W.S. WORKS AT MILLS HILL (Middleton Junction),

(D) FRUIT TRAFFIC for HARTLEY'S SIDING (Preston Road).

(E) FRUIT ex L. & N. E. LINE (G. E. SECTION), via DONCASTER,

(F) GREEN PEA TRAFFIC ex AXHOLME JOINT LINE, GOOLE, DONCASTER, AND BRANCHES.

(G) FRUIT TRAFFIC from WISBECH DISTRICT AND M. & G. N. LINE.

Intimation will be given by Divisional Control, Manchester, as to the date when the workings set out in this notice will actually come into operation.

GREEN PEA TRAFFIC ex AXHOLME JOINT LINE, GOOLE, DONCASTER, AND BRANCHES.

Green pass from the Axholme Joint Line, Goole, etc., to Cardiff (L.N.W.) and South Wales must be worked as follows:—

7-45 p.m. Goole to Heaton Lodge.
1-30 a.m. Heaton Lodge to Crewe.
5-55 p.m. Edge Hill to Abergavenny (from Crewe).

Green peas from Knottingley, etc., to Scarborough and Bridlington must be worked by the following services:—

6-45 p.m. Goole to Oldham Road (to Wakefield).
9-30 p.m. Normanton to Rose Grove (Wakefield to Horbury).
Trip Horbury to Healey Mills.
12-25 a.m. Healey Mills to Normanton.

1-45 a.m. Goole to Wakefield will convey green peas from branch stations to Newcastle, etc., to connect with 4-30 a.m. Wakefield to Normanton, which must make connection when advice received that traffic is passing.

When required, the 5-10 p.m. through freight Goole to Hunslet Sidings S will run under Fitted Freight regulations. Wakefield Control will advise Leeds Control particulars of the vehicles for London.

	arr	dep
	p.m.	p.m.
Goole Mineral Junction		5 10
Rawcliffe Bridge Junction	pass	5 17
Hensall Junction	...	5 32
Knottingley	5 52	6 30
Pontefract	pass	6 25
Methley Junction	...	6 40
Stourton Junction	6 40	...

Connecting trains:—
9-30 p.m. Stourton to St. Pancras **S**
8-55 p.m. Stourton to Birmingham **S**
10-30 p.m. Stourton to Nottingham **S**
10-45 p.m. Stourton to Leicester **S**
11-38 p.m. Stourton to Chadlseden **S**

(New) 6-10 p.m. Fully-fitted Freight Goole to Carlton Sidings stopping at Knottingley to attach. Limited to 39 wagons and brake:—

	arr	dep
		p.m.
Goole Marshalling Sidings		6 10
Goole Junction	pass	6 13
Rawcliffe Bridge Junction	...	6 18
Hensall Junction	...	6 31
Knottingley	6 48	7 8
Pontefract	pass	7 13
Crofton Fond Junction	...	7 20
Carlton Sidings	7 45	...

5-15 p.m. **S** Rawcliffe to Wakefield to start at 5-8 p.m., Snaith arr. 5-20, dep. 6-12, Hensall arr. 6-25 p.m., forward as hooked.

(New) 6-20 p.m. "Q" Fitted Freight Goole to Carlton Sidings, stopping at Knottingley to attach:—

	arr	dep
		p.m.
Goole Marshalling Sidings		6 20
Goole Junction	pass	6 26
Rawcliffe Bridge Junction	...	6 30
Hensall Junction	...	6 44
Knottingley	7 2	7 22
Pontefract	pass	7 27
Crofton Fond Junction	...	7 40
Carlton Sidings	7 50	...

(New) 7-15 p.m. "Q" Fitted Freight Knottingley to Stourton:—

	arr	dep
		p.m.
Knottingley		7 15
Pontefract	pass	7 27
Methley Junction	...	7 33
Stourton	7 50	...

When not more than 10 London's from all points, the 6-10 p.m. ex Goole will run to Stourton to connect with the 8-30 p.m. London; also convey provincials ex Axholme Joint Line.
When over 10 London's from all points the 7-10 p.m. Goole to Stourton must not convey London's, and the 6-10 p.m. ex Goole to run to Carlton and also convey provincials from Axholme Joint Line thereto.

When 39 London's ex the 6-10 p.m. to run to Carlton, detach provincials at Knottingley; provincials to be worked from Knottingley to Stourton by new "Q" 7-15 p.m. Knottingley to Stourton.
When there are over 39 and not more than 49 London's from all points, 39 to be worked on 6-10 p.m. ex Goole and remainder on 7-15 p.m. Knottingley to Stourton, including provincials ex Axholme Joint Line.
When over 49 from all points, 39 on 6-10 p.m. Goole to Carlton; remainder an additional train to

Left page

From	Conveys green peas and perishables for
Goole ... ... Knottingley	Green peas and perishables for L.N.E. Line (via Knottingley)
Rawcliffe	
Snaith	
Hensall Junction	
Hensall	
Whitley Bridge	
Wakefield	Green peas and perishables for Wakefield, Bradford, Huddersfield, Halifax, and L. & N. E. Line (via Normanton)
Goole ... ... Todmorden	East Lancashire District and P. and W. Line
Rawcliffe	
Hensall Junction ... Smithy Bridge	Bacup, Mills Hill, Middleton, and Middleton Junction.
Hensall ... ... Rochdale	Todmorden, Oldham, Bury, Rams-bottom, Bacup, and Bolton districts.
Whitley Bridge	
Knottingley	Green peas and perishables for exchange thereat
... ... Miles Platting	Green peas and perishables for exchange that place
... ... Oldham Road	General traffic for exchange for that place
Wakefield	General traffic for that place
... ... Miles Platting	
... ... Oldham Road	

Present 6·45 p.m. M O Goole to Oldham Road will leave at 6.30 p.m.—

	arr p.m.	dep p.m.
Goole		6 30
Goole Junction	pass	6 35
Rawcliffe Bridge Junction	pass	6 40
Hensall Junction	7·0	7·30 forward as booked

When there are not more than 8 wagons of green peas, the 6·45 p.m. ex Goole may terminate at Wakefield.

	S arr p.m.	S dep p.m.
Goole		6 45
Rawcliffe Bridge Junction	pass	
Rawcliffe	7 2	7 12
Snaith	7 20	7 28
Hensall Junction	7 36	
Hensall	8 8	8 20
Whitley Bridge	8 58	9 11
Knottingley	pass	9 45
Pontefract	10 12	10 45
Crofton Junction	pass	
Wakefield	11·9	
Horbury Junction	11 29	
Mirfield	11 25	
Heaton Lodge Junction	11 30	
Bradley Wood Junction	11 50	
Brighouse		
Sowerby Bridge	11 44	12 7
Eastwood	pass	
Todmorden	12 34	12 50
Smithy Bridge	12 50	1 25
Rochdale	pass	
Middleton Junction	1 46	
Thornham Bridge Junction	1 57	
Miles Platting		2 20
Oldham Road	2 25	

Knottingley shunt engine will make a trip from Knottingley Depot to Knottingley at 4.25 p.m.

Engine and guard to be at Todmorden at 11.55 p.m. to work a new perishable train—12·15 a.m. M Todmorden to Blackpool (Talbot Road), calling at Rose Grove and Kirkham:—

	dep a.m.
Todmorden	12 15
Copy Pit	12 33
Burnley (Manchester Road)	12 34 Brakes
Rose Grove	1 15 / 1 36
Accrington	pass
Blackburn	1 53
Bamber Bridge	2 10
Preston (E.L.)	2 32
Preston No. 5	2 45
Kirkham	3 8 / 3 30
Poulton	3 45
Blackpool (Talbot Road)	3 55

Right page

		arr p.m.	dep p.m.
Shaftholme Junction		pass 5 10	4 35
Knottingley		arr 5 50	dep 6 25
Shaftholme Junction		pass	

5·50 p.m. Knottingley to Doncaster S conveys green pea traffic from Knottingley to Doncaster for that place and south thereof.

Pontefract shunt engine will when required work green pea traffic from Methley Branch stations and Pontefract to Knottingley in time to connect with the 5·10 p.m. train and later trains.

Engine usually working 4–5 p.m. Ackers to Knottingley will work green pea and vegetable traffic from Doncaster Branch stations to Knottingley in connection with 5·10 p.m. and 6·45 p.m. trains ex Goole. In the event of its running out of course must run specially to Knottingley with green pea traffic only, and return for booked workings.

Freight train workings on the Axholme Joint Line will be as under:—

		A 6·0 a.m. Goole to Fockerby	B 8·30 a.m. Goole to Haxey Junction	O C 10·20 a.m. Goole to Belton	L.E. 11·50 a.m. Goole Shed to Reedness Junction Goole Sled	Wednesdays excepted F. & V. 2·10 p.m. Reedness Junction to Fockerby	Wednesdays only E. & V. 2·10 p.m. Reedness Junction to Fockerby
		a.m.	a.m.	a.m.	a.m.	p.m.	p.m.
Goole (L.M.S.)	dep	6 20	8 30	10 20	11 50		
Potter's Grange	dep	6 30	8 44	10 38	noon 12 0		
Marshland Junction	"	6 32	9 1	10 46	12 x		
Reedness Junction	arr	6 45	9 15	10 56			
Reedness Junction	dep	7 30				1 0	2 10
Eastoft		7 40					
Luddington		8 5				1 30	2 30
Fockerby	arr						
Reedness Junction	dep		9 40	11 10			
Crowle	arr			11 24			
"	dep		10 0	noon 12 0			
Ealand Depot	"			p.m. 12 15			
Belton			10 30	12 30			
Epworth	arr		10 40				
Epworth	dep		11 20				
Sandtoft			11 40				
Hatfield Moor	arr		11 50				
Epworth	dep		1 35				
Haxey Town			2 2				
Haxey Junction	arr						

A—Makes a trip between Reedness Junction and Peat Works 10·5 a.m. to 10·25 a.m., and between Reedness Junction and Goole Fields 11·10 a.m. to 11·55 a.m. Conveys traffic from Goole (L.M.S) and Goole Junction for Reedness Junction and Fockerby Branch; also Haxey Junction tranship wagon.

B—Conveys traffic from Goole (L.M.S.) and Goole Junction for Belton, Epworth, Burnham Siding, Haxey Town, Haxey Junction, and Hatfield Moor Branch. On Saturdays follows 9.32 a.m. passenger ex Goole from Reedness Junction, and performs shunting where necessary in lieu of 10.20 a.m. goods.

C—Conveys traffic from Goole (L.M.S.) and Goole Junction for Spilman's Siding, Crowle, Ealand Depot, Hagg Lane Siding, and Belton; also picks up Haxey Section tranship wagon at Reedness Junction and forwarded traffic at Spilman's Siding and Hagg Lane Siding.

Q—When required—Saturdays excepted.

WORKING OF GREEN PEA TRAFFIC—continued.

	L.F. 12·13 p.m. Reedness Junction to Goole Shed	Wednesdays excepted. 2·15 p.m. Pockerby to Reedness Junction	Wednesdays only. 2·40 p.m. Pockerby to Reedness Junction	4·55 p.m. Goole (L.M.S.) to Potter's Grange	2·5 p.m. Belton to Goole	12·30 p.m. Haxey Junction to Goole	5·30 p.m. Potter's Grange to Goole (L.M.S.)	7·40 p.m. Reedness Junction to Goole
	p.m.	p.m.	p.m.	p.m.	p.m.	p.m.	p.m.	p.m.
Haxey Junc. ...dep	..	..	..	..	..	12·30	..	..
Haxey Town	..	..	..	..	..	12·30	..	..
Epworth	..	..	..	..	..	12·40	..	..
Hatfield Moor.dep	..	..	..	..	..	12·55	..	..
Sandtoft	..	..	..	..	..	..	..	..
Epworth ......arr	..	..	..	..	..	..	..	..
Epworth ....dep	..	..	..	..	..	2·20	..	..
Belton ....arr	..	..	..	..	..	2·45	..	..
Ealand Depot. ...	..	..	..	..	2·25	2·55	..	..
Crowle ....dep	..	..	..	..	2·30	..	..	..
	..	..	..	..	2·30	3·25	..	..
	..	..	..	..	3·0	3·40	..	..
Fockerby .....dep	2·15	2·40	..	..	..	3·55	..	..
Luddington	2·40	2·0	..	..	..	..	..	..
Eastoft	3·10	3·30	..	..	3·20	4·0	..	7·10
Reedness Junc. ..arr	3·45	4·0	..	4·58	4·35	4·35	..	7·25
Marshland Junc. ..	12·13	..	..	..	4·50	5·18	..	7·33
Potter's Grange.arr	12·21	..	..	..	4·56	5·34	5·30	7·53EV
Goole (L.N.E.).arr	..	..	..	..	5·23	5·39	..	8 5EV
Goole (L.M.S.).arr	12·33	..	..	5 5	5·44EV	5·58EV	5·40	..
					5·51EV	6 8EV		

C—On Saturdays runs 15 minute earlier Reedness Junction to Goole (L.M.S.).

S X—Saturdays excepted.

Q—When required.

† Runs to Goole Fields Siding for traffic 3·30 p.m. to 4·0 p.m. when required.

Wakefield Control to arrange for shunt engine to leave Goole Junction at 4·35 p.m. and 5·5 p.m. for Potter's Grange Junction, arriving there at 4·45 p.m. and 5·15 p.m. ex Belton and 12·30 p.m. ex Haxey Junction.

2·30 a.m. Normanton to Bradford M will convey green pea traffic for Bradford from Normanton to Wakefield to connect with 9·25 p.m. Hull to Bradford.

3·45 a.m. Normanton to Halifax will convey green pea traffic for Huddersfield and Halifax from Normanton and Wakefield.

11·30 p.m. Normanton to Windsor Bridge S will, in addition to present classification, convey green pea and perishable traffic to Todmorden East for Todmorden East and East Lancashire.

12·45 a.m. Wakefield to Mirfield M will convey green pea traffic from Wakefield and Thornhill for Huddersfield and be extended to Huddersfield. Will not stop for traffic purposes between Mirfield and Huddersfield.

12·50 a.m. Normanton to Rose Grove M will convey green pea traffic from Normanton green pea traffic for Hebden Bridge, when required, and stop at the latter place to detach.

				E. & B.	dep. p.m.
Crofton Junction					3·45
Featherstone Station					4·30
Pontefract					5 0
Knottingley					..

and when required will work a trip Knottingley to Carlton with fruit and vegetable traffic as below:—

	arr p.m.	dep p.m.
Knottingley	..	6·50
Crofton East Junction	pass	7 22
Oakenshaw North	pass	
Carlton	..	7·38

The 4·30 p.m. Featherstone to Knottingley will convey vegetable traffic from Featherstone and Pontefract to Knottingley in connection with the various fruit and vegetable trains therefrom.

Bolton engine will leave shed at 1·15 a.m. M, depart E. & V. 1·20 a.m. Bolton to Rochdale, and work new train 2·30 a.m. Rochdale Bay Sidings to Bolton. The train will be classified and timed as under:—

Conveys traffic from	To	For
Rochdale Bay Sidings ... { Bury	Green pea and perishable traffic for Bury to Bacup and Haslingden
{ Bolton	That place

	E. & V. M arr a.m.	dep a.m.
Bolton	..	1·30
Bury	pass	1 33
Castleton	..	1 43
Rochdale	1 50	..

Traffic for stations Ramsbottom to Bacup and Haslingden to be trippled to Tottington Junction for booked trains forward.

This train will also run in fruit season in connection with the 7·55 p.m. Hull to Aintree. When 11·30 p.m. Normanton to Windsor Bridge is conveying fruit for Bury and Bolton engine and van will return to Rochdale for second trip. Manchester Control to arrange.

Green peas for Nelson arriving Rose Grove after departure of 4·5 a.m. Rose Grove to Colne will be worked to Nelson by 11·30 p.m. Bolton to Colne, which will call at Rose Grove when required, or other suitable service. Manchester Control to arrange on receiving advice from Rose Grove.

The agents on Goole Branch, Doncaster Branch, and Methley Branch stations must telephone Wakefield Control each day, 4·30 p.m., daily the number of wagons they have for the 6·15 a.m. Goole to Oldham Road, and Control will arrange for the latter to be assisted if required.

Stations Goole to Featherstone (Askern Branch inclusive) must telephone Wakefield Control nightly the number of wagons of green peas for Western and Midland Divisions and lines beyond ; also for L.N.E. Line, giving number of wagons and destination.

Wakefield Control must wire " Y Decoy" (Doncaster) the departure of the 5·50 p.m. and 7·40 p.m. Knottingley to Doncaster trains, giving destination and number of wagons of green pea traffic.

The Yard Master at Doncaster will advise Wakefield Control as early as possible daily quantity and destination of green pea traffic for L. M. S. Line.

The agents at stations where green peas are loaded must arrange for Manchester traffic to be loaded together ; also traffic for London (L. M. & S.) Stations to be loaded together, and for vacuum pipes to be coupled.

Stations on Axholme Joint Line must advise Goole not later than 3·0 p.m. each day, giving destination of green pea traffic being conveyed to Goole.

Guards of trains working green pea traffic must show in separate columns on their train reports number of wagons of green peas, which column heading to be altered to " Green Peas."

Green pea traffic for London and South must be confined to the booked services laid down, and be loaded sufficiently early to enable such trains to run on time.

It is essential that the trains and traffic concerned be smartly dealt with, and goods agents, yard masters, station masters, inspectors, and all staff concerned must give the working their special attention, and in the event of any difficulty arising must immediately

AXHOLME JOINT RAILWAY
L.N.E. and L.M.S. Joint
GOOLE to FOCKERBY, HATFIELD MOOR and HAXEY JUNCTION—Weekdays

	1	2	3	4	5	6	7	8	9	10	11	12	13	14	15	16	17	18	19	20	21	22	23	24	25	26	27	28	29	30
DOWN	D Goods	D Goods		D Goods	D Goods		D Goods	D Goods		D Goods	D Goods		D Goods	D Goods		Light Engine	Engine and Van		D Goods	D Goods		Light Engine		D Goods	Engine & Van	D Goods	Light Engine			
	SX			SX			SO			SX			SX			SX	SX		SX					SO	SXQ	SXQ	SX			
	a.m.	a.m. F		a.m.	a.m.		a.m.	a.m.		a.m.	a.m.		a.m.	a.m.		noon	p.m.		p.m.	p.m.	p.m.			p.m.	p.m.	p.m	p.m.			
le Eng. Shd. dep.	–	6⁴⁵	7⁵⁵	–	a.m		a.m.	a.m.		a.m.	a.m.		a.m.	a.m.					–	–	1 40			–	–	–	–			
ole (L.N E.) arr.	–	6⁵⁰	7⁵⁸	–			–	–		–	–		–	–					–	–				–	–	7 7				
dep.	–	7 0	8A13	–			–	–		–	–		–	–					–	–				–	–	7112				
ole (Min. Jct.) dep.	6 10	7 12	8A28	–			7 30	9 18		9 18	–		10 40	–					–	–				–	–					
ole Engine arr.	6 15	–	–	–			7 55	9 23		9 23	–		10 45	–					–	–				–	–					
Shed Junction dep.	6 p17	–	–	–			7 p57	9 p23		9 p25	–		10 p47	–		12 0			–	–	1 45			–	–					
tter's Grange arr.	6 p22	–	–	–			7 p18	9 p30		9 p30	–		10 p52	–		12 5			–	–				–	–					
Junction dep.	6 25	–	–	–			7 50	9 35		9 35	–		10 54	–		12 8			–	–	1 47			–	–					
rshland arr.	–	–	–	–			1 0	9 45		–	–		11 1	–		12 13			–	–				1 56	–					
Junction dep.	6 33	–	–	–				9 45		9 45	–			–					1 30	–				1 10	–					
o're Fields Sdg. dep.	6 48	–	–	–				–		–	10 55			12 0					1 35	–				1 15	–					
dness Jn. dep.	7 p20	–	–	8 50			10 p25	10 28		10 10	11 0		11 10	12 5		12 23				–				–	3 38	4 50				
astoft dep.	7 p32	–	–	–			10 p45	–		10 10	11 23						12 45			–				–						
ddington dep.	7 p40	–	–	–			11 p0	–		11 p0									–	–				–	–					
ockerby arr.	7 p45	–	–	–			11 p5	–		11 p5									1 5	–				–	–					
at Works dep.	8 p0	–	–	–			11 p15	–		11 p15									–	–				–	–					
Siding dep.	8 p5	–	–	8 55			11 p20	–		11 p20									–	–				–	–					
owle arr.	–	–	–	–			–	10 42		10 42	10 22		11 37						–	–				3 18	–					
dep.	–	–	–	–			–	11 2		11 2	10 27		12 2						–	–				–	–					
land Depot arr.	–	–	–	–			–	–		–	–		–	–					–	–				–	–					
dep.	–	–	–	–			–	–		–	–		–	–					–	–				–	–					
ton arr.	–	–	–	–			–	11 22		11 22	10 44			–					–	–				–	–					
dep.	–	–	–	–			–	11 45		11 45	11 4		11 17	–					–	–				–	–					
worth arr.	–	–	–	–			–	12 6		12 6	11 25		12 27	–					–	–	2 15	2 20		–	–					
dep.	–	–	–	–			–	12 31		12 31	11 40		12 42	–					–	–	2 40	–		–	–					
andtoft Depot arr.	–	–	–	–			–	12 42		12 42	11 53			–					–	–				–	–					
dep.	–	–	–	–			–	12 52		12 52	12 5			–					–	–				–	–					
Hatfield Moor arr.	–	–	–	–			–	1 2		1 2	12 15			–					–	–				–	–					
dep.	–	–	–	–			–	–		–	–			–					–	–				–	–					
rnham Sdgs. arr.	–	–	–	–			–	–		–	–		12 47	–					–	–				–	–					
dep.	–	–	–	–			–	–		–	–		12 55	–					–	–				–	–					
xey Town arr.	–	–	–	–			–	–		–	–		1 2	–					–	–	2 55			–	–					
dep.	–	–	–	–			–	–		–	–		1 12	–					–	–				–	–					
xey Jctn arr.	–	–	–	–			–	–		–	–		1 17	–					–	–	3 15			–	–					

A—Transhp Van   F—6.40 a.m. Light Engine from Goole Mineral Junction.   p—Propel Train.   ‡—Shed.

AXHOLME JOINT RAILWAY
L.N.E. and L.M.S. Joint
HAXEY JUNCTION, HATFIELD MOOR, and FOCKERBY to GOOLE—Weekdays

	1	2	3	4	5	6	7	8	9	10	11	12	13	14	15	16	17	18	19	20	21	22	23	24	25	26	27	28	29	30	31	32
UP	Engine & Van	D Goods		D Goods	D Goods		Light Engine		D Goods		D Goods	D Goods		Light Engine		D Goods		D Goods	D Goods	D Goods	D Goods	D Goods		D Goods		D Goods						
	SX	SX		SX	SX		SX		SO		SO							SX	SXQ	SXQ	SO	SX		SX								
	a.m.	a.m.		a.m.	p.m.		p.m.		p.m.		p.m.	p.m.		p.m.		p.m.		p.m.	p.m.	p.m.	p.m.	p.m.		p.m.		p.m.						
Jct. dep.	–	–		–	–		–		–		–	–		–		–		–	–	3 45				3 15		3 45						
Town arr.	–	–		–	–		–		–		–	–		–		–		–	–	3 55				3 20		3 50						
dep.	–	–		–	–		–		–		–	–		–		–		–	–	3 58				4 10		4 25						
ld Moor dep.	–	–		–	–		–		12 40		–	–		1 30		–		–	–					–		–						
oft Depot arr.	–	–		–	–		–		12 48		–	–		1 L38		–		–	–					–		–						
dep.	–	–		–	–		–		1 10		–	–		2 0		–		–	–					–		–						
a dep.	–	–		–	–		–		1 23		–	–		2 15		–		5 40						4 25		4 40						
dep.	–	–		–	–		–		1 45		–	2 25		2 40		–		5 30						5 30		5 15						
dep.	–	–		–	–		–		2 11		–	–		–		–		5 40						5 40		5 40						
dep.	–	–		–	–		–		2 30		–	–		–		–		5 55						6 0		6 0						
Depot arr.	–	–		–	–		–		3 2		–	–		–		–		–						–		–						
dep.	–	–		–	–		–		3 15		–	–		–		–		–						–		–						
dep.	–	–		–	–		–		3 20		–	–		–		–		–						–		–						
orks arr.	–	9 5		–	–		–		3 50		–	–		–		–		–	4 35	5 10				6 17		6 17						
dep.	–	–		–	–		–		–		–	–		–		–		–	–					–		–						
rby dep.	8 15	–		–	–		–		12 50		–	–		–		–		1 45						–		–						
ngton dep.	–	–		–	–		–		12 56		–	–		–		–		1 51						–		–						
dep.	–	–		–	–		–		12 45		–	–		–		–		2 5						–		–						
ate arr.	–	–		–	–		–		–		–	–		–		–		2 9						–		–						
dep.	–	–		–	–		–		12 50		–	–		–		–		2 20						–		–						
Xt dep.	–	–		–	–		–		1 5		–	–		–		–		2 24						–		–						
gifts Sdgs. arr.	–	–		–	–		–		*		–	–		–		–		2 50						–		–						
dep.	–	–		–	–		–		–		–	–		–		–		3 0						–		–						
ers Sdgs. arr.	–	–		–	–		–		*		–	–		–		–		3 4						–		–						
dep.	–	–		–	–		–		–		–	–		–		–		3 22						–		–						
ss Jct. arr.	8 30	9 10		11 25	12 30		12 30		1 35		4 0			–		–		3 28	4 40	4 45	5 10			6 27		6 27						
elds Sdg. arr.	–	10 20		11 30	12 35		12 35		1 30		4 20			2 50		–		5 40	6 0					6 47		6 47						
and arr.	–	10 25							1 50							–		–						6 15		–						
tion dep.	–	–		12 40					2 45		4 35		2 50			–		5 53	6 25					7 6		7 6						
Grange arr.	–	–		12 46					2 55		4 43		3 4			–		5 59						7 6		7 6						
tion arr.	–	–		12 48					2 55		4 45		3 7			–		6 p5	6 43					7p12		7p12						
(Min. Jct.) arr.	–	–		12 53					3 10		5 0		3 12			–		6 17						7 24		7 24						
(L.N.E.) arr.	–	–														–		–	6 46													

‡—Shed   p—Propel train.

The Freight-only Working Timetable for July 1937

goods agent, Claud Baines', were published in the May 1993 *Railway Observer*.

How true was the comment in the extract from the *RO* of March 1941, to the effect that 'The Axholme Joint Line must be a part of the British Railways [*sic*] least affected by the war, everything still seems to carry on in a leisurely style that it would take an earthquake of major proportions to upset'. This extract brought back vivid memories to me, as I was, at the time, nearing the end of what was to be a twelve-month stint in the employ of the LMS at Epworth station, as a general clerical factotum and assistant to the goods agent, Claud Baines.

The passenger service having ceased prior to the war, all that was left was a daily freight service from Goole to Haxey Jct. (on the GN&GE Joint line heading south east from Doncaster) and a separate one to Fockerby, at the end of a branch which diverged eastwards at Reedness Jct., situated in the wilderness a few miles south of Goole. The Haxey Jct. goods also handled traffic on a short sub-branch to Hatfield Moor which headed westwards towards Doncaster from Epworth. Coal, fertilisers and, in the season, seed potatoes from Scotland formed the backbone of the inwards traffic, together with the occasional consignment of agricultural machinery (I remember seeing an invoice for a tractor from Ayot, next door to what is now my home town of Welwyn Garden City) whilst outward traffic included grain, potatoes, green peas (for which the Isle of Axholme was noted) hay, straw, and the odd cattle wagon load of pigs. For loading hay and straw, we tried to obtain an ex-L&Y long wheelbase open wagon, but were not always successful!

The day's activity would start with Belton, the next station to the north, offering the daily goods on the single line tablet instrument located in the goods office, any time after 10.30 am. Some fifteen minutes later, the goods would trundle in, always headed by a small ex-L&Y 0-6-0 (12037/41/2/4/7/56 from Goole shed shared the work). We would open the LMS goods van next to the engine - the sliding door was invariably difficult to move; the hinged doors fitted to GWR vans were much to be preferred - from which we would extract our mail and 'smalls' traffic, both passenger and goods rated. Meanwhile the regular guard, 'Old Sharpy' with his rubicund visage, would amble up from his brake van and point out the wagons to be put off in our yard.

The engine having run round would then pull the train out of the platform and proceed to shunt the yard. Incoming wagons had to be positioned, empties knocked out and traffic from the Hatfield Moor and Haxey branches segregated. Shunting was a slow process, as both the drivers and their mounts were 'feeling their age', and the latter was not equipped with lever reverse. Eventually the goods would depart for Hatfield Moor, tender first, where peat moss litter was the staple outwards traffic.

On return from Hatfield Moor, about 1 pm, the wagons would be stabled and wagons for the Haxey branch coupled up, before departure, engine first, some half an hour later. The final burst of activity took place in mid-afternoon when the goods returned from Haxey, picked up outwards traffic from the yard and that previously brought in from Hatfield Moor and finally made its slow journey back to Goole.

The only variation in this routine took place during the summer green pea season (this traffic was invariably worked in cattle wagons, to provide good ventilation) when a light engine would arrive from Goole at lunch time and change places with

DOWN

Distance from Goole M C	Description	No. 2150	2152	2154	2156	2158	2158	2162	2160	2164
	Class	D	D	D	D	D	D	D	D	D
		SX	D	SX	SO	SO	SX	SO	SX	SX
		am	am	am	am	am	am	am	am	am
	Previous Times on Page									
M C	Goole Engine Shed		6 45							
	Goole		6 50							
	Goole (Min. Jct.)	5 55	7 25		7 0	7 50	8 28	8 50		10 40
	Goole Engine Shed Jct.	6 0	7 40		7 5	7 55	8 33	8 55		10 45
0 38	Goole Engine Shed Jct.	6p 2			7p 7	7p57	8p35	8p57		10p47
	Potters Grange Junction	6p 7			7p12	8p 2	8p40	9p 2		10p52
2 35	Marshland Junction	6 10			7 20	8 7	8 45	9 6		10 54
4 60	Goole Fields Siding	6 18			7 30	8 17	8 55	9 14	10 20	11 1
5 48	Reedness Jct.	6 33			7 45	8 32	9 10	9 26	10 25	11 13
8 55	Reedness Jct.			8 50		3 52	9 40	9 45		11 25
	Eastoft	7p20			10p25					
9 70	Eastoft	7p32			10p38					
	Luddington	7p40			11p 0	9 4	9 52	9 59		11 37
11 24	Luddington	7p45			11p 5	9 9	9 57	10 5		12 2
	Fockerby	8p 0			11p15	9 26	10 14	10 35		12 32
6 51	Moores Farm	8p 6			11p21	9 51	10 44	10 45		12 47
8 50	Peat Works Siding			8 55			10 49			
	Crowle					*	10 59	10 55		12 58
	Crowle					10 10	11 5			
12 77	Ealand Depot					10 35	11 30	11 13		1 15
	Ealand Depot					10 48	11 43			
	Belton					11 0	11 55			
14 77	Belton					11 10	12 5			
	Thomas Siding									
	Thomas Siding									
17 54	Epworth									
	Epworth							* 11 33		1 35
19 63	Sandtoft Depot									
	Hatfield Moor							11 56		1 45
	Burnham Sidings							12 3		1 52
17 78	Burnham Sidings									
	Haxey Town									
19 42	Haxey Town									
	Haxey Jct.									
	Forward Times on Page									

Nos. 2150, 2156, 2158, 2162, 2164—p Propel train. No. 2162—Hagg Lane *

DOWN (continued)

Distance from Goole	Description	No. 2166	2168	2170	2172	2174	2176	2178	2180
	Class	D	LE	D	D	D	LE	LE	D
		SX	SX	SX	SO	SX Q	SX		
		PM	noon	PM	PM	PM	PM	PM	PM
1–2	Goole Engine Shed / Goole		12 0					8 4	9 5
3–4								8 10	9 15
5–6	Goole (Min. Jct.) / Goole Engine Shed Jct.						7 7		
7–8			12 5				7 12		
9–10	Potters Grange Junction / Marshland Junction		12 8						
11–12		12 15	12 20		2 10				
13	Goole Fields Siding / Reedness Jct.	12 20	12 35		2 15				
14–15	Reedness Jct. / Eastoft					4 30			
16–17	Eastoft / Luddington			12 45					
18–22	Luddington / Fockerby / Moores Farm / Peat Works Siding / Crowle			12 57		4 33			
23–24	Crowle / Ealand Depot			1 2					
25–26	Ealand Depot / Belton			1 7					
27–28	Belton / Thomas Siding			1 12					
29–30	Thomas Siding / Epworth			1 18					
31–32	Epworth								
33–35	Sandtoft Depot / Hatfield Moor / Burnham Sidings								
36–37	Burnham Sidings / Haxey Town								
38–39	Haxey Town / Haxey Jct.								

Working timetable for September 1949.

UP

M C	Description	2151	2153	2155	2157	2161	2159	2163
	Class	E & V	D	D	LE	D	D	D
		SX	SX	SX	SX	SO	SO	SO
		am	am	am	PM	PM	PM	am
	Previous Times on Page							
—·44	Haxey Junction ⊕							
	Haxey Town							
	Haxey Town							11 40
	Hatfield Moor							11 48
	Sandtoft Depot							12 10
4 45	Sandtoft Depot							12 22
	Epworth ⊕							12 40
	Epworth							
	Thomas Siding							12 50
6 45	Thomas Siding ⊕							1 15
	Belton							1 29
	Belton							
	Ealand Depot							1 39
10 72	Ealand Depot ⊕							1 44
12 71	Crowle		9 5					2 0
	Crowle							
	Pest Works Sidings							
	Moorns Farm	8 15						
	Fockerby							
	Luddington					12 20		
	Luddington					12 26		
	Boltgate							
	Boltgate					12 45		
	Eastoft							
	Eastoft					12 50		
	Whitgifts Sidings					U		
	Whitgifts Sidings						U	
	Blackers Sidings							
13 74	Blackers Sidings ⊕	8 30	9 10			1 35		2 12
14 62	Reedness Jct.		9 25	11 20	12 40	1 45		2 30
17 7	Goole Fields Siding		9 30	11 25		1 50		
19 4	Marshland Junction ⊕				12 48			2 45
	Marshland Junction				12 54			2 53
	Potters Grange Junction				12 56			2p55
19 42	Goole				1			3 10
	Forward Times on Page							

No.	2165	2167	2171	2169	2173	2175
Class	D	D	D	D	D	D
	SX	SX	SO	SX G	SX	SX
	PM	PM	PM	PM	PM	PM
1 Haxey Junction			12 50			3 0
2 Haxey Town			12 55			3 8
3 Haxey Town		12 40				
4 Hatfield Moor		12 48	1 10			3 45
5 Sandtoft Depot		12 10				
6 Sandtoft Depot		1 22	1 25			4 0
7 Epworth						
8 Epworth	1 45	1 45	1 55			4 45
9 Thomas Siding	1 51	1 51				*
10 Thomas Siding	2 5	2 6	2 5			4 55
11 Belton	2 9	2 11	2 10			
12 Belton	2 20	2 48				5 5
13 Ealand Depot	2 24	3 2				5 5
14 Crowle	2 44	3 15	2 27			5 25
15 Crowle	2 50	3 20	2 32			5 30
16 Pest Works Sidings		3 50		4 40		
17 Moorns Farm						
18 Fockerby						
19 Luddington						
20 Luddington						
21 Boltgate						
22 Boltgate						
23 Eastoft	3 0					
24 Eastoft	3 4					
25 Whitgifts Sidings	3 22					
26 Blackers Sidings	3 28					
27 Blackers Sidings						
28 Reedness Jct.						
29 Reedness Jct.		4 2	2 44	4 43	5 30	5 42
30 Goole Fields Siding		4 20	3 0			6 10
31 Marshland Junction					6 5	
32 Marshland Junction		4 35	3 15			6 50
33 Potters Grange Junction		4 43	3 23			6 55
34 Potters Grange Junction					6 15	
35 Goole (Min. Jct.)		4p45	3p25		6 20	6p59
36 Goole		5 0	3 39			7 11

the engine that brought in the goods from Hatfield Moor, which would then return to Goole. Sometimes I operated the ground frame to carry out this manoeuvre and fancied myself a signalman!

At that time, my home was in York; at weekends I used to cycle to Doncaster and hoist my bike into the front van of the wartime 20-coach equivalent of 'The Flying Scotsman'. On Monday morning I would return to Epworth in the same manner, with the difference that I caught a local all stations train from York to Doncaster which originated at Darlington and was invariably hauled by an NER 'R' class 4-4-0; arrival in Doncaster could be up to half an hour late.

One Saturday in May 1941 I said goodbye to Epworth, lifting my cycle on to the verandah of 'Sharpy's' brakevan for a lift to Hatfield Moor and cycling the significantly reduced distance from there into Doncaster.

A detailed account of the train operations appeared in the March 1941 *Railway Observer* and read as follows:

The line is worked by engines from Goole LMS shed, and for practically a year only six different engines have been seen on the branch, namely Nos. 12037/41/3/4/7/56, all power class '2', ex-L&Y, and all possessing a metal plate on the central splasher bearing the interesting information 'Beyer Peacock, Ltd, Manchester, 1887'. For all their age, however, they are well liked by their drivers, most of whom are as old as the steeds they mount; the class '2s' have hardly ever failed in service - in this respect they are reputed to be more reliable than the larger 0-6-0 class '3' engines ex-L&Y.

There are wagon exchanging facilities with the GN&GE Joint Line at Haxey Junction and once a day an engine off the Axholme Joint Line has to go the water column at the end of the up platform on the LNER line. There are only 3 water columns on the Axholme Joint Line proper, at Reedness Jct., and the other situated near to Sandtoft station, which is the only intermediate station on a 6 mile branch leading from Epworth to a peat works on Hatfield Moors.

The usual train service on the branch is as follows. A goods train leaves Goole about 6 am for Reedness and the Fockerby branch, the engine and brake returning light to Reedness about 9 am to shunt Reedness yard and to fetch the loaded wagons out of a peat works about a mile south of Reedness. About 12 noon another trip is made up the Fockerby branch to fetch out the loaded wagons, and the train then returns to Goole, leaving Reedness about 2.30 pm. On Saturdays there is only one service up the Fockerby branch, leaving Goole about 8 am. Meanwhile, another goods train leaves Goole at 9.18 am for Reedness, Epworth and the branch to Hatfield Moor, reaching Hatfield Moor about 12 noon, and returning about 1 pm, and reaching Goole any time about 5.30 pm. Finally a goods train leaves Goole at 10.40 am for Haxey Jct., stopping to shunt at all stations on the way except Belton. Haxey Jct. is reached about 2 pm and left again about 3.30 pm, Goole being reached anywhere round 7 pm. In summer the latter trips are amalgamated into a combined working from Goole at 9.18 am (traffic being lighter), the trip up to Hatfield Moor being made first, and a relief engine and men are sent from Goole about 1 pm, the changeover being effected at Epworth after the train has returned from the Hatfield Moor branch about 2.15 pm, the early turn engine and men going straight back to Goole.

The Axholme Joint Line must be a part of British Railways least affected by the war as everything still seems to carry on in a leisurely style that it would take an earthquake of major proportions to upset. Of course, it has had its 'evacuees', in the shape of strange brake vans of all vintages, ranging from the ex-North British 'Black Maria' brakes to a Southern Railway 23 ton brake designated to work between Hastings and Tonbridge, and to a GWR brake from Cardiff equipped with sanding apparatus, which is of course a novelty for these parts; a greater change in physical features would be hard to imagine in this country than the comparison afforded between the dead flat areas which stretch for miles around here, and the mountainous valleys of South Wales. The LMS brakes are rostered to all trips on the Axholme Line, as are LMS engines, but often nowadays the LMS brake fails to turn up, and a substitute has to be found. The severe weight restrictions prevent any engine larger than an ex-L&Y class '2' 0-6-0 goods working on the Axholme Line.

Other reports on the freight operations on the AJR were published in the *Railway Observer*. A visitor on 21st December, 1954 found that traffic was fairly brisk, apart from the Epworth-Haxey Junction section which was under the threat of total closure. Fifteen wagons of sugar beet were worked out via Haxey Junction to the British Sugar Corporation's factory at Brigg.

The daily goods train from Goole to Haxey Junction was being worked by class '2' 2-6-0 No. 46408. The engine of this train also works the five-mile Epworth-Hatfield Moor Peat Works branch. During the day several unconventional methods of operating were noticed in this somewhat remote part of Lincolnshire. The Hatfield Moor train, consisting of four wagons and a brake, was propelled up the branch by No. 46408. Shunting at Eastoft Depot added a further three wagons which were attached in front of the brake van! From a point near Eastoft to the terminus the line is still laid with Light Railway flat-bottomed track.

From Epworth to Haxey Junction propelling was again the order of the day. No. 46408 propelled fifteen loaded wagons of beet and a brake, whilst behind the engine were three wagons for Haxey Town! This facilitated easy shunting as the yard at Haxey Town is in a trailing direction.

The yard at Haxey Junction has now become overgrown and the platform loop points have been removed. Although the station buildings are no longer occupied, the GPO have recently installed a modern coin-operated public telephone. The reason for this is not quite clear and one imagines that it must have very limited use.

On 30th October, 1957, it was observed that the section closed on 1st February, 1956 from Epworth to Haxey Junction had been used for the storage of wagons. Traffic was being worked by class '2' 2-6-0 No. 46409 and a ballast special for track relaying on the Hatfield Moor branch was in the hands of class 'J10' 0-6-0 No. 65417. 'Traffic on this system has declined very considerably during the past years and now consists of little more than peat from Hatfield Moor and seasonal sugar beet traffic'.

By May 1962, when the small Hunslet diesels had taken over, there was a daily goods train from Goole to Reedness Junction. If traffic demanded, it

The reason for the AJR track being left down to Belton as late as 1972. The nearby Keadby power station needed much of its large generating equipment to be taken away to be serviced regularly and due to the weak road canal bridge at Crowle, these were loaded on to the AJR at Ealand depot, transported by rail over the canal and unloaded at Belton (as seen in the photograph) to continue their journey by road. When the new road bridge was installed in 1973 there was no longer a reason for the railway to be left, as everything could then be moved by road.   *Mrs Grace Johnson*

The last freight train in 1965 consisting of a load of 11 rotor-spreaders and a New Holland Bailer (from Aylesbury *via* Goole) destined for John Harris of Epworth, who were situated just down the road from Epworth station. Nearly all the machinery and spare parts for this company came in by train.   *Courtesy John Harris*

Special arrangements were made at Epworth station on 21st November, 1959, when Scottish farmer William Doig moved all of his farm and family 346 miles from Brechin to Epworth. A mobile crane and additional road lorries were needed to unload the 32 wagon train and move the contents 1½ miles to Melwood Grange. Here Mr Doig waits as the special pulls-up.

Mrs Grace Johnson

The special train hauling just one passenger coach within its make-up, transported this family (including dog) to Epworth in November 1959. From left to right: the four sons Bruce, Dennis, Billy and Ian, next Mrs James Doig (brother's wife), Mrs William Doig, Brother James and farmer Doig himself. The family left the area in the late 1960s

Mrs Grace Johnson

than ran to Fockerby and Epworth but only rarely did it venture down the branch to Hatfield Moor, which succumbed to closure on 30th September,1963: The AJR passed into history on 5th April, 1965 when the remaining sections, Marshland Junction to Epworth and Reedness Junction to Fockerby were officially closed. The single line from Marshland Junction to Ealand Sidings did however remain until 1972 and was worked (when needed) as a 'long siding' as stated in the 1969 British Railways Sectional Appendix. The Central Electricity Generating Board entered into an agreement with BR to pay for the maintenance of the line so that they could use the section from Ealand to Belton on occasions when the huge stators from Keadby power station needed to be taken away for maintenance. These would be transported by road from the power station to Ealand depot, loaded onto a train (brought in from Goole) and then taken over the canal via the swing bridge to Belton station, where they would be loaded onto low loader lorries and taken away. All this was to avoid the weak and narrow canal bridge on the A161 at Crowle. However in 1970, Lindsey County Council replaced the old bridge with a new one and so in 1972 the remaining rails of the AJR were lifted and another railway passed into history.

The Last Passenger Train

In the later years of the AJR rail tours occasionally traversed the branch, including brake van specials. The last was a 4-car dmu chartered by the North Axholme Secondary School at Crowle (*see next page*) on 1st April, 1965. Many people turned out to watch or ride on the last passenger train over the line. Included below is a report of the trip by Mr B.J. Hastings (the Geography Teacher) in the April 1965 issue of the *Lincolnshire Transport Review*.

Promptly at 11.30 am on Thursday 1st April, the 4-car multiple unit provided for the North Axholme Secondary School's 'Farewell Special' glided out of Goole station. Aboard were 184 children, members of the school staff, invited guests, newspaper reporters and TV cameramen. If it was a sad occasion, one would have scarcely noticed it! Brisk trade in light refreshments was done by senior pupils, maps and itineraries were being studied and excitement ran high.

A fast sprint down to Marshland Junction was only a prelude to our gentle meander through the northern part of the Isle. A 15 mph speed limit was in force on the 'Axholme', all facing points not fitted with point locks had to be clamped, and all wagons standing on adjacent lines whose points were not protected by 'traps' had to be scotched securely.

Four farmers' sidings were noted between Marshland Jn and Reedness Jn where the Axholme system forks into two routes; these were Corner Siding, Glossop's, Smith's and Goole Fields. A bridge over the Swinefleet warping drain brought us into Reedness Junction where 'platforms' were provided on both routes. It should be added that Axholme platforms are nothing elaborate and involve only a low 'Kerb' and a slight elevation above the normal trackside formation. Consequently steps were always necessary in the days of passenger service. We carried scaling ladders on board the train, but we noted that the original steps were still available at Reedness and at Crowle.

We toured the northern Isle branch first. Blacker and Whitgift sidings were passed before Eastoft where TV covered the gates being opened across the A161 road. On then to Bramhill Siding and Luddington. The Burton Hills Escarpment showed up clearly now as we continued almost to the Trent at Fockerby, passing one more siding - Pinder's Siding. Here a welcome awaited us from villagers and Garthorpe C.P. School brought down by their headmistress.

After 15 minutes or so we returned to Reedness and took the main line southwards to Crowle and Epworth. The Divisional Movements Officer (Mr Earnshaw from Hull) was present at Reedness with the station master to bid us welcome; his limousine and chauffeur we noted parked in the yard.

On then past Crowle Peat Works and Spilman's Siding over the Lincs border and down to Crowle. Another short break and then on past Crowle Primary School where children not on the trip were lined up to greet us. At Ealand an anxious moment occurred whilst we cleared a transformer on a railway wagon parked on

This 4-coach dmu, seen here at Epworth station, was hired by the North Axholme Secondary School, Crowle and used to say 'farewell' to the AJR. It ran on 1st April, 1965 and was carrying passengers on a line which had been officially closed to passengers for 32 years! Many people turned out to see it pass. The gentleman on the extreme left is Alan Wise; Reg Fletcher, Chairman of the then Isle of Axholme Rural district Council stands at the door of the dmu's cab whilst by the buffers stands Alan Rowbottom. *Courtesy Edwin Harrison*

the adjacent siding. These out-of-gauge loads have been a regular job on the 'Axholme'. This example was being removed from Keadby Power Station to the manufacturers for attention. Rail haulage is employed over the 3 miles 7 chains from Ealand to Belton because it would not pass over the narrow road swing bridge at either Goole or Crowle. Pickford's haulage therefore conveyed it from Keadby to Ealand, BR handle it on the 'Axholme' to Belton and Pickford's reload it for road haulage to destination.

Passing over the Doncaster-Grimsby main line, the Stainforth-Keadby Canal and the A18 main road, we continued to Hagg Lane siding and Belton, where the village constable was waiting with his camera. Here we met the penultimate Axholme goods train drawn by D2600. This was unexpected as it was understood the branch goods was to be cancelled that day. On again we trundled, up the rise over the A161 road and Richard Thomas & Baldwin's brick works siding to Epworth, capital of the Isle and our terminus. We noted the lifted remains of the Hatfield Moor branch and the main line to Haxey which were photographed afresh and we began the return journey to Crowle, setting down passengers at Ealand siding (an innovation since it was never a station!) and at Crowle. The 32 miles 50 chains from Goole had taken 4 hours - an average of 8.1 mph! A gentle trip, however, full of interest and made thoroughly pleasurable by the courtesy and friendliness of the railway staff who accompanied the train or were employed at the Axholme stations. The two district inspectors were exceedingly helpful enabling us to see everything yet maintain the timings laid out for progress. We also carried two drivers, one guard, one p.w. inspector and one lengthman to clamp points.

Some Other Legal Agreements

Whilst on the operational aspects of the Joint line, it is of interest to browse through the many other legal agreements between the railway and local personalities or businesses. Most railway histories only cover the railway operations as seen from the railway, such as the running of trains and associated technical aspects; but many other facets of the day to day running are interesting.

Remembering the sparsely populated area of the Isle, it is strange to see the well known company of newsagents, W.H. Smith & Son Ltd, plying for the right to 'sell and loan newspapers, books, periodicals, pamphlets, prints, stationery, cutlery, travelling caps, wrappers and straps for the same'. By an indenture executed on 10th March, 1905, the NER and L&YR granted them the exclusive right for three years from 1st January, 1905, to sell newspapers and to advertise (in proper frames) on station walls, fences, hoardings, overbridges etc; which would probably have been more lucrative than the selling of books! For this privilege, W.H. Smith's were to pay five per cent of the total sales receipts (including library subscriptions) each year, and fifty per cent of the advertising revenue. They were to keep legible books of accounts; they were not to offer immoral or illegal publications for sale, however they were to make available for sale NER/L&YR timetables and guidebooks when produced. The return of unsold newspapers etc. to London was free of charge, as long as the original forwarding journey had been paid for. Free passes on the AJR were available to Smith's agents to tend to the bookstalls! The stations covered by this agreement were Belton, Crowle, Eastoft, Epworth, Fockerby, Haxey Town, Luddington, Haxey Junction and Reedness Junction.

From all the photographs studied, nowhere can a bookstall as such be seen, so one has to presume that if Smith's did ply their trade on the AJR, they probably did so in space made available in the booking offices. The author approached Messrs. W.H. Smith & Co. Ltd to check their records as to the establishment of bookstalls under this agreement, but sadly they have failed to reply.

On 18th February, 1910, the NER/L&YR granted the British Automatic Company Ltd the sole rights for ten years (from 1st January, 1910) to place automatic sweetmeat machines on the premises of the AJR. The machines to be supplied would sell cigarettes, matches and chocolates and would be kept supplied by the station masters, who would also collect the money. This money (plus any base coins or articles pushed into the machines) would be sent to the company, less 5 per cent commission for the station master or agent. The rent, payable quarterly for siting these machines was to be 20 per cent of the gross takings, except for the Nestle's chocolate or Peters' chocolate machines, which were fixed at 10 per cent of the gross revenue, with a minimum annual rental of four pounds, ten shillings [£4.50p]. No advertisements were allowed regarding the machines, of which the following were placed on the stations: Crowle had one column and one chocolate machine; Epworth, one column and one chocolate machine; Haxey Junction just one chocolate machine and Haxey Town, one chocolate machine and one 'hanger' machine.

During March 1930, the LNER became concerned about rabbits and entered into an agreement in April, with David Stubley a local farmer as 'to the destruction of rabbits on lineside at Crowle'. Apparently Stubley rented five acres of railway land between bridges 9 and 10 near to Crowle and his crops were being decimated by these rabbits. He was allowed to walk along the line and embankments to snare the 'said rabbits', all for the sum of one shilling [5p] per annum. Although this was fairly common practice for the railways, this is the only 'rabbit' AJR agreement that has been found in the records, so one must presume that all the other 'AJR rabbits' were poached!

From 1st July, 1931 the Church of England were permitted to place collecting boxes for 'waifs and strays' at two of the stations, namely Haxey Town and Haxey Junction. These two boxes were fixed on the wall 'left of the Booking Office Ticket Window' at an annual rent of 2s. 6d. [12½p] each, payable in arrears on the 1st July. Lastly an agreement entered into on 14th August, 1930 between the LNER/LMSR and Anthony Blackbourn of Crowle (a carter) is worthy of a glance as it shows the rates and duties of a local businessman, working for the AJR. The agreement actually took effect from 1st June, 1930, when a previous agreement with the late Anthony Howard

Blackbourn was cancelled. The carter was commanded to accept and deliver all parcels and goods, and other articles (conveyed by passenger or goods train) for delivery to the Crowle area. He also had a list of consignors from which he had to collect and deliver the goods to Crowle railway station. He was paid 1d. for each object up to 56lb. weight and 2d. on consignments over 56lb. (if over one ton, then 2s. 6d. was paid). For this he had to supply all the rulleys (carts), ropes and other equipment and be available during the total opening hours of the railway. One wonders if it was worth it!

Signalling

The whole length of the AJR was single track. The section from Marshland Junction to Reedness Junction was worked by electric staff until 1956, when it was converted to electric tablet*. The remainder of the main line from Reedness Junction to Haxey Junction had always been worked by electric tablet, with intermediate block posts at Crowle, Epworth and Haxey Town where trains could pass (*see NER 1905 Appendix next page*). In 1907, a loop was established at Belton and this of course became a block post, which shortened the long section between Crowle and Epworth. Haxey Town ceased to be block post about April 1930.

The following detailed list of signal boxes is from information supplied by Chris Woolstenholmes and John Foremen (supplied by Noel Coates); and details of lever frames are listed for the Joint Line by T.T. Sutcliffe in his informative signalling books. In all there were six signal boxes, 34 ground frames and three crossing huts maintained by the NER (later LNER).

Marshland Junction to Reedness Junction

All the following were single-lever ground frames built by the Railway Signal Co. Ltd (RS Co.) and installed in 1903. All were released by an Annett's key attached to the train staff: Marshland Siding (Plum Tree Siding), Dougherty's Siding, Corner's Siding, Smith's Siding, Glossop's Siding and Goole Field's Siding (sometime called Brownyee Siding).

Reedness Junction was a 13-lever wooden McKenzie & Holland box installed in 1903 (closed 5th April,1965). There were also two ground frames, both single-lever RS Co. installed in 1903, again released by Annett's key. They were called Reedness Yard siding GF and Reedness Junction GF.

Reedness Junction to Fockerby (Branch)

All the following were single-lever RS Co ground frames installed in 1903, released by Annett's key attached to the train staff: Blacker Siding, Whitgift Siding, Eastoft Station, Bramhill Siding, Luddington Station, Pinder's Siding and Fockerby Station.

*In April 1905, the electric staff repeatedly failed on three occasions, once because a rat ate the wires of the batteries at Reedness Junction. This was treated as a 'severe problem' and became the subject of Board discussions.

Single Lines on which Passenger Trains run.

Staff or Tablet Stations, Sections, Passing Places, and †Preceding Places, and Spec Instructions with regard thereto.

These lines are worked in accordance with the regulations for Train Signalling Block Telegraph System on Single Lines of Railway ; and under the Train Sta or Train Staff and Ticket System, or under the Electric Train Staff System, under the Electric Train Tablet System, except where stated to the contrary.

† See Regulation 5, Single Line Regulations for working by Train Staff and Ticket, page 4.

(1).—Trains must not be allowed to approach from opposite directions at the sa time at " Line Clear," except as shown in the " Remarks " column, and th under Clause 4 of the Block Telegraph Regulations.

(2).—Trains not conveying passengers may be accepted from opposite directions und Regulation 5 of the Block Telegraph Regulations where they cannot be accept at " Line Clear " unless stated to the contrary in the " Remarks " column.

(3).—Where trains are allowed to pass each other, and they cannot be accepted fr opposite directions at the same time, the first train must be drawn clear on the loop line, or shunted clear of the running line before the other is allow to leave the next Block Station.

NOTES.—Passing Places are denoted thus *
The Term " Goods Trains " means all trains not conveying passenge

STAFF STATIONS AND SECTIONS.	WORKED BY	Description of Trains which may pass each other.	REMARKS.
Axholme Joint	(L. & Y. & N.E.	Railways).	
1. Marshland Junction *Reedness Jc. Station	} Electric Train Staff	}	One goods and one passenger, Fock-erby Section only
2. *Reedness Jc. Station *Crowle Station ..	} ELECTRIC TABLET	} Passenger or goods	
3. *Crowle Station .. Epworth Station ..	} ELECTRIC TABLET	} Passenger or goods	
4. *Epworth Station .. *Haxey Junction ..	} ELECTRIC TABLET	Passenger or goods	

Extract from the NER Appendix dated 1st January, 1905

Reedness Junction to Crowle

All the following were single-lever RS Co. ground frames installed in 1904 and released by tablet/token: Moor Farm Siding, Peat Moss Siding and Spilman's Siding. Crowle Yard ground frame was an 8-lever McKenzie & Holland wooden box of 1904.

Crowle to Epworth

Crowle level crossing ground frame was a 4-lever McKenzie & Holland wooden box installed in 1904. Ealand Depot was a single-lever RS Co. ground frame installed in 1904 and this was released by tablet. Crowle Swing Bridge Engine Cabin was a 5-lever McKenzie & Holland box of 1904 and built on a gantry. Crowle Swing Bridge was a 12-lever RS Co. wooden signal box of 1904. Hagg Lane Siding was a single-lever RS Co. ground frame of 1904 released by tablet. Belton Station was a 7-lever McKenzie & Holland wooden signal box of 1904 and Belton level crossing was a single-lever RS Co. ground frame of 1904, released by tablet. Epworth was an 8-lever McKenzie & Holland wooden signal box of 1904.

Epworth Junction to Hatfield Moor(Branch)

All the sidings on this branch were worked by single-lever RS Co. ground frames installed in 1904 and released by tablet. These were Hatfield Moor Goods, Allerton's Siding and Sandtoft Goods.

Epworth to Haxey Junction

Again all the sidings were worked by single-lever RS Co. ground frames built in 1904 and released by tablet. They were Burnham Lane Siding, Haxey Town North Ground Frame, Haxey Town South Ground Frame, Haxey Junction North Ground Frame and Haxey Junction South Ground Frame.

Between the two Haxey Town ground frames was Haxey Town station level crossing which had a 2-lever McKenzie & Holland frame installed in 1904 and again released by tablet. The latter and all the ground frames were positioned out in the open. The tablet/staff stations were Marshland Junction, Reedness Junction, Crowle Yard Ground Frame, Belton station, Epworth station and Haxey North Ground Frame.

In the case of foggy weather or falling snow, the following instructions were to be applied as issued by the L&YR in November 1919 (*see next page*).

The Fockerby branch was worked on the one engine in steam principle using a train staff. This method made it unnecessary to provide loops at the intermediate stations; the train staff was provided with a key for unlocking the points leading into sidings *en route*. A train staff was also used on the Hatfield Moor branch.

Signals were provided at Reedness Junction, Crowle, Crowle Swing Bridge, Belton, Epworth, and Haxey. They followed the pattern employed by the North Eastern Railway, which favoured the signal arm in a slotted

NOTES. D.—Day Turn. N.—Night Turn. F.—Foreman Platelayer.

NOTES.
M—Signals fogged by Machine.
*—Denotes Signals connected to Indicators.

Note.—Where Indicators are not provided a Detonator must be placed on the rails except when a Signal marked thus * is lowered.

AXHOLME JOINT RAILWAY.

Signal Box	Name of Signal	No. of Men.	Position of Fogman.	Names of Fogmen. First Turn.	Names of Fogmen. Second Turn.	When the object named below is obscured by Fog, etc., the Fogmen must be called out.	Person to call out Fogmen.	Persons to visit Fogmen at Posts.
MARSHLAND JUNC.	Up distant from Reedness Junction	1	Up Side	W. Sims (P.W.)	...	Home Signals	Signalman, Marshland Jun.	P. Way Ganger, H. Scott.
REEDNESS JUNC.	To work to Station Master's instructions	1		C. Richardson (P.W.)	...	Home Signals	Station Master	Station Master.
CROWLE	To work to Station Master's instructions	1		J. Meggit (P.W.)	...	Home Signals	Station Master	Station Master.
CROWLE (SWING BRIDGE)	To work to Steersman's instructions in connection with Home Signals at each end of bridge	1		J. Sharp (P.W.)	...	Home Signals	Steersman, Crowle Swing Bridge	Steersman, Crowle Swing Bridge.
BELTON	To work to Station Master's instructions	1		P. Picksley (P.W.)	...	Home Signals	Station Master	Station Master.
EPWORTH	To work to Station Master's instructions	1		C. Elvidge (P.W.)	...	Home Signals	Station Master	Station Master.

post. At Crowle, Belton, Epworth and Haxey there was a home and starting signal for each direction. There was a host of signals at Reedness Junction: for trains coming from Goole there was a home signal before the Swinefleet Warping Drain was reached, followed by a main and branch starter for the junction. In the reverse direction the main line and the Fockerby branch each had an outer home as well as the home signal protecting the junction, and the starter was situated beyond the Warping Drain. There were no distant signals at Reedness Junction; in fact there were very few on the line, as the Light Railways Act requires the provision of these only when the home signal cannot be seen from a distance of ¼ mile.

Consequently distant signals were used only where required such as the one provided for northbound trains at Crowle, where the approach to a level crossing was concealed by a curved cutting. Most of the NER signals were replaced in later years by modern upper quadrants, but the old North Eastern type was still to be found when the line closed.

At all the stations where there were signals the block instruments and single-line apparatus were kept in the booking office which was either in the station master's house or in the station buildings; but the levers working the signals were housed in a separate cabin, in some instances quite a distance away.

As Crowle and Belton both had level crossings adjacent to the station, the signals protecting the crossing were slotted so that they could not show 'off' unless not only the signalman, but also the gate operator, had pulled a lever after closing the gates to road traffic. At Crowle the gates were interlocked with the protecting signals by a special lever frame provided by the crossing gates.

Until 1955 Crowle swing bridge was protected in each direction by outer home signals which were interlocked with the opening mechanism of the bridge. A signal box was provided, and in addition to the signals for the railway there were two special signals on the canal bank, each about 200 yards from the bridge, for the purpose of indicating to those in charge of vessels on the waterway whether the bridge was open to them or not. These canal signals had a ring at the end of a special type of arm which was characteristic of signals used by the North Eastern Railway for controlling water traffic at swing bridges.

The Isle of Axholme Light Railway Order laid down that signals should be fixed both for rail traffic and for users of the canal, the latter being to inform or warn barge-owners using the Navigation during foggy weather when the bridge was closed to them.

When the signalling installations at Crowle swing bridge were removed, protection was provided by key interlocking between the bridge gear and the approach signals at Crowle and Belton, which were the block posts on either side of the bridge.

LIST OF SIGNAL BOXES, ADDITIONAL RUNNING LINES, LOOPS AND REFUGE SIDINGS—continued

Description of Block System on Main Lines	SIGNAL BOX	Distance between Signal Boxes M.	Yds.	Additional Running Lines* Up	Down	Up Description†	Up Standage in wagons in addition to E & V	Down Description†	Down Standage in wagons in addition to E & V	Hours Signal Box Open	REMARKS *Broken line indicates lines worked by Permissive or No Block Regulations. †PL—Passenger Loop GL—Goods Loop RS—Refuge Siding
	GOOLE AND HAXEY (AXHOLME JOINT LINE)										
	Goole										
	Boothferry Road ...										
	to			} See Staddlethorpe and Thorne Table							
Electric Token	Marshland	0	0								
	Reedness										
	Station	2	1682							6.0 am (7.0 am T) to 8.0 pm M to S	
	Crowle										
	Station	2	1065							7.0 am to 7.0 pm M to S	
	Belton										
	Station	4	354							7.0 am to 6.30 pm M to S	
	Epworth										
One engine in steam	Station	1	1703							7.0 am to 6.0 pm M to S	
	Haxey Junction										
	Station	4	1434							7.0 am to 5.0 pm M to S	
	REEDNESS AND FOCKERBY										
	Reedness										
One engine in Steam	Station	0	0							See Goole and Haxey Table	
	Estoft										
	Station	2	1688							6.0 am to 7.30 pm M to S	
	Luddington										
	Station	2	338							6.0 am to 7.30 pm M to S	
	Fockerby										
	Station	1	671							6.0 am to 7.30 pm M to S	
	HATFIELD MOOR BRANCH										
One engine in Steam	Epworth										
	Station	0	0 See Goole and Haxey Table								
	Hatfield Moor										
	Station	5	220								
	(Not a Block Post)										

ROUTE AVAILABILITY OF LOCOMOTIVES

Sections of the Line over which N.E.R. Engines normally work have been classified according to the classes of Engines which are permitted to work over them, and N.E.R. Locomotives have been correspondingly grouped for Route Availability purposes.

Following are the Engine Groups for Route Availability purposes, and pages 71 to 73 are shown the Sections of Line and groups of Engines permitted to run over them.

Only Engines up to and including the group in which a section is placed may be worked over than Section of Line, except in those cases where additional classes are shown to be permitted.

ROUTING GROUPS

Group No.		Classes of Tender Engines		Classes of Tank Engines
3	B	12	F	2 (G.E.), 3, 4, 5
	D	3, 41	J	66, 67/2, 68, 69, 88
	J	3, 4, 10, 21, 25, 36	N	9, 10, 11

Item No.	Section of Line	Route Availability Group
—	Haxey Junction to Marshland Junction (Goole)	3
—	Epworth to Hatfield Moor	3
—	Reedness Junction to Fockerby	3

Extract from the North Eastern Region Working Timetable September 1949.

Chapter Eight

Closure and Lifting the Line

In this brief chapter, a full account is given of how the northern section of the AJR was abandoned as recorded by the railway engineer responsible at the time, Mr John Addyman. This element of railway history has probably never been recorded in so much detail before and especially by the person concerned.

Within six months of the closure of that part of the AJR north of Epworth, a contract was let for the recovery of the track and other assets. 1965 and 1966 were the peak years for post-Beeching branch line abandonments and a well established procedure was used. Basically two different types of contract were employed, one for small abandonments like station sidings on lines to remain open and the other for most branch lines and large marshalling yards. For political reasons passenger branches generally had to wait a year before abandonment could commence, but the track on freight lines like the AJR could be taken up as soon as some basic procedures had been fulfilled. Once clearance had been given by the Regional General Manager, the Civil Engineer prepared the abandonment drawing on which the branch was represented in diagrammatic form. This was drawn to scale with all the running lines, sidings, buildings, signal boxes, bridges and level crossings being shown. Copies of the drawings were sent to the various railway departments with requisition instructions for the item for which they were responsible. The Public Relations & Publicity Officer was reminded about contracts for advertisements on stations or bridges; the Bridge Engineer was given the opportunity of saving any serviceable bridge girders; the Architect was asked about gas and water supplies and whether any dwellings were supplied with water from the locomotive tanks; the Signal & Telegraph Engineer decided if all his remaining equipment could be considered as scrap; the Estate & Rating Surveyor decided which buildings, including signal boxes, he did not wish to be demolished; and the Chief Mechanical & Electrical Engineer was asked about water cranes and other equipment. Estimates of the net profit which should accrue from the abandonment were sent to the General Manager. Net credits of around £2,500 per mile for the 18 miles were expected after paying the demolition contractor and making good the highways at the level crossings. Also taken into account was the cost of removing the points and crossings, and installing plain line at Marshland Junction where the AJR connected with the main line from Goole to Doncaster.

The General Manager issued an order and simultaneously the Supplies & Contracts Manager in Derby was asked to arrange for the branch recovery to be let to tender. He invited about six contractors from a select list to tender for the work and to attend a site meeting with a representative of the District Engineer. Prior to this meeting, it was practice for the District Engineer's representative to either walk the whole branch or as much as necessary to determine any special requirements.

John Addyman who was in charge of York District abandonment in 1965 recalls the pre-contract inspection of the branch.

I arrived at Reedness with two permanent way inspectors with the intention of each of us walking one of the three lines in each direction. We had the keys to various railway buildings and the first we opened was the rail motor shed, where we found the petrol-engined bogie trolley intact and well cared for. We had brought a four gallon can of petrol which we put into the vehicle and the permanent way inspectors (who were experts at coaxing rail motors into action) soon had the engine running. The special rails and turntable were in a shed and we manhandled the trolley on to the running line. The prospect of our long walks had disappeared! We went as far as the home signal at Marshland Junction and then as we had the keys to the level crossing gates on the A161 at Eastoft, I decided to return and go through up the branch to Fockerby. We returned to Reedness Junction about mid-day and although it was a pleasant early autumn day, it had become obvious to me why these machines were called 'pneumonia bogies' as we were fairly cold when we garaged the motor trolley; we must have been the last 'passenger train' from Marshland to Fockerby. The remainder of the branch received a more cursory inspection from the roads that crossed or ran near it.

At Epworth, we opened the station buildings and it was like walking into a time capsule. The office had been closed for some months, but it was clean with everything neatly positioned as if someone was still working there. Besides a few fairly recent working timetables and special traffic notices, most of the books and papers dated from the 1930's and 1940's and some even earlier. There were stacks of LNER wagon tickets for livestock, other agricultural produce and explosives (the latter for the Hatfield Moor branch). We had become hardened to vandalism and filth at most other disused railway buildings and we were totally amazed at the wonderful condition at this office. Perhaps the fact that Epworth was John Wesley's birthplace had a lasting effect on the residents! We gently closed the door and I later arranged for the Divisional Manager to clear the papers.

The special requirements dealt with on our preliminary inspection included marking with paint rails and chaired sleepers considered to be serviceable and which would be retained for use elsewhere; and details like deciding where fencing was required behind the abutments of abandoned bridges. The pre-tender inspection was held in October 1965 and a procession of contractors cars visited various locations. The special items relating to the branch were pointed out, such as the buildings and bridges to be demolished and whether telegraph poles were to be removed or not. Any questions by the contractors were answered and all the information was confirmed to them in writing. The contractors had about a fortnight in which to submit their tenders to Derby and the contract was always awarded to the lowest bidder. Competition was fairly tough and a local firm - Eagre Construction Co. Ltd of Scunthorpe - won this one. The costs were normally £500 to £600 per single track mile, but large bridges, steep gradients or narrow cuttings/embankments could increase the price; but none of these applied to the AJR.

It was British Rail's responsibility to supply the right number and type of wagons ordered by the contractor for each day's work. Bogie wagons were required for the serviceable rails, but the remainder of the scrap usually went out in high goods wagons. Obviously work started from the remote end of the branches and it was normally possible to replace the full wagons from the previous day by empty wagons, with little delay to the contractor, by utilising existing sidings to pass the wagons. Only very occasionally were two train movements required in a day. British Rail were liable for claims from the contractor for late or non-delivery of wagons. No problems were encountered on the AJR and work proceeded very smoothly entailing the removal of all sidings between Marshland Junction and Belton; the Fockerby branch completely; Epworth to Belton completely and the Hatfield Moor branch.

Scrap rails were torched into furnace lengths of about 5 ft and the chairs were removed from the sleepers by using compressed air driven tools to extract the chair-screws. All the contractors had standardised on the use of a tracked Drott or bull-dozer with two prongs formed from old rails protruding forward from the front of the blade. The furnace lengths of old rail were placed across the prongs by the labourers and when a safe number had been collected the Drott lifted them into the wagon. The full length serviceable rails were dragged by a chain from the Drott alongside the bogie wagon and then lifted by the prongs onto the wagon. The sleepers were moved by digging the prongs slightly into the ballast (just below the sleeper) and as the machine moved forward, the sleepers rolled onto the prongs and 10 to 15 sleepers could be loaded at once. The Drott also acted as a shunter to move the wagons as work progressed, however none of these operations had ever been envisaged when the makers designed the machine!

Obviously all these movements were made easier if the line was level and had wide flat areas between the fences as on the AJR. On a good day, half a mile of track could be removed and the necessary work on the AJR was completed in under two months. Thos. W. Ward Ltd of Sheffield acted as British Rail's agents for the disposal of the scrap and obtained the best possible prices from the steelworks or foundries. At that time British Rail were flooding the market and steel rails fetched about £15 to £18 per ton and the cast chairs around £10 to £12 per ton.

The only problem that arose on the AJR abandonment was when a former employee of the contractor decided to go into the scrap business on his own account. Copper was making a good price at the time and he decided to take down the telegraph wires, not knowing they were rented to the GPO. When some local farmers had their phones cut off, he was soon apprehended by the police.

When the abandonment was completed, all that remained was for British Rail to agree with the County Council the cost of reinstating the road surface at each of the public road level crossings. The usual price paid was between £100 to £300 per crossing in rural areas, depending on the width and status of the road. The Estate Surveyor then disposed of the land and buildings as profitably as possible and in so doing tried to relieve BR of any maintenance responsibility for bridges, drains, culverts that remained.

As regards the southern section of the AJR between Epworth and Haxey Junction, this was lifted before the northern section by BR, using their own direct labour in 1962.

So all that was left of the AJR, was a single line, running from a facing connection on the up Doncaster main line at Marshland Junction down to Belton station, and BR treated this in their Working Appendices as a long siding. The reason for this section remaining has been stated earlier and by 1972 this too had gone: this really was the end of the AXHOLME JOINT RAILWAY.

All that remained of the trackbed at Haxey Junction AJR station site on 25th August, 1969, with the back of the GNR main line station building on the left.   *John R. Bonsor*

The semi-derelict site of Belton station on 25th August, 1969 with signal and track still *in situ;* classified as a long siding by BR, this was used by the Central Electricity Board.
John R. Bonsor

Heads of Agreement: 27th January, 1900

HEADS OF AGREEMENT dated the Twenty Seventh day of January one thousand nine hundred, NORTH EASTERN RAILWAY (herein after called the North Eastern Company) and the GOOLE AND MARSHLAND LIGHT RAILWAY COMPANY (herein after called the Marshland Company), with reference to Goods, Mineral and Live Stock Traffic passing between the two systems of the two Companies.

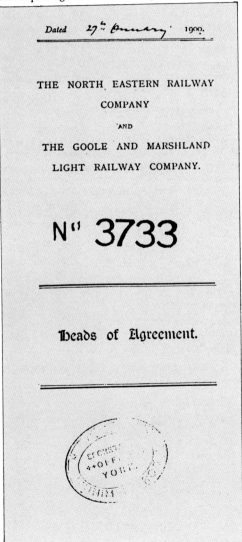

Dated 27ᵗʰ *January.* 1900.

THE NORTH EASTERN RAILWAY

COMPANY

'AND

THE GOOLE AND MARSHLAND

LIGHT RAILWAY COMPANY.

N⁰ **3733**

𝔥𝔢𝔞𝔡𝔰 of 𝔄𝔤𝔯𝔢𝔢𝔪𝔢𝔫𝔱.

Heads of Agreement dated the *Twenty-seventh* day of *January* one thousand nine hundred, between the NORTH EASTERN RAILWAY COMPANY (hereinafter called the North Eastern Company) and the GOOLE AND MARSHLAND LIGHT RAILWAY COMPANY (hereinafter called the Marshland Company), with reference to Goods, Mineral and Live Stock Traffic passing between the systems of the two Companies.

1. The Marshland Company to work the traffic on their own line.

The necessary exchange sidings at Marshland Junction to be provided at the joint cost of the two Companies.

No engine or vehicle of the Marshland Company at any time to pass on to the North Eastern Company's lines unless the same be approved as fit to run with safety thereon by the Locomotive Superintendent of the North Eastern Company, and the user of the North Eastern Company's line by the Marshland Company to be subject to the rules and regulations of the North Eastern Company from time to time in force.

2. The rates on all through Traffic to, from, or *via* the North Eastern Railway, to be fixed and quoted by the North Eastern Company, the rates on Traffic between Goole and stations on the Marshland Railway to be based on the North Eastern Company's Local Scales.

3. The through rates referred to in Clause 2 to be compiled on the following basis :—

(*a*) LOCAL AND FOREIGN CLASS RATES.—GOODS.

On the Goole rates, plus the amounts shewn on the attached table marked Appendix No. 1, for the extra distance from Goole.

(*b*) LOCAL AND FOREIGN SPECIAL RATES.—GOODS.

On the Goole rates, plus the following sums per ton as nearly as practicable.

	REEDNESS AND SWINEFLEET. Per ton.	EASTOFT. Per ton.	LUDDING- TON. Per ton.	ADLING- FLEET. Per ton.
Town Manure	9d.	10d.	1/-	1/-
Roadstone	9d.	10d.	1/-	1/-
Ashes	9d.	10d.	1/-	1/-
Other Traffic in Class "A"	9d.	1/-	1/3	1/3
Traffic in Class "B"	9d.	1/-	1/3	1/3
Traffic in Class "C"	1/-	1/3	1/6	1/6

(*c*) COAL AND COKE RATES.

On the North Eastern Scales of Rates applicable, assuming the traffic delivered through railway sidings.

These scales to be modified in the case of rates to and from stations beyond the North Eastern Railway where competitive rates or group rates in force by other routes render it necessary.

4. Live Stock Rates to be based on the North Eastern Local Scale for Local Stations, and on Railway Clearing House Scale for Foreign Stations.

5. Returned empties to be charged on the ordinary scale on total distance.

6. The North Eastern Company to provide wagons, sheets, and ropes on the same system as on their own railway for the conveyance of traffic to and from stations on the Marshland Railway.

7. The Marshland Company to be credited through private settlement with the following proportions:—

	REEDNESS AND SWINEFLEET. Per ton.	EASTOFT. Per ton.	LUDDING-TON. Per ton.	ADLING-FLEET. Per ton.
Coal and Coke and Traffic in Classes "A" and "B"	1/-	1/3	1/6	1/6
Not Carted Traffic	1/9	2/-	2/2	2/4
Carted Traffic	4/3	4/7	4/10	5/-

Live Stock:—
> Full Wagons, 3/6 per Wagon.
> Half Wagons, 3/- per Half Wagon.

On Smalls (through or local), consignments under 1 cwt. to be treated as 1 cwt. Returned empties to be divided as "collected and delivered" traffic.

' The above proportions are based on the application to the Marshland Company's business of the existing North Eastern Company's local scales of rates for Live Stock, Agricultural Traffic, and Town Manure, and are subject to revision in the event of these scales at any time being withdrawn.

8. The proportions to be credited to the Marshland Company set out in Clause 7 not to apply to traffic to or from stations beyond the North Eastern Company's system conveyed *via* the Lancashire and Yorkshire route *via* Goole Junction.

The proportions to be credited to the Marshland Company upon traffic so conveyed to be as follows:—

	REEDNESS AND SWINEFLEET. Per ton.	EASTOFT. Per ton.	LUDDING-TON. Per ton.	ADLING-FLEET. Per ton.
Coal and Coke and Traffic in Classes "A" and "B"....	9d.	1/-	1/3	1/3
Not Carted Traffic	1/3	1/6	1/8	1/10
Carted Traffic	3/3	3/7	3/10	4/-

Live Stock to and from all stations :—

> Full Wagons, 2/6 per Wagon.
> Half Wagons, 2/- per Half Wagon.

9. Settlement of Traffic receipts between the two Companies to be made monthly, the balance due to either Company to be paid within a month from the date of settlement.

10. The Marshland Company to be responsible for any damage occurring on their railway to rolling stock and sheets.

11. Each Company to be responsible for damage to goods occurring on their respective railways, but claims for damage incurred during transit (it being impossible to say at what part of the transit the damage occurred) to be borne by mileage, or in such proportions as may be agreed in any particular case.

12. The Marshland Company to be responsible for the payment of demurrage charges debited to the North Eastern Company for foreign vehicles and sheets detained on the Marshland Railway beyond the recognised time in accordance with the Railway Clearing House Regulations for the time being, but with regard to North Eastern stock and sheets so detained the following reduced scale will apply :—

> Wagons, 1/- per day.   Sheets, 3d. per day.

13. The North Eastern Company to provide the Marshland Company with the requisite supply of station books, abstracts, stationery, etc., at cost price.

14. If North Eastern vehicles are used for the conveyance of traffic arising and terminating on the Marshland Railway, such traffic being otherwise exempt from the operation of this Agreement, the charge to be 1/- per vehicle per day.

15. The Marshland Company to be responsible for any loss or damage due to the action of their servants in charge of trains whilst running over the North Eastern line.

16. This arrangement to be for twelve months certain from the opening of the railway, and thenceforward subject to three months' notice on either side.

George S. Gibb

> *For the North Eastern Railway Company.*

Seb. W. Nagle

> *For the Goole and Marshland Light Railway Company.*

APPENDIX No. I.

Table of additions to Goole rates in fixing Class rates to and from Stations on the Marshland Company's Railway.

	A	B	C (2 Tons)	C (Under 2 Tons)	1	2	3	4	5
From or to Stations on North Eastern or beyond up to 10 miles from Goole									
Add for Reedness and Swinefleet	7d.	7d.	10d.	1/3	1/3	1/3	1/8	2/1	2/1
,, Eastoft	10d.	11d.	1/3	1/3	1/8	2/1	2/1	2/11	2/11
,, Luddington	11d.	1/-	1/8	1/8	1/8	2/1	2/6	3/4	3/4
,, Adlingfleet	1/1	1/3	2/1	2/1	2/1	2/6	2/11	3/9	4/2
From or to Stations on North Eastern or beyond from 10 to 30 miles from Goole.									
Add for Reedness and Swinefleet	7d.	8d.	10d.	10d.	1/3	1/8	1/8	1/8	2/1
,, Eastoft	11d.	11d.	1/3	1/3	1/8	2/1	2/6	2/6	3/4
,, Luddington	1/-	1/1	1/8	1/8	1/8	2 6	2/11	2/11	3/9
,, Adlingfleet	1/2	1/3	1/8	1/8	2/1	2/11	2/11	3/4	4/2
From or to Stations on North Eastern or beyond from 30 to 50 miles from Goole									
Add for Reedness and Swinefleet	6d.	6d.	10d.	10d.	10d.	10d.	1/3	1/3	1/8
,, Eastoft	8d.	9d.	1/3	1/3	1/3	1/8	2/1	2/1	2/6
,, Luddington	8d.	10d.	1/3	1/8	1/8	1/8	2/1	2/6	2/11
,, Adlingfleet	9d.	1/-	1/3	1/8	1/8	2/1	2/6	2/11	3/9
From or to Stations on North Eastern or beyond over 50 miles from Goole									
Add for Reedness and Swinefleet	4d.	4d.	10d.	10d.	10d.	10d.	10d.	1/3	1/8
,, Eastoft	6d.	7d.	1/3	1/3	1/3	1/8	1/8	2/1	2/6
,, Luddington	6d.	7d.	1/3	1/3	1/3	1/8	1/8	2/1	2/6
,, Adlingfleet	7d.	9d.	1/3	1/3	1/3	2/1	2/1	2/6	3/4

Appendix Two

North Eastern Railway Act, 1902

An Act to confer additional powers upon the North Eastern (AD 1902) Railway Company and upon that Company jointly with the Lancashire and Yorkshire Railway Company for the construction of new railways and other works and the acquisition of lands and jointly with the Midland and Lancashire and Yorkshire Railway Companies in respect of their Normanton Station and for vesting in the Company and the Lancashire and Yorkshire Railway Company the Goole and Marshland Light Railway and the Isle of Axholme Light Railway and for other purposes.

(31st July, 1902)

Whereas it is expedient that the North Eastern Railway Company (in this Act called 'The Company') should be empowered to make and execute the new railways and other works by this Act authorised and to acquire the lands in this Act described and that the other powers in this Act mentioned should be conferred on the Company: And whereas it is expedient that the Company and the Lancashire and Yorkshire Railway Company (in this Act called 'the Joint Companies') should be empowered to make and execute the new railways and other works by this Act authorised and that the other powers in this Act mentioned should be conferred on the Joint Companies :

And whereas it is expedient that the Company, the Midland Railway Company and the Lancashire and Yorkshire Railway Company (in this Act called 'The Three Companies') should be empowered to acquire the lands and execute the works in this Act described in that behalf:

And whereas plans and sections showing the lines and levels of the said works and plans of the said lands and also books of reference containing the names of the owners and lessees or reputed owners and lessees and of the occupiers of the said lands.

Vesting of Goole & Marshland and Isle of Axholme Companies undertakings in Joint Companies and dissolution of light railway companies.	52. Subject to the provisions of this Act and of the agreement set forth in the Second and Third Schedules to this Act which are hereby confirmed the undertakings of the light railway companies shall be and are hereby transferred to and vested in the Joint Companies as part of the joint undertaking and as from the respective dates of such transfers or the passing of this Act whichever shall last happen the light railway companies shall be and are hereby dissolved except for the purpose of winding up their undertakings for which purpose they may exercise all such powers and authorities as are necessary.
Payment to Goole & Marshland Light Railway Company	53. The Joint Companies shall pay to the directors of the Goole and Marshland Light Railway Company the purchase money mentioned in the agreement between that company, and the Joint Companies set forth in the said Second Schedule out of which the said directors shall pay and discharge all the debts and obligations of the Goole and Marshland Light Railway Company and the balance of

which they shall distribute rateably amongst the proprietors of the said company.

Payment to Isle of Axholme Light Railway Company

54. The Joint Companies shall pay to the directors of Payment to Isle the Isle of Axholme Light Railway Company the purchase-money mentioned in the agreement between that company and the Joint Companies set forth in the said Third Schedule out of which the said directors shall subject to the provisions of the said agreement pay and discharge all the debts and obligations of the Isle of Axholme Light Railway Company and the balance of which they shall distribute rateably amongst the proprietors of the said company.

For protection of Great Northern and Great Eastern Joint Committee

57. The following provision for the protection of the Great Northern and Great Eastern Joint Committee (hereinafter in this section called 'the joint committee') shall unless with the consent in writing of the joint committee under their common seal apply and have effect: The Joint Companies shall at their own expense provide at or near the junction of Railway No. 1 (A) (authorised by and described in the Isle of Axholme Light Railways Order 1898) with the sidings of the joint committee all necessary and proper sidings for the reception of and dealing with traffic coming on to the lines of the Joint Companies from the lines of the joint committee at the junction aforesaid.

Provisions as to sidings on Goole & Marshland Light Railway

58. The Joint Companies shall as part of the Goole and Marshland Light Railway undertaking make and maintain the sidings coloured red on the plan signed in triplicate by the Right Honourable the Earl of Morley the Chairman of the Committee of the House of Lords to which the Bill for this Act was referred or other equally convenient sidings or accommodation and shall afford reasonable facilities for the reception and delivery of goods traffic thereat.

Appendix Three

Facsimile Copy of Selected Pages From Sebastian Meyer's 1903 Tender

NORTH   EASTERN

a n d.

L A N C A S H I R E   a n d   Y O R K S H I R E

R A I L W A Y S.

----------------0----------------

October 1903.

I S L E   O F   A X H O L M E   L I G H T   R A I L W A Y.

A R C H I T E C T U R A L   W O R K S.

--------------000000--------------

T E N D E R   F O R   W O R K S.

S. W. Meyer   Leeds

To the Directors of the

North Eastern & Lancashire & Yorkshire   £ 4231. 8. 5

Railway Companies.

GENTLEMEN,

    I hereby offer and agree to execute in a -
workmanlike manner, and with materials of the best quality, the -
whole of the Buildings required in the erection of the -
Architectural Works on the Isle of Axholme Light Railway for
the above Railway Companies, according to the Conditions of
Contract, Specifications, Plans, Elevations, Sections and -
Detail Drawings prepared by the Architect to the North Eastern
Railway Company, and according to drawings and instructions to
be given in explanation thereof by the said Architect, and on
the terms and conditions mentioned and contained in the Draft

of the Architect for the time being to the North Eastern Railway
Company, and will complete the works without extra charge,
according to the true intent and meaning of the Specifications,
Drawings and Conditions of Contract, subject to the explanation
of the Architect in any case of doubt or dispute, and will,
within one week after been required to do so, give the Architect
a copy in detail of the Quantities and Prices by which the -
following sums have been ascertained. And in case this Tender
is accepted I hereby undertake to execute a Deed of Contract
to be prepared by the Companies according to the Draft before
referred to, within a month from this date.

    The whole of the works to be done in SIX MONTHS
from orders to start, and it is to be understood that the Works
are to be let in one Contract.

    The following statement shews the work proposed to
be done by own workmen, also the names of the Tradesmen (all of
whom have examined the Drawings, Specifications and Conditions
of Contract, and agree to abide thereby) to whom I propose
to sub-let the remainder, if approved by the Architect.

Excavation, Masonry and Brickwork	By	
Carpenter's and Joiner's Work	By	
Slaters Work	By	James Bryant
Plasterer's Work	By	Sons
Plumber's and Glazier's Work	By	

and Lancashire Yorkshire Railway

ISLE OF AXHOLME

LIGHT RAILWAY.

SPECIFICATION

AND

BILLS OF QUANTITIES

FOR

Architectural Works.

ARCHITECT'S OFFICE

YORK.

SEPTEMBER, 1903.

SUMMARY.

	£		
BILL No 1. General Conditions.	200	.	.
BILL No 2. Haxey Junction Station Buildings, Weigh Office & Station Master's House.	966	6	11
BILL No 3. Haxey Station Buildings &c.	982	3	9
BILL No 4. Epworth Station Buildings &c.	959	2	1
BILL No 5. Belton Station Buildings &c.	947	19	8
BILL No 6. Two Weigh Offices at Sidings.	175	16	.
TOTAL AMOUNT OF TENDER	4231	8	5

AS WITNESS my hand this 19 day of October One Thousand Nine Hundered and three.

ESTIMATE for Station Buildings, Weigh Offices, and Station Masters' Houses on the Isle of Axholme Light Railway.

SEPTEMBER. 1903.

Bill No. 1.

General Conditions applying throughout the Contract.

The Contractor is referred to the General Conditions of Contract the Drawings and the Sites for further particulars.

The Contract includes all trades required in the erection of buildings as follows and is divided into No. 5 Bills, as shewn:—

Bill No. 2.—HAXEY JUNCTION.
Station Buildings.
Weigh Office.
Station Master's House.

Bill No. 3.—HAXEY.
Station Buildings.
Weigh Office.
Station Master's House.

Bill No. 4.—EPWORTH.
Station Buildings.
Weigh Office.
Station Master's House.

Bill No. 5.—BELTON.
Station Buildings.
Weigh Office.
Station Master's House.

According to the plans sections elevations and details numbered 1 to 19 together with any further drawings and particulars which may be given from time to time by the Architect.

The Contractor for the Architectural work must not interfere with the Contractor for the Engineering works or damage the works executed by him and must so arrange to carry on the buildings as the ground and sites and the convenience of working will allow.

The works are to be carried out in such order as the Architect shall direct and the whole completed in ten months from the date of the acceptance of tender.

The Contractor will be required to confine his operations within the spaces set apart for the use keeping the approaches and platforms free from materials scaffolding, etc. also arrange for the delivery of materials and the removal of debris at such times as will be convenient to the working of the traffic.

Fix all barriers and provide and maintain all lights and notices for the safety of the public.

Erect all hoardings and fences as directed. (See Clause No. 10 General Conditions.)

Brought forward £

Allow for Sunday work or overtime as may be necessary. (See Clause No. 29).

Allow for maintaining the work six calendar months after completion. (See Clause No. 40).

Allow for insuring the works as directed. (See Clause No. 42).

The Contractor's workmen will be subject to the Company's Bye-laws whilst on the Company's premises and the Contractor is to prevent their trespassing or entering the Company's premises and crossing the line unless on business.

No travelling or other expenses will be allowed to the Contractor or men as during the Contract and terms of maintenance they will be looked upon as having a local habitat notwithstanding any rules in connection with his trade to the contrary.

Any instructions or orders given to the Sub-Contractor (if any) by the Clerk of Works or Architect must be accepted as if given to the main Contractor and such orders and instructions will not render the Company responsible to the Sub-Contractor as in giving such orders the Sub-Contractor is looked upon as the Contractor's Agent.

Allow for the delivery and carriage of materials (See Clause No. 6), and arrange with Engineering Contractor for carriage of material over new line and pay all charges.

Allow for water for the works in all trades including all temporary plumbing tanks, etc. required.

The Contractor is to keep an approved foreman constantly upon the works.

The Contractor is to set out the works and be responsible for the correctness of same.

All prime cost (P.C.) values quoted are to be taken as exclusive of all trade discounts and the invoices of all such items are to be produced if so required by the Architect.

All provisional items and amounts are to be the subject of special orders in writing by the Architect and are to be used and expended as he may direct or are to be deducted in whole or part if so ordered by the Architect.

The Contractor must conform to the Bye-laws of the Local Authorities so far as they have jurisdiction over the works and he must give all notices and pay all fees legally demandable.

Clear away all surplus excavation materials and rubbish as they may accumulate and at the completion of the Contract leave the premises clean and perfect in every respect.

The Directors do not bind themselves to accept the lowest or any tender.

The Contractor is to peruse the General Conditions of Contract and allow for any expenses arising out of the stipulations contained in the clauses not mentioned above.

Carried to General Summary, page 64 £

Station Buildings.

EXCAVATOR, BRICKLAYER AND MASON.

Should the foundations in excavation be carried to a greater or less depth than that shewn on plans the value of such variation will be added to or deducted from the quantities at the schedule rates.

Bale or pump out and remove all water that may arise or settle in the foundations etc. and keep same free from water until completion of the contract.

Remove all offensive soil or other matter and where the vegetable soil comes near to the level of the proposed floors or under pavings the same to be removed.

Such of the materials from the foundations that may prove suitable can be used in filling up.

The price for excavation to include for any planking and strutting that may be necessary.

The cement to be of the best quality Portland finely ground and weighing not less than 112lbs. to the struck bushel and capable of sustaining a tensile strain of 125lbs. at seven days and 425lbs. at fourteen days to the square inch. The Contractor to keep on hand a sufficient quantity so that samples taken by the Clerk of Works may be tested before the bulk is required for use and no cement to be used until authority has been given.

Drains.

The drain pipes to be best quality the best quality one-tenth thickness salt glazed inside and out socket jointed fireclay pipes the joints luted in cement cleaned off on the inside and made perfectly tight with a broad splay collar of Portland cement on the outside.

The trenches for drains to be cut circular on bottoms and cut down for sockets of pipes so that the pipes may bed the whole length to have regular falls from point to point and to be dug to the depths indicated on the drawings and include for any planking and strutting necessary.

The drains are to be smoke tested at the Contractor's expense prior to covering in any drain failing this test to be taken up and relaid at Contractor's expense.

No drain to be covered in until inspected by the Clerk of Works and written authority given.

Bricklayer.

The lime mortar to be composed of one part freshly burnt lime of quality approved by the Architect mixed with two parts clean fresh sand and one part clean clinker ashes measured dry in proper boxes all to be ground under rollers and thoroughly tempered with a proper quantity of pure fresh water to a tough paste. All mortar (either lime or cement) to be freshly mixed for use and none in any case to be used after it has been permitted to dry or partially set.

The cement mortar to be composed of one part cement to three parts clean sharp fresh water sand measured dry in proper boxes.

The bricks to be good hard sound well shaped and thoroughly burnt free from lime and other defects uniform in size. Samples of common bricks to be submitted for approval previous to commencing.

The external facework to be select with several coloured common bricks free from chips and other imperfections and pointed and jointed with a neat cut weather joint.

All bricks to be wet in a humid state. Each bed and joint thoroughly flushed through with mortar laid with as thin joints as practicable and no four courses when walled to rise one inch more than four courses laid dry.

All rough brickwork to be walled old English bond. The facework to be walled three courses of stretchers and one course headers and stretchers alternately.

Broken bricks or pieces will not be allowed except such as are necessary to form proper bond.

All work to be protected during wet or frosty weather and any injured by frost or from any other cause must be replaced by the Contractor at his own cost.

The price for brickwork is to include for plumbing all angles forming reveals and building in ends of timbers etc.

Mason.

The stone to be best hard Bradford from the best beds in the quarry free from vents discolorations slate and other defects and set on its natural bed.

N.B.—See the Conditions of Contract the Drawings and Site for further descriptions and information applying to these trades.

Foundations.

Description	Quantity	Rate	£	s	d
Excavations in trenches 2ft deep part returned filled in and rammed remainder carted and led deposit ...	35 cub yds	1/9	3	1	3
Excavation on made bank to platform for front wall of building and plank and strut bank and fill in after and form tank inside wall (subject to measure) ...	13 cub yds	1/9	1	13	3
Filling in to raise ground level under pavings with hard dry material well rammed in layers of 6in each ...	1 cub yds	2/-		18	0
9in reduced brickwork in mortar (to ground floor line) ...	118 sup yds	5/6	32	9	0
Half-brick walls in mortar (ditto) ...	45 sup yds	2/9	6	3	9
Extra only for external facing with selected bricks jointed with a neat cut weather joint ...	28 sup yds	1/9	2	9	0
Amount of Foundations		£	46	16	3

Drains.

The following drains to be measured and to instructions hereafter given.

Description	Quantity	Rate	£	s	d
4in drain pipe as described and digging average 2ft deep ...	24 lin yds	2/-	2	8	1
4in ditto ditto 3ft deep ...	24 lin yds	2/6	3	1	1
4in ditto ditto 4ft deep ...	24 lin yds	3/-	3	1	1
6in ditto ditto 4ft deep ...	20 lin yds	3/3	3	5	1
Extra only for 4in bends ...	No. 3	6	1	6
Ditto 4in quadrant bends ...	No. 3	6	1	6
Ditto 4in junctions ...	No. 2	9	1	6
Connect 6in drain to engineers main drain insert junction and make good ...	No. 1	4/-	4	0
Connect and make good down pipes to drains ...	No. 3	2/-	6	0
Carried forward		£	59	1	9

Isle of Axholme Light Railway.

Bill No. 2.—Haxey Junction.

SECTION No. 1.

Station Buildings.

SLATER.

The roofs to be covered with firsts Veinhulli (new quarry) 16in × 10in slates all to be sound and truly squared and laid on 1¼in × ⅜in (root) railway laths on spars and 1¼in × ⅜in lath on boarded roofs free from sap shakes and large loose or dead knots secured with strong galvanized iron nails.

The eaves course to be doubled throughout and to overhang eaves spouts sufficient to deliver water into same.

Each slate to have 3in bond or overlap and to be secured with two copper nails each weighing 5lbs per thousand.

Cut slating up the gables to project over moulds on large boards etc. and to have a slight fall to roof.

N.B.—See the Conditions of Contract Drawings and Site for further particulars applying to this trade.

Description	Qty	Rate	£	s	d
Slating as described on 1¼in × ⅜in laths pointed on underside with lime and hair mortar ...	109 sup yds	3/9	20	6	9
Extra only for double course at eaves ...	125 lin ft	6	3	7	1
Mastic cement fillet neatly pointed between large board and slating ...	31 lin ft	4		10	4
Blue Staffordshire plain ridge tile with lap joints bedded in mortar and pointed in colored cement ...	53 lin ft	1/6	4	6	6
Fixing only lead soakers ...	No 8½ doz	9		5	1

Attend upon and make good after other trades make good breakages and leave roof perfect and drop-dry as completion of the Contract.

Carried to Abstract, page 19 ... £ 28 19

SECTION No. 1.

Station Buildings.

CARPENTER AND JOINER.

The whole of the woodwork exposed to the weather and also internally where not otherwise specified to be the best red St. Petersburg fir. Panels drawer bodies etc. to be in Country wood. Moldings and similar work in yellow pine. The 'Strudes' to framings etc. joists spars purlins principals and other roof timbers to be firsts D.M. quality. The whole to be thoroughly seasoned and free from sap shakes large loose or dead knots. All unwrot timbers to be sawn die-square.

All woodwork intended for varnishing to be selected clean and bright free from knots and finished with the iron; wall beading to be in selected Carolina pine free from knots and in narrow widths and secret nailed.

All machine prepared joiner's work shall if required be dressed off by hand.

The framed work to be prepared and put together at least a month before required for fixing but not wedged up until instructions are given by the Clerk of Works.

All joists spars sheeting and similar work to be fixed 16in centre to centre unless otherwise stated on drawings. Include for spikes nails glue wedges pins keys firring pieces grounds ridges fillets etc. necessary for the well and efficient fixing of all joiner's work also tenon mitre pocket splay notch warp half dovetail etc. where required in carpenter's work.

All framed work and where one piece of woodwork is fixed over another exposed to weather to have one coat of white lead paint at all joints tenons crossings etc. previous to being put together.

No woodwork to be fixed nearer than 3in from inside face of flue or fire-clock.

All items of ironmongery to include for all necessary screws and fixing complete.

N.B.—See the Conditions of Contract the Drawings and Site for further particulars and descriptions applying to these trades.

Description	Qty	Rate	£	s	d
Centering to semicircular arches including setting strutting and striking ...	26 sup ft	6		10	-
Turning piece to segmental arch 4½in soffit ditto ... ditto ...	17 lin ft	8		4	3

Roofs, Floors, etc.

Description	Qty	Rate	£	s	d
Deal in lintels and wall plates including halved joints (scantlings 4½in × 14in 4½in × 3in 3in × 3in) ...	21 cub ft	3/-	3	12	-
Deal in floor joists including all trimming (scantling 4½in × 3in) ...	44 cub ft	3/1	6	15	8
Labor planing deal ...	6 sup ft	1		6	9
3in sarking under lead ...	3 sup yds	1/6		4	6
3in west grooved tongued and painted one side sarking to eaves ...	21 sup yds	1/9	1	16	9
Ditto ditto in short lengths to gables ...	4 sup yds	1/9		7	-
3in west grooved tongued and V jointed one side slade beading with 3in grounds plugged to wall ...	3 sup yds	2/-		15	-

SECTION No. 1.

Station Buildings.

PLASTERER.

The mortar to be composed of best fresh burnt and approved lime suitable for Plasterer's purposes and clean sharp fresh water sand; the lime to be well boiled and run through a fine sieve and a suitable quantity of well beaten long pile cow hair to be worked into it while in a liquid state and to have the requisite quantity of sand mixed with it so that it will set hard.

The mortar to be prepared as soon as instructions are given and to lie until required.

The lathwork is to be done with strong Baltic redwood rent laths lath and a half in thickness and not exceeding 1in in width and to have the joints broken every two feet; the ends of laths are to be butted and nailed singly upon the joists.

The ceilings to be lathed laid floated and set. The walls (of Booking Office and Ladies' Rooms) to be rendered floated and set. Each coat to be allowed time to dry before the next is applied and the first coat to be well scratched so a to give as good key for the next coat the finishing coat of both walls and ceilings to be worked up smooth and even with a steel trowel.

N.B.—See the Conditions of Contract Drawings and the Site for further particulars and descriptions applying to this trade.

			£	s.	d.
Lath lay float and set ceilings	...	62 sup yds	1/9		6
Render float and set walls	...	93 sup yds	1/4		1
Render in Portland cement ¾in thick to back of urinal finished smooth	...	6 sup yds	2/-		1
Ditto to sides of E.C. pit	...	3 sup yds	1/9		3
Render in plaster behind dado boarding and counter ¾in thick	...	14 sup yds	9		6
Counter lathing lintels	...	12 sup ft	3		
Labor to rounded angle in plaster 3in girth	...	10 lin ft	2		1
Moulded stop to ditto	...	No 1	9		6
Labor cut splay quirk in plaster to head on door and window frames	...	120 lin ft	1¼	15	
Labor chamfer on edge of cement rendering	...	20 lin ft	1		
Attend upon and make good after all trades make good all damage and leave all plastering smooth and perfect at completion.					
	Carried to Abstract, page 19	**£**	14	5	

BILL No. 2.—Haxey Junction.

Abstract of Section No. 1.

Station Buildings.

		Page.	£	s.	d.
Excavator, Bricklayer and Mason	...	7	2 11	13	4
Carpenter and Joiner	...	12	11 9	13	5
Slater	...	13	25	19	2
Plasterer	...	14	14	5	6
Plumber and Glazier	...	16	14	16	1
Painter	...	18	12	5	11
	Carried to Summary of Bill No. 2, page 46		**£ 401**	**16**	**3**

BILL No. 2.—Haxey Junction.

Abstract of Section No. 3.

Station Master's House.

	Page	£	s.	d.
Excavator, Bricklayer and Mason ...	33	265	14	7
Carpenter and Joiner ...	39	110	14	5
Slater ...	40	30	5	
Plasterer ...	41	35	15	6
Plumber and Glazier ...	43	15	1	-
Painter ...	44	13	7½	11

BILL No. 2.—Haxey Junction.

Abstract of Section No. 2.

Weigh Office.

	Page	£	s.	d.
Excavator, Bricklayer and Mason ...	21	0 3	-	6
Carpenter and Joiner ...	23	14	3	11
Slater ...	24	5	6	2
Plasterer ...	25		16	6
Plumber and Glazier ...	26	3	6	9
Painter ...	27	1	4	-

Carried to Summary of Bill No. 2, page 46.

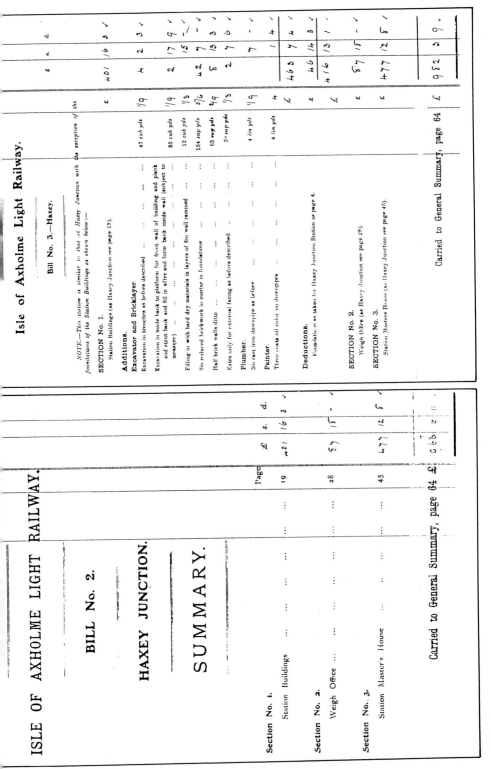

Isle of Axholme Light Railway.

Bill No. 3.—Haxey.

NOTE.—This station is similar in that at Haxey Junction with the exception of the foundations of the Station Buildings as shewn below:—

SECTION No. 1.

		£	£	s.	d.
Station Buildings (as Haxey Junction see page 19).			401	16	3
Additions.					
Excavator and Bricklayer.					
Excavation in trenches as before described	47 cub yds	1/9	4	2	3
Excavation in made bank to platform for front wall of building and plank and strut bank and fill in after and form bank inside wall (subject to measure)	83 cub yds	1/9	2	17	9
Filling in with hard dry materials in layers of 6in well rammed ...	12 cub yds	1/3		15	-
9in reduced brickwork in mortar in foundations	154 sup yds	5/6	42	7	-
Half brick walls ditto	63 sup yds	2/9	8	13	3
Extra only for external facing as before described	3+ sup yds	1/3	1	7	6
Plumber.					
3in cast iron downpipe as before	4 lin yds	1/9	1	-	-
Painter.					
Three coats oil colour on downpipes	4 lin yds	4		1	4
			465	4	4
Deductions.					
Foundations as taken for Haxey Junction Station as page 4.			46	14	3
			416	13	1
SECTION No. 2.					
Weigh Office (as Haxey Junction see page 28).			5	15	-
SECTION No. 3.					
Station Masters House (as Haxey Junction see page 45).			477	12	3
	Carried to General Summary, page 64	£	952	5	9

ISLE OF AXHOLME LIGHT RAILWAY.

BILL No. 2.

HAXEY JUNCTION.

SUMMARY.

		Page	£	s.	d.
Section No. 1.					
Station Buildings		19	401	16	3
Section No. 2.					
Weigh Office		28	56	15	-
Section No. 3.					
Station Masters House		45	477	12	5
	Carried to General Summary, page 64	£	9 68	8	11

ISLE OF AXHOLME LIGHT RAILWAY.

BILL No. 4.—Epworth.

Abstract of Section No. 1.

Station Buildings.

	Page	£	s.	d.
Excavator, Bricklayer and Mason ...	50	150	17	6
Carpenter and Joiner ...	56	251	2	11
Slater ...	57	35	5	9
Plumber and Glazier ...	58	18	11	10
Painter ...	59	25	6	5

Isle of Axholme Light Railway.

Bill No. 4.—Epworth.

SECTION No. II.

Station Master's House.

NOTE.—This building is similar to that at Haxey Junction Station.

	£	s.	d.
To amount of Station Master's House at Haxey Junction (see page 45).	277	12	5

Carried to Summary of Bill No. 4, page 62

Isle of Axholme Light Railway.

Bill No. 5—Belton.

NOTE :—This station is similar to that at Haxey Junction with the exception of the foundations of the Station Buildings as shewn below :—

				£	s.	d.
SECTION No. 1.						
Station buildings (as Haxey Junction see page 19.)			£	401	16	3
Additions.						
Excavation in trenches as before described	65 cub yds	1/6		4	17	6
Excavation over site under floors 12in deep and cart away and find deposit	29 sup yds	6			14	6
9in reduced brickwork in mortar in foundations	75 sup yds	5/-		18	15	-
Half-brick walls in mortar in foundations	24 sup yds	2/6		3	-	-
			£	429	3	3
Deductions.						
Foundations as taken for Haxey Junction Station see page 4.)			£	46	14	3
			£	382	9	-
SECTION No. 2.						
Weigh office (as Haxey Junction see page 28.)			£	87	18	-
SECTION No. 3.						
Station Master's House (as Haxey Junction see page 45.)			£	477	12	8
Carried to General Summary, page 64			£	947	19	8

SEPTEMBER, 1903.

GENERAL SUMMARY.

	Page	£	s.	d
Bill No. 1. General Conditions	2	200	-	-
Bill No. 2. Haxey Junction Station Buildings, Weigh Office and Station Master's House	46	966	6	11
Bill No. 3. Haxey Station Buildings, etc. ...	47	982	3	9
Bill No. 4. Epworth Station Buildings, etc. ...	62	959	2	1
Bill No. 5. Belton Station Buildings, etc. ...	63	947	19	8
		175	16	-
Total Amount of Tender	£	4231	8	5

Bill No. 6 [illegible] Weigh [illegible] Office [illegible] £87. 18/- [illegible]

The Specification and Bills of Quantities contained in this and the preceding 63 pages are the Specification and Bills of Quantities referred to in [illegible] Contract dated the nineteenth day of November 1903 and made between me of the one part and the North-Eastern Railway Coy and the Lancashire & Yorkshire Railway Coy of the other part.

Witness [illegible]

[illegible]

3.11.03

List of Firms and Sidings on the AJR

Extracted from the L&NW, Midland and L&Y Railways book of places, works, firms and sidings dated 1917.

Name of person	Siding name	Nearest station	Name of person	Siding name	Neare stati
Allen J.	Allerton	Hatfield Moor	Hodgson T.	Blackers	Easto
Austwick T.	Whitgift	Eastoft	Jacques T.	Burnham	Epwor
Backhouse B.	Corners	Reedness	Johnson T.	Burnham	Epwor
Darley F.	Corners	Reedness	Laister J.	Burnham	Epwor
Blacker J.	Eastoft		Leeman C.	Blackers	Easto
Bletcher J.H.	Hagg Lane	Belton	Lockwood T.	Burnham	Epwor
Bramhill W.J.	Boltgate	Luddington	Maples W.	Blackers	Easto
British Moss Litter			Martinson T.	Goole Fields	Reednes
Company	Peat Moss	Reedness	Middlebrook A.	Whitgift	Easto
Brunlee W.	Goole Fields	Reedness	Moorfoot S.	Blackers	Easto
Bruster J.	Burnham	Epworth	Moors Farm	Moors Farm	Reednes
Cawkwell A.	Goole Fields	Reedness	Nothand A.	Blackers	Easto
Corner J.	Goole Fields	Reedness	Oates Thomas	Hagg Lane	Belto
Cowling H.	Blackers	Eastoft	Oldridge Mrs	Goole Fields	Reednes
Dougherty G.	Corners	Reedness	Pepper M.	Goole Fields	Reednes
Dougherty G.	Dougherty	Reedness	Pindar J.T.	Pindar	Luddingto
Duckles T.	Dougherty	Reedness	Purvis R.	Goole Fields	Reednes
Featherby W.	Goole Fields	Reedness	Reed Mrs P.	Belton	Belto
Fillingham G.	Burnham	Epworth	Rusling F.	Hagg Lane	Belto
Fillingham W.	Spilmans	Crowle	Smith W.	Smiths	Reednes
Firth J.	Dougherty	Reedness	Spillman	Spillmans	Crowl
Fowler W.	Burnham	Epworth	Stones C.	Spillmans	Crowl
Glew Mrs	Blackers	Eastoft	Stubley D.	Hagg Lane	Belto
Gossop B.	Hagg Lane	Belton	Thompson Col	Goole Field	Reednes
Hill J.	Hagg Lane	Belton	Wroot George	Corners	Reednes

Advert in the Saturday
1st April, 1933 edition of
the *Epworth Bells*.

Appendix Five

Chronology

16th August, 1898	Goole & Marshland Light Railway Order, 1898, confirmed by the Board of Trade.
11th March, 1899	Isle of Axholme Light Railway Order, 1898, confirmed by the Board of Trade.
8th January, 1900	Marshland Junction to Reedness opened for goods, and worked by contractors' locomotives.
31st July, 1902	North Eastern Railway Act, 1902, received Royal Assent, which authorised the North Eastern and the Lancashire & Yorkshire Railways to purchase jointly the Goole & Marshland and Isle of Axholme Light Railways.
1st October, 1902	The Lancashire & Yorkshire and the North Eastern Railways acquired the Goole & Marshland and Isle of Axholme Light Railways, and the joint undertaking was named 'Axholme Joint Railway'.
1st July, 1903	Working of traffic by the contractors' locomotives ceased.
10th August, 1903	Marshland Junction to Crowle, with the branch to Fockerby, opened for all traffic.
14th November, 1904	Crowle to Haxey Junction section opened for goods traffic.
2nd January, 1905	Crowle to Haxey Junction section opened for passenger traffic.
5th August, 1905	Axholme Joint Railway (Hatfield Moor Extentension Light Railway) Order, 1905, confirmed by the Board of Trade.
5th January, 1909	Hatfield Moor branch partially opened for goods traffic.
22nd February, 1909	Hatfield Moor branch fully opened for goods traffic.
1st January, 1922	The Lancashire & Yorkshire Railway Company was merged into the LNWR, so for one year it became NER/LNWR Joint.
1st January, 1923	Grouping of Railways. Axholme Joint Line vested jointly in the LMS & LNE Railways.
17th July, 1933	Passenger services from Goole to Haxey Junction, together with the branch to Fockerby, withdrawn.
1st January, 1948	Nationalisation of Railways: Axholme Joint Railway became part of the North Eastern Region of British Railways.
1st February, 1956	Epworth to Haxey Junction section closed completely, track lifted 1962.
30th September, 1963	Hatfield Moor branch ceased operation.
2nd April, 1965	Last goods train ran
5th April, 1965	Epworth to Marshland Junction closed.
1972	Remaining track lifted.

Appendix Six

Details of Mileages on the Axholme Joint Railway

Main Line	Miles	Chains
Marshland Junction to Corner Siding	1	20
Corner Siding to Smith's Siding		29
Smith's Siding to Glossops Siding		13
Glossops Siding to Goole Fields Siding		68
Goole Fields Siding to Reedness Junction		43
Reedness Junction to Reedness station		3
Reedness station to Peat Moss Works Siding	1	0
Peat Moss Works Siding to Spilman's Siding		68
Spilman's Siding to Crowle station	1	11
Crowle station to Crowle (Ealand Depot)	1	20
Crowle (Ealand Depot) to Hagg Lane Siding	2	6
Hagg Lane Siding to Belton station	1	1
Belton station to Epworth Junction	1	66
Epworth Junction to Epworth station		11
Epworth station to Burnham Lane Siding	1	27
Burnham Lane Siding to Haxey Town station	1	57
Haxey Town station to Haxey Junction	1	44
Haxey Junction to Haxey Junction station		5
	17	**12**

Fockerby Branch	Miles	Chains
Reedness Junction to Reedness station		10
Reedness station to Blacker Siding	1	24
Blacker Siding to Whitgift Siding		31
Whitgift Siding to Eastoft station	1	22
Eastoft station to Bramhill Siding		46
Bramhill Siding to Luddington station		49
Luddington station to Pinder's Siding		29
Pinder's Siding to Fockerby station	1	5
	5	**56**

Hatfield Moor Branch	Miles	Chains
Epworth Junction to Sandtoft Goods station	2	71
Sandtoft, Goods station to Allerton's Siding	1	29
Allerton's Siding to Hatfield Moor Goods station		58
	4	**78**

Total Mileage	27	66

Appendix Seven

Accidents on the AJR

The following is a complete record of all incidents that occurred between 1905 and 1916 on the AJR

The following list of Accidents reported upon since October 1st, 1904, was submitted, and the various recommendations approved, viz. :—

Date.	Place of Accident.	Nature of Accident.	Train.	Recommendation.
1904. Oct. 1st......	Eastoft—Facing point for Goods Yard.	Engine and L. & Y. Horse Box derailed.	6-47 p.m. Passenger Fockerby to Reedness Junction.	Acting Fireman Oliver fined a day's pay.
Oct 22nd ...	Crowle — Up facing points.	Engine, Wagons, and Horse Box derailed.	5-45 p.m. Passenger Goole to Haxey Junct.	Acting Fireman Caukill severely reprimanded.
Oct. 29th ...	Reedness Junction ...	Wagon derailed	11-0 a.m. Engine and Van Fockerby to Reedness Junction.	Porter Mason reprimanded.
Dec. 16th ...	Fockerby	Wagon derailed	2-0 p.m. Goods Reedness Junction to Fockerby.	Guard Coultish reprimanded.
1905. Jan. 6th ...	Reedness Junction ..	Engine and Wagon derailed.	3-0 p.m. Goods Fockerby to Goole.	Guard Coultish suitably cautioned.
Feb. 1st. ...	Epworth	Engine derailed	9-15 a.m. Goods Goole to Haxey Junction	Guard Shillito reprimanded.
Mar. 11th ...	Fockerby	Carriage derailed	8-42 a.m. Passenger Fockerby to Reedness Junction	Guard Coultish fined 5s

The following list of accidents reported upon since April 1st, 1905, was submitted, and the various recommendations approved. viz. :—

Date.	Place of Accident.	Nature of Accident.	Remarks.
1905. April 25th..	Reedness Junction ...	Private wagon off the road.	Accidental, owing to temporary slewing of road.
May 3rd ..	Reedness Junction ..	L & Y. engine mounted rails.	Accidental, due to temporary alteration of road during fixing of new wagon weighbridge.
May 5th ...	Eastoft.........	N. E. wagon drawbar broken.	Defective drawbar.
May 24th...	Epworth	N. E. wagons (2) off road. Door of one wagon broken.	Door of one of wagons collided with cattle wagon standing on short line used for loading.
June 5th ...	Haxey Town	Goods brake van derailed, footboard and axle box damaged.	Engine left No. 1 siding whilst wagons were being run past, and collided with brake van. Acting Driver Watson severely reprimanded.
July 10th...	Haxey Junction	L. & Y. engine derailed.	Points not properly set. Porter Coggon reprimanded.
July 21st..	Reedness Junction ..	L. & Y. 3rd Class carriage brasses displaced and drawbar slightly bent.	Carriage struck points which were sprung by leading vehicle.
July 26th...	Eastoft	Dock buffer stops damaged.	Points set for dock instead of for coal siding. Guard Brooksbank reprimanded and cautioned.

Aug. 5th ...	Haxey Town	L. & Y. wagon door damaged and telegraph pole displaced.	Door of wagon was resting on dock, and when engine commenced shunting, it collided with telegraph pole. Porter Drinkall reprimanded
Aug. 22nd	Reedness Junction ..	L. & Y. engine derailed	Leading wheels left rails when engine was putting carriages into siding round the curve. Road has been examined and found to be in good order.
Aug. 26th	Epworth	N. E. wagon off road and damage to brakes on two N. E. wagons.	Wagon was derailed by colliding with another wagon standing foul of siding points. Error of judgment of Guard Johnson.

MISHAPS AT CROWLE SWING BRIDGE.

Date.	Nature of Accident.	Remarks.
1905.		
April 19th	Keel "Kathleen" when passing through caught her sail on handrail and rotary box of bridge end, carrying her sail away and breaking her mast.	Bridgeman attempted to close bridge before keel was clear. Claim for £26 0s. 10d. made by owners has been dealt with by Mr. Cudworth.
May 27th	Keel "Industry" ran aground	Owners state that keel had to run aground to avoid colliding with bridge, which was closed against them after signal had been given to pass through. Bridgemen say bridge had to be closed for a train to pass, after waiting 20 minutes for keel, which had stuck in channel. No damage was done.
June 8th.................	Keel "Rambler" sail caught on bridge pier, tearing the sail away.	Bridge fully open. Keel unable to steer straight course on account of high wind prevailing at time.
June 30th	Keel "Dora" ran aground in order to avoid colliding with the bridge.	Signal against keel. No damage done.
August 23rd	Stone lock broken. Abutments placed 2½in. out of position at side. Parapet wall had to be rebuilt for distance of 13ft. along with brickwork.	When swinging bridge too much way allowed when releasing lever controlling lock. Bridgeman Davis severely reprimanded.

The following list of accidents reported upon since September 1st, 1905, was submitted, and the various recommendations approved, viz :—

Date.	Place of Accident.	Nature of Accident.	Remarks.
1905.			
Sept. 2nd...	Haxey Junction	Point rod bent.	Acting Fireman Appleyard discharged in connection with another offence.
Sept. 21st..	Crowle..................	Loading gauge broken.	Porter Mason reprimanded.
Oct. 3rd ...	Crowle..................	Point rod and switch rail bent.	Guard Johnson reprimanded.

Oct. 20th...	Haxey Junction	Engine 954 off road and damaged slightly. Point rod connections broken.	Driver Cooper and Porter Coggon reprimanded.
Oct. 21st...	Hagg Lane Crossing	Crossing gate broken.	The staff were engaged in the yard and did not hear the bell. It is recommended that a loud sounding gong be provided (*vide* minute 123).
Oct. 25th...	Reedness Junction...	N.E. wagon derailed. L. & Y. wagon buffer rod bent.	Porter Shannon reprimanded.
Oct. 28th...	Crowle...............	Points run through, locking apparatus broken and switch bent.	Mr. Watkins, Stationmaster, cautioned.
Nov. 2nd...	Haxey Town	Wagon conveying crane 2,046 end damaged and one rail clip broken off chain.	G. O'Brien, fitter, Hydraulic department, Goole, discharged.
Nov. 16th ..	Corner's Siding (Goole Fields)	Siding points run through. Stretcher rod bent and crank broken.	Fireman Ibberson severely reprimanded.
Nov. 14th ..	Crowle...............	Two wagons derailed, three chairs broken, locking apparatus damaged.	Porter Taylor cautioned.
Nov. 24th ..	Reedness Junction...	Engine 145 off road with leading wheels. Three chairs broken.	Accidental.
Nov. 28th ..	Reedness Junction .	N.E. wagon derailed. One axle guard bolt. one axle clip bolt. and coupling link broken. Four chairs broken.	Accidental.
Dec. 13th...	Crowle...............	N.E. wagon derailed. Two chairs broken.	Guard Taylor reprimanded.
Feb. 21st...	Crowle...............	Loading gauge broken.	Porter Taylor cautioned.

MISHAPS AT CROWLE SWING BRIDGE.

Date.	Nature of Accident.	Remarks.
1905.		
November 1st.........	Keel "Jupiter" of Hull was being towed during thick fog and collided with bridge, breaking her mast.	The bridge signals were at danger. Keelman to blame.

The following list of accidents reported upon since March 1st, 1906, was submitted, and the various recommendations approved, viz.: —

Date.	Place of Accident.	Nature of Accident.	Remarks.
1906. Feb. 22nd..	Reedness Junction...	Loading gauge pulled out of position.	Porter Fields (Luddington) cautioned.
Feb. 27th...	Epworth	L. & Y. cattle wagon end boards and uprights broken. L.&Y. van brake bent, buffer stops bent.	Driver Cooper and Fireman Burn cautioned.

March 30th	Burnham Siding ...	Crossing gates run through and broken to pieces.	Run through by 7-18 a.m. passenger train ex Goole during slight fog.
May 5th ...	Epworth	N. E. wagon brake lever bent and guard broken.	Guard Coultish cautioned.
May 11th ..	Crowle.............	Points run through, rod broken, and switch bent.	Porter Taylor cautioned.
May 11th ..	Reedness Junction...	Buffer stops slightly damaged...	Guard Parsisson and Porter Troop cautioned.
May 18th ..	Crowle..................	Engine 962 derailed, three sleepers broken.	Driver Taylor and Porter Taylor cautioned.
May 28th ..	Haxey Junction	Engine 956 off road with leading wheels. One chair broken.	Ganger Emmerson cautioned.
June 30th...	Luddington	Points run through and damaged Crank cracked.	Fireman Codd reprimanded.

MISHAPS AT CROWLE SWING BRIDGE.

Date.	Nature of Accident.	Remarks.
1906. March 31st......	Keel " Onward " collided with bridge.	The bridge signals were at danger. Keelmaster to blame.
April 5th.........	Sloop " Mizpah " fouled the North Pier and broke her bowsprit shackle.	The bridge signals were at danger. Keelmaster to blame.
June 6th	Yacht " Ailie " collided with bridge ...	Accident due to want of judgment on the part of the owner who did not lower the mast, thinking it would clear the bridge.
July 30th	Keel " Star " collided with bridge ...	The mishap was due to the Keelmaster not making fast to a proper post provided for the purpose on the opposite bank.

The following list of accidents reported upon since July 30th, 1906, was submitted and the various recommendations approved : —

Date.	Place of Accident.	Nature of Accident.	Remarks.
1906. Aug. 17th..	Eastoft	Crossing gates run through and damaged.	Driver Pettinger fined.
Aug. 30th. .	Crowle	Loading gauge damaged	Guard Blaydes cautioned.
Sept. 1st ...	Crowle	Buffer stops broken	Guard Johnson cautioned.
Oct. 24th...	Haxey Junction	Catch points run through. Rod bent.	Fireman Barker cautioned.

Nov. 27th.	Crowle	Ealand and Mill Road crossing gates run through and broken up.	Clerk Townend cautioned.
Dec. 10th.	Luddington	N. E. wagon 84,355 off road. Two rods broken, switches and two rods badly bent.	Guard Ash cautioned.
1907. Jan. 21st ...	Between Peat Works and Spilman's Siding.	Horse killed. Brake fittings of engine tender damaged.	Joint Companies not responsible.
Jan. 25th...	Reedness Junction ...	Dock buffer stops damaged.	Guard Scholes cautioned.

The following list of accidents reported upon since March 1st, 1907, was submitted and the various recommendations approved.

Date.	Place of Accident.	Nature of Accident.	Remarks.
1907. March 4th.	Fockerby	Train divided when running between Luddington and Fockerby. Wagons collided with buffer stops. L. & Y. wagon 13,517, N. E. wagon 28.384, broken up.	Accidental.
April 12th.	Smith's Siding.........	L. & Y. engine 956 off road ...	Accident attributed to defective sleeper at place of derailment.
May 24th.	Eastoft	N. E. wagon 29,110 derailed. Coupling link broken.	Porter Prendergast fined 2/6.
May 27th.	Haxey Junction	Points run through and rods bent.	Fireman Swindlehurst reprimanded.

The following list of accidents reported upon from July 1st to December 31st, 1907, was submitted, and the various recommendations approved:—

Date	Place of Accident.	Nature of Accident.	Remarks.
1907. August 7th.	Haxey Town	Wath Main wagon 19 derailed. Six ordinary and 3 p.c.chairs broken.	Accident attributed to defective condition of siding.
Nov. 8th...	Goole....................	L. & Y. third 1537 footboard split and panel grazed. Crossing gates damaged.	Driver S. Johnson suspended for one week for passing signal at danger.
Dec. 19th and 23rd	Epworth	Metal stays of buffer stops broken.	Guard Johnson cautioned.

The following list of accidents reported upon from January 1st. 1908, to June 30th. 1908, was submitted, and the various recommendations approved: —

Date	Place of Accident.	Nature of Accident.	Remarks.
1908. Jany. 6	Reedness Junction	Points run through bolt broken and switches bent	Porter Broomhead cautioned.
Jany. 31	Reedness Junction	Points run through, one switch broken, one switch and two rods bent	Guard Jeeves reprimanded.
Feby. 27	Epworth	Points run through, rods and locking apparatus damaged	Porter Bramhill cautioned.
April 22	Epworth	Points run through, rods bent.	Porter-clerk Johnson cautioned
May 16	Haxey Junction	Points run through. switches strained and rods badly bent	Fireman Longhorn reprimanded.
June 1	Epworth	Engine 984 off road with leading wheels, nine ordinary chairs broken	Porter Bramhall cautioned.
June 1	Crowle	Points run through, one rod and one casting broken, one switch bent	Guard Johnson cautioned.
June 22	Crowle	N.E. van 90707 door knocked off and damaged	Guard Johnson and Porter Sharp cautioned.

The following list of accidents reported upon from July 1st to December 31st. 1908, was submitted, and the various recommendations approved: —

Date.	Place of Accident.	Nature of Accident.	Remarks.
1908. Sep. 17th.	Fockerby	Engine 1064 derailed.	Fireman Ibbetson fined 2s. 6d.
Oct. 27th.	Crowle	Field-lane crossing gates run through.	Mrs. Meggitt, gatekeeper, attending sick child and omitted to observe signals. Matter dealt with by Engineer
Nov. 18th.	Between Crowle and Reedness Junction	Engine vacuum cylinder slightly damaged owing to platelayer throwing down small lever between running lines.	Platelayer Meggitt severely reprimanded.
Dec. 5th.	Reedness Junction	L. & Y. wagon 11637 and N.E. wagon 103067 damaged, also 16 sleepers and 12 chairs broken owing to rough shunting.	Guard Coultish reprimanded.

Date.	Place of Accident.	Nature of Accident.	Remarks.
1909. Aug. 11th.	Reedness Junction ...	Buffer stops knocked down. L. & Y. Brake Van No. 25089 derailed, 8 sleepers, 4 chairs and 2 bolts broken, 3 point rods bent.	Engine collided with buffer stop during shunting operations.
Sep. 14th...	Fockerby	Engine 969 derailed, 3 sleepers and 3 chairs broken.	Driver Blackburn fined 5/-
Sep. 20th...	Reedness Junction ...	Ramskir & Co.'s wagons 35 and 51 derailed and damaged. 4 ordinary chairs, 1 p.c. chair, 2 lead chairs, 2 check chairs and 3 sleepers broken. Switch damaged and rod bent.	Leading wagons left rails at points. Cause not ascertained.
Nov. 23rd...	Epworth	Points run through. Switch bent, rod bent and stud broken.	Porter Picksley cautioned.
Dec. 9th ..	Haxey Junction	G. C. wagon 27911 end damaged. N. E. wagon 96620 derailed.	Wagons collided during shunting operations owing to slippery state of rails.
Dec. 20th....	Reedness Junction ...	Engine 954 tender derailed. 8 lead chairs, 6 bolts, 1 switch and 2 point rods broken.	Tender came off road at points. Cause not ascertained.

PERSONAL ACCIDENTS.

The following list of accidents to the public and to Joint Line Servants during the half year ended December 31st, 1909, was submitted.

Date.	Place of Accident.	Nature and Cause of Accident.
1909 July 10th...	Haxey Junction	Mrs. Sharp was alighting from the 5-30 p.m. passenger train at Goole, when she missed the bottom step and fell on her side on the platform.
Sep. 17th...	Haxey Junction	Mrs. Hornby was alighting from the 6-34 p.m. train, when she fell from the top step on to the platform injuring her left elbow.
Nov. 20th..	Haxey Town	Miss Coggan was letting the window down when she trapped her finger between the door light and the door.
Dec. 8th ...	Crowle	Porter Sharp was ascending a ladder with a sheet on his back, for the purpose of sheeting L. & Y. wagon 12578 loaded with peat moss, when, owing to the frosty state of the ground, the ladder slipped out at the foot, and he fell heavily.
Dec. 8th ...	Reedness Junction ...	Guard Coultish thrown over end of wagon when shunting owing to sudden start of engine.

The following list of accidents, reported upon from January 1st to June 30th, 1910, was submitted, and the various recommendations approved.

Date.	Place of Accident.	Nature of Accident.	Remarks.
1910. Jan. 6th. ...	Haxey Junction	Points run through, rods broken, and switch bent	Fireman Dale cautioned.
Jan. 27th. .	Crowle	L. & Y. wagon 29591 derailed	Porter Sharp reversed the points when the wagon was passing over them. He has been suitably cautioned.
Feb. 9th...	Haxey Junction	Points run through, rodding bent, and compensator moved out of position	Through a misunderstanding between the Driver and Fireman, the latter reversed the points when the engine was approaching them. Driver Gowland fined 2/6. Fireman Hall fined 2/6.
Apl. 7th. ...	Ealand Depot	L. & Y. vans 31329 and 33596 roofs damaged.	Caused through one van standing slightly foul of the points during shunting operations. Porter Fields cautioned.
May 10th. .	Reedness Junction ...	N.E. wagon 83985 safety loop and end pillar broken. ...... N.E. wagon 83938 end plank damaged.	Caused by the Guard allowing a shunt of wagons to come into sharp contact with those that were standing in the siding. Guard Taylor reprimanded.
May 18th. .	Reedness Junction ...	N.E. wagon 69037 derailed, axlebox broken, axleguard bent, sole plate bent, and bearing spring shoe displaced. L. & Y. engine 969, buffer wrenched off	The damage occurred through the wagon running back foul of the points while the engine was in the adjoining siding. Porter Thompson cautioned.
June 16th. .	Reedness Junction ...	L. & Y. goods brake 25089, both upright iron hand rails broken off on one side	The hand rails were torn off by a wagon which was standing foul of the points. Guard Coultish reprimanded.
June 18th. .	Epworth	Points run through, rod broken, and switches bent	Driver Cooper and Fireman Gibson suspended one day each.

PERSONAL ACCIDENTS.

The following list of accidents to Joint Line servants during the half-year ended June 30th, 1910, was submitted :—

Date.	Place of Accident.	Nature and Cause of Accident.
1910. January 12th	Belton	Platelayer Everatt was assisting Foreman Wilson to fix a crane when the jib fell, causing the handle to spin round quickly. Everatt was hit in the chest and knocked off the wagon. He received injuries to his head, chest, and right leg.
March 1st	Reedness Junction	Porter John Webster was lighting one of the platform lamps and had the lamp glass in his left hand, when his foot slipped off the wood block on which he was standing and he fell to the ground. His right hand came in contact with the lamp glass, breaking the glass, and cutting his hand badly.

The following list of Accidents reported upon from July 1st to December 31st, 1910, was submitted and the various recommendations approved :—

Date.	Place of Accident.	Nature of Accident.	Remarks.
Aug. 10th ...	Epworth	Points run through. Switch bent and locking damaged.	Caused through Guard Johnson' pulling wrong lever whilst working ground frame. Johnson cautioned.
Aug. 18th .	Epworth	Third class carriage No. 1537 buffer bent.	Engine detached to pick up filled wagon of perishable traffic and on returning came sharply in contact with the standing vehicles thus causing damage. Driver Raddings fined 2/6.
Sept. 28th..	Reedness Junction ...	8 L. & Y. wagons derailed and damaged, 18 chairs broken, two 30 feet rails bent, fish plate bent.	Attributable to defective sleepers.
Sept. 29th .	Fockerby	Engine No. 950 derailed. Five sleepers and four chairs broken.	Caused through Fireman Brown calling the engine forward before reversing the lever. Fireman Brown dealt with by L. & Y. Loco Dept.
Oct. 14th...	Reedness Junction ...	Colliery wagon derailed. One point rod and two chairs broken.	Cause not ascertainable.
Oct. 28th...	Crowle	Points run through. One point rod broken.	Caused through a misunderstanding between the Driver and Porter Sharp who was working the ground frame; the latter reversed the points when the engine was approaching them Porter Sharp severely reprimanded.
Nov. 17th..	Haxey Town.	Station house on fire. Hole burnt through middle bedroom floor. Two beams partly burnt, bedroom ceiling blackened, and bedroom paper spoiled.	A fire was lit in the bedroom of the empty house on the date of the Station Master's removal from Haxey Junction and at about 1·25 p.m. the bedroom floor was discovered by a charwoman, who was cleaning the house, to be on fire.
Nov. 21st..	Between Dutch River and Marshland Jun.	L. & Y. brake third No. 496 and third class carriage No. 1537 damaged. N.E. 12-ton covered goods van No. 19133 (empty) damaged.	Caused by the doors of N. E. wagon 19133 swinging open whilst travelling. Responsibility rests with the Goods Dept., Goole (L. & Y.), and suitable notice has been taken of the matter.
Nov. 29th...	Eastoft	Engine No 969 derailed, leading and driving wheels, right-hand driving spring broken. Four chairs broken, one rail bent, and point switch bent.	Joint Inquiry held at Eastoft January 5th. 1911. Unable to agree as to the ends.

The following list of accidents reported upon from January 1st to June 30th, 1911, was submitted, and the various recommendations approved :—

Date.	Place of Accident.	Nature of Accident.	Remarks.
1911. Feb. 21st...	Eastoft	L. & Y. wagons 33971 & 13132, buffer-locked. Wooden buffer plank broken and wooden stops displaced.	Attributed to greasy state of rails. Wagons gained speed and came into violent contact with the dock end. Accidental.
Mch. 15th..	Reedness Junction ...	L. & Y. wagons 14016 & 32495 derailed and damaged. One sleeper damaged and 15 chairs broken.	Caused by defective sleepers.
April 6th...	Goole Fields Siding (Reedness Junction)	L. & Y. van 31350 derailed and damaged.	Attributed to defective sleepers.
May 17th...	Luddington	Twelve fence rails and one platform lamp post damaged.	Caused through Porter Fields omitting to put the door of a wagon up again after transhipping. Fields severely reprimanded.
June 1st ...	Reedness Junction ..	L. & Y. flat 20699 forced over the wheel chock. Brake rodding bent.	Siding only holds 21 wagons and Guard Coultish explains that he was tightening them up to prevent fouling other siding. Accidental.
June 6th...	Epworth	Points run through. Switch and rods bent.	Caused through Guard Johnson omitting to pull No. 5 points over whilst working the ground frame. Johnson suitably cautioned.

The following list of accidents reported upon, from July 1st to December 31st, 1911, was submitted, and the various decisions approved :—

Date.	Place of Accident.	Nature of Accident.	Remarks.
1911. July 31st....	Haxey Junction	Point rods bent	Fireman Needham reversed points before engine clear. Needham reprimanded.
Sept. 12th..	Epworth	Points run through ; switches badly bent and rods damaged.	Clerk F. B. Webster, who was working the ground frame, inadvertently reversed the points before engine clear. Webster suitably cautioned.
Sept. 14th..	Haxey Junction	Points run through and rods badly bent.	Fireman Phillipson reversed points before engine clear. Phillipson reprimanded.
Sept. 18th..	Sandtoft	Motor car in collision with gate-post, level crossing.	Post knocked slightly out of position, but no further damage done.

Oct. 3rd ...	Crossing, Boltgate Siding	Farm cart smashed in pieces...	Horace Shipley, aged 12 years, was in charge of a horse and empty cart, and whilst crossing the line the cart was caught by the engine of an approaching train. No injury to boy or horse. Mr. W. J. Bramhill, the owner of the cart and employer of the boy, has impressed upon all his employees the necessity for exercising every care when using the crossing in future.
Oct. 4th ...	Crowle	Points run through	Porter Sharp took hold of No. 6 instead of No. 5 lever and attempted to reverse the points. The train was passing over at the time and did not leave the rails. Porter Sharp suitably cautioned.
Oct. 12th...	Reedness Junction ..	Engine 959. Leading wheels derailed and 8 chairs broken.	Engine was proceeding into No. 8 siding when the leading wheels appear to have struck the points. Cause unknown.
Nov. 3rd...	Reedness Junction ...	Engine 956. Leading wheels derailed at points and 6 chairs broken.	Cause not ascertainable.
Nov. 25th..	Reedness Junction ...	Points strained	Porter Revill pulled points in error when the engine was upon them. Revill suitably cautioned.
Dec. 7th ...	Haxey Junction	Points run through and bent...	Fireman Fox reversed points before engine had passed over the trailing end. Fox suitably cautioned.
Dec. 13th ..	Belton	Points run through and casting broken.	Porter Taylor reversed lever before wagons clear of points. Taylor suitably cautioned.

394. MISHAPS ON JOINT LINE.

The following list of accidents reported upon from January 1st to June 30th, 1912, was submitted and the various decisions approved :—

Date.	Place of Accident.	Nature of Accident.	Remarks.
1912. Jan. 5th ...	Ealand Crossing	Gate broken	Gate bolt of one of the gates worked loose as a train was slowly approaching Porter Fields instructed to see that the socket is well cleaned out in future.
Jan. 6th ...	Reedness Junction ...	N.E. wagon 2218 derailed	Guard Johnson was endeavouring to prop wagon clear of points but in doing so caused the two leading wheels to leave the rails. Tool van arrived 12-0 midnight and wagon rerailed 12-35 a.m.

Jan. 6th ...	Reedness Junction ...	Buffer stops at the end of loop damaged	Engine ran into buffer stops owing to Fireman J. H. Hewson closing the points in mistake. Fireman cautioned for reversing the points without instructions from the Guard to do so.
Feb. 5th ...	Reedness Junction ...	N.E. crane and guard wagon O4926 buffers damaged	Crane and wagons found in Reedness Junction yard with buffers damaged. They had apparently been buffer-locked and damage had occurred when being moved. No evidence of rough shunting.
Feb. 9th ...	Eastoft	Sleeper buffer stops shifted and broken	During shunting operations Guard Coultish knocked 4 wagons into the dock. 1 brake was pinned down but owing to the greasy state of the rails the wagons gained speed and hit the buffers. Guard suitably reprimanded and cautioned.
Feb. 16th...	Belton	No. 6 facing points strained ...	Porter Taylor reversed No. 6 points before engine clear. Taylor suitably cautioned.
Feb. 17th...	Reedness Junction ...	No. 2 siding chock damaged ...	On Feb. 17th it was found that the chock of No. 2 siding had been forced back and 1 sleeper broken. Unable to ascertain exactly when and how damage occurred.
Feb. 27th...	Eastoft	Pair cattle hurdles broken	Pair of young horses attached to dray load of straw owned by Mr. J. Brambill took fright in the goods yard through some cause unknown and smashed two cattle hurdles.
Mch. 2nd...	Reedness Junction ...	Buffer stops broken..........	During shunting operations 4 wagons knocked into No. 3 siding. Wagons were properly braked down but, on examination, it was found that the upright castings had broken off owing to an old flaw.
Mch. 4th ...	Epworth	No. 6 points run through, 3 ordinary chairs broken, 1 point rod broken. Switches and locking damaged	Guard Johnson pulled over No. 6 instead of No. 4 points, causing G.C. wagon 23179 to be derailed one pair of wheels. Guard suitably cautioned.
Mch 11th..	Reedness Junction ...	Loading gauge broken down ...	During shunting operations after dark wagon N.E. 106106 containing loose straw loaded by Messrs Major Bros. struck the gauge and broke the upright post about 4 or 5 feet from the top. Porter Revill states he tested the ends with the hand gauge but not the centre. Porter Revill severely reprimanded.
Apl. 16th...	Reedness Junction ...	N.E. wagon 66833 forced on buffer stops	Whilst shunting 4 wagons into No. 3 siding, Porter Thompson braked the wagons down but owing to the heavy gradient and the frosty state of the rails the wagon came in contact with L. & Y. 33647 loaded

| | | | with potatoes and N.E. 26999 loaded with a binder causing them to be buffer-locked and forcing empty N.E. wagon 66833 on to the buffer stops. The buffer plank was broken off previously and 4 sleepers and an old tree were placed on the rail for a wheel chock, and these enabled the wagon to mount the stops. No rough shunting. |
| May 20th... | Reedness Junction ... | Engine derailed .... | Whilst propelling an empty coach into the N.E. siding the bogie carriage cleared the points but the engine leading wheels came off the road. Engine rerailed at 9-0 p.m. There was no manipulation of the points whilst the engine was passing over them. Cause unascertainable. |

412. MISHAPS ON JOINT LINE.

The following list of accidents reported upon from July 1st to December 31st, 1912, was submitted and the various decisions approved :—

Date.	Place of Accident.	Nature of Accident	Remarks.
1912. September 6th	Reedness Junction.	Engine 950 derailed.	Whilst drawing wagons out of the Goods yard the engine became derailed. No manipulation of the points whilst the engine was passing over them. Cause unascertainable.
September 7th	Reedness Junction.	Engine 950 derailed.	Trailing wheels of engine left the rails whilst making a shunt into the yard through No. 7 points with 8 wagons. No staff in the signal cabin at the time. Cause unascertainable.
October 9th	Reedness Junction.	Engine 950 brake failed and Mid. van 114195 damaged and derailed.	Engine vacuum brake failed to act and engine travelled down the gradient at excessive speed and derailed and damaged Midland van 114195.
November 22nd	Luddington.	Ramskir Co.'s coal wagon No. 9 Door broken off.	Wagon stood foul during shunting operations. Porter Wardle responsible and suitably reprimanded.
December 5th	Reedness Junction.	Two empty cattle wagons Nos. 15603 and 1585 derailed at points.	All points and signals in connection with cabin disconnected. N.E. Signalling Dept. have matter under enquiry.
December 6th	Luddington.	Empty passenger bogie brake coach No. 2646 drawbar hook broken.	Goods engine backing to train on main line with coach attached to engine. Application of brakes caused the hook to snap. Slight flaw in drawbar.

The following list of accidents reported upon from January 1st to June 30th, 1913, was submitted, and the various decisions approved :—

Date.	Place of Accident.	Nature of Accident.	Remarks.
1913. January 30th ...	North end new siding, Reedness Junction	Engine 957 derailed	... Whilst drawing out of siding with N.E. traffic, engine jumped switch with leading wheels which took road to Stop Block, remainder of wheels taking proper road. Cause unascertainable.
March 28th ...	Crossing Gates, Haxey Town Main Road	Crossing Gate broken	... Porter Simmons opening gate to let road traffic over, and pushing gate on to one of engine buffers. Top and bottom bars and one stay of gate broken. Porter Simmons suitably reprimanded.
April 17th ...	Reedness Junction Siding	Engine 969 derailed	... Engine was propelling two wagons of coal into dock siding. Wagons passed over points but leading wheels of engine took other road, the remainder of the engine taking proper road. Cause unascertainable.
May 15th ...	Epworth No. 6 points, Sandtoft Sidings to Main Line	Goods Brake 20650 derailed	Whilst goods train was coming off Hatfield Moor Branch Porter Johnson, working ground frame, pulled over No. 6 points but reversed them before van was completely over, causing derailment of goods brake. Porter Johnson suitably reprimanded.

Date.	Place of Accident.	Nature of Accident.	Remarks.
1915 Mar. 12th ..	Reedness Junction ...	Load Gauge knocked by jib of crane of tool van.	Break down van train was employed here loading a damaged wagon, and during shunting operations jib of crane, which had been raised, caught top of gauge, knocking it out of position. The Loco. Dept. Staff are responsible and the Chief Mechanical Engineer states matter has had attention.
Mar. 22nd .	Reedness Junction ...	Engine Tender off road, all wheels, at points.	Points set in proper direction and cause unascertainable.
April 8th ...	Field Lane Crossing, Crowle	Crossing Gate damaged. Passenger brake 2186 lamp stand bent and van side slightly damaged.	Whilst goods train was approaching crossing the gate was blown across rail, and engine could not be brought to a stand in time to avoid damaging gate.

			After examination Goods Guard considered it safe and would not cause further damage, but as 1-30 p.m. Haxey Junction to Goole passenger train was passing, one of the projecting pieces caught side of passenger break-van 2186, slightly damaging it. Goods Guard Thurston suitably cautioned.
May 29th ..	Reedness Junction ...	Wagon 10148 knocked over stop block. Brake gear bent.	Wagons collided violently during shunting operations Guard Dixon suitably cautioned.
June 1st ...	Eastoft Goods Yard...	Wood Buffer stops smashed.	During shunting operations L. & Y. van 6734 was standing against buffers in dock when two wagons were shunted into siding causing damage. Due to defective break on wagon 6734.
June 16th ..	Reedness Junction ...	Third Class Six-Wheeled Coach No. 1234. One pair wheels derailed.	While placing coach into back road one pair of wheels came off road. Coach examined and found true to gauge. Caused by defective sleepers.

The following list of accidents reported upon from July 1st to December 31st, 1916, was submitted, and the various decisions approved :—

Date.	Place of Accident.	Nature of Accident.	Remarks.
1916 Oct. 23rd...	Reedness Junction ...	Engine 960 derailed.	Shunter Thompson was holding the points whilst the engine was passing from loop line to weigh line. The tender was first and the two leading pairs of wheels and also the first pair of engine wheels came off the road owing to Shunter Thompson failing to hold lever firmly. Thompson cautioned.
Nov. 13th..	Belton Coal Siding ...	Buffer Stops broken.	Error of judgment on the part of Guard Johnson when controlling entrance of train into sidings. Johnson cautioned.
Dec. 6th ...	Epworth Goods Yard.	Axle of Agric: Pole-Wagon broken.	Shunter Sharp failing to satisfy himself that all clear prior to releasing wagons during shunt. Shunter Sharp cautioned.
Dec. 11th...	Reedness Junction ...	Fockerby Passenger Coach derailed and damaged.	Porter Vaux moving points between wheels of coach, causing derailment. Porter Vaux cautioned.

The following list of accidents reported upon from January 1st to June 30th, 1916, was submitted, and the various decisions approved : —

Date.	Place of Accident.	Nature of Accident.	Remarks.
1916 Jan. 3rd ..	Reedness Junction ..	Engine 956 derailed, leading wheels.	Engine split No. 8 points through some cause unascertained
Jan. 6th ...	Epworth	No. 6 points run through. Rodding displaced and connecting rod bent.	Caused through Porter Myatt inadvertently setting wrong points. Myatt cautioned.
Jan. 21st...	Field Lane Crossing, Crowle	Two sheep killed.	Caused through sheep straying on to line at level crossing.
Feb. 2nd ...	Belton	Points run through. Two point rods broken.	Caused by Porter Arrand setting points prematurely. Arrand cautioned.
Feb. 16th ..	Blacker's Siding	Coal wagon blown off road...	Mishap occurred at safety points during heavy gale.
Feb. 21st...	Haxey Junction	Partial derailment of engine No. 956. Two chairs broken.	Mishap occurred at trap points. Cause unknown.
Mar. 25th..	Eastoft	Gates run through.	Due to Clerk Bramhill omitting to take action on receipt of advice of Special train. Bramhill cautioned.
Mar. 27th..	Eastoft	Yard gates slightly damaged	Porter Cook on coming on duty at 7-0 a.m. found the yard gates wide open and damaged ; there were traces of wagon wheels in the yard, evidently caused by a runaway horse and wagon. Unable to fix responsibility.
April 18th..	Epworth	No. 3 points run through. Point rod broken and switch bent.	Driver Royston passed No. 7 signal at danger and in consequence ran through No. 3 points. Porter Myatt also responsible for not placing points in proper position and lowering the signal. Royston and Myatt cautioned.

PERSONAL ACCIDENTS.

The following accidents which occurred during the half-year ended December 31st, 1916, were reported :—

Date.	Place of Accident.	Nature and Cause of Accident.
1916. July 18th ...	Crowle (Goods Yard) ...	John Naylor, head cut. Fall from cart.
Sept. 13th...	Haxey Junction	Shunter Sharp. Right eye damaged by spark from engine.
Nov. 30th ...	Reedness Junction ...	Porter R. Vaux. displacement of muscles of knee. This man was loading hay for the Military Authorities and accidentally slipped down on the top of the truck.

Appendix Eight

The Line Today: Walks and Nature Reserves

About 12 acres of the old railway between Belton and the Belton picnic site, can be reached from Jeffrey Lane in Belton or from the east side of the road opposite the picnic site. This area consists of grassland and scrub with hawthorn, blackthorn, ash, dog rose, privet and hop. There is good grassland flora with creeping cinquefoil, ribbed melilot, meadow vetching, flixweed, common knapweed and perforate St John's wort. Butterflies include Ringlet and Meadow Brown. Among the bird life are whitethroat, dunnock and linnet.

A further 34 acre site is situated to the north of Haxey on the old AJR line with the main access point in Low Street, Haxey about 150 metres west of the Kings Arms and Butter Cross; the line runs some one and half miles northwards. A car park is available close to the junction of Blackmoor and Marlborough Roads. This reserve provides a level walking route for the disabled and elderly. The southernmost mile of the line is in a deep cutting, whilst the remaining northern section is on an embankment. The cutting slopes carry ash, dog-rose, elder, aspen, oak and field maple. The speciality of the reserve is the green-winged orchid which grows in considerable numbers on the banks and in the ballast. Eighteen butterfly species have been recorded, including the Dingy Skipper. The area is also alive with birds especially the long-tailed tit, bullfinch, redwing (winter) and willow warbler (summer) whilst barn and long-eared owls hunt the area. From the embankments, the walker has spectacular views over the Isle.

Other stretches of the old AJR remain unspoilt, some being SSSI's with rare plants growing but sadly these are in private ownership.

The picnic site between Belton and Epworth situated on the infilled cutting of the old AJR. The Hatfield Moor branch ran away to the left of this photograph, c. 1993.

Author

The fine structure of the AJR station master's house at Haxey had been extended when photographed in 1980. The old level crossing gate opens on to the site of the trackbed running north (now a nature reserve), with the photograph being taken from the site of the down platform. *Alf Ludlam*

A view taken from the AJR trackbed in 1981 of the former station master's house at Belton with the level crossing gates still *in situ*. *Alf Ludlam*

One of the underbridges between Haxey and Epworth showing the substantial brick construction to take the proposed double track   *Author*

The trackbed between Belton and Epworth cutting in 1993 where it crossed the main road. The bridge has long been demolished and the embankment this side taken away, now being a car park and picnic area. The brick works of Richard Thomas & Co. Ltd, once had a siding running into their premises capable of holding 10 wagons, with a run-round facility.   *Author*

The AJR trackbed n
walkway near to Bur
Lane siding, south
Epworth in 1993.   A

The remains of the
mencement of the Ha
Moor branch as it cu
away from the main
north of Epworth cutt
                    A

The infilled, north en
Epworth cutting show
still a large area not fi
The hill is the height o
surrounding fields nor
Epworth station area.
                    Au

Index

Bold type indicates photographs

Tailpiece

Odd lot finds its way under hammer!
Extract from the Axholme Herald, 18th February, 1993

Auctioneers are used to selling some odd 'lots' but Lot 558 at Dickinson, Davy and Markham's Brigg sale yesterday will take some beating for curiosity.

It was, simply, a lump of earth - in an old cigar box mind, and, it was averred, a lump with a distinguished past.

For this was the first sod cut by one William Halkon on September 22, 1895, when construction work began for the Goole and Marshland Light Railway.

This was one of the first lines of its type to be built in England - lightly laid lines for slow speed trains for sparsely populated places.

Six more miles followed in 1902 and another eight to Haxey in 1904. The first section shut down in 1965 and all of it had gone by 1972.

However, yesterday, in Brigg it got a mention, post mortem, and the clod of earth in its box made a handsome £8.